AMERICAN DEMAGOGUE

Critical Essays on the Trump Presidency

For Maria + John
Long live the American
Republic!

Ray Smock
Former Historian,
U.S. House of Representatives

D1367380

For all the dedicated public servants of the
Federal Government, both civilian and military.

Thank you for your service in maintaining
and defending this great republic.

The shortest way to ruin a country is to give power to demagogues.
Dionysius of Halicarnassus, *Antiquities of Rome*, VI, circa 20 BC

A new race of men is springing up to govern the nation;
they are the hunters after popularity, men ambitious,
not of the honor so much as the profits of office—the
demagogues, whose principles hang laxly upon them,
and who follow not so much what is right as what leads
to a temporary vulgar applause.
Joseph Story, *Commentaries on the Constitution of the United States*, 1833

Table of Contents

Introduction

Until Donald Trump, the United States had never elected a president who had no experience in government at any level, who never held elective office of any kind, or never served in the military. Trump was, and is, a flamboyant New York real estate tycoon and celebrity television personality. He swaggered into the presidential debates in 2015 with a brash style of insulting and degrading his opponents. He could never talk seriously or in depth on policy issues, but he said that he would fix America's problems and that he, being a billionaire businessman, would make a better president than any politician.

He would make America great again. In short, he ran as a demagogue whose appeal was emotional and guttural. The campaign had very little to do with national policy or the Republican Party platform. He ran as Trump. He was his own brand, a brand he had cultivated for years before entering politics with his name in big gold letters on hotels, casinos, and skyscrapers around the world.

Trump tapped into the anger and frustration over stagnant wages, lost jobs, and a hollowing out of many American cities and towns. He exploited the genuine feelings of many Americans that they were left behind by elite politicians in a far-off swampland called Washington, DC. He used blatant racism against our first black president, beginning with his "Birther movement" even before he decided to run for president. He claimed President Barack Obama was not qualified to be president by birth and demanded to see his birth certificate. His campaign relied on fear that "illegal aliens" were flooding across the border with Mexico bringing with them, crime, drugs, and disease. In one of his opening campaign salvos he claimed Mexicans coming to America were rapists. To show he was fair and balanced, he said not all of them were bad people.

At rallies across America Trump told his supporters that he would build a big beautiful wall to keep out the alien hordes. It became his signature issue. It exploited our complex and unresolved immigration policy. Immigrants became his chief scapegoat for the ills of the nation. This is textbook demagoguery.

As I write this introduction, the government is in its longest shutdown, with more than 800,000 government employees affected because President Trump will not sign necessary appropriations bills to keep the government running, unless he gets money to build his wall on the border with Mexico.

On the evening of January 8, 2019, the president spoke to the nation from the Oval Office for the first time in his presidency. His short, stilted message, read from a Teleprompter, centered on the need for border security. But his examples focused on gory details of grizzly crimes committed by illegal immigrants in an appeal to emotion rather than reason. Government statistics show that immigrants commit dramatically less crimes of all kinds than do citizens of the United States, but facts fly out the window when the tactic is demagoguery.

I call this book of critical essays American Demagogue because I see Donald Trump as a classic example of this type of political personality. Demagogue is a word applied most often to politicians who run for office by using a combination of fearmongering, lies and half-truths, identifying an enemy to hate, and by making promises to fix problems that only the demagogue can fix.

Trump did not invent demagoguery. It has been a common practice used throughout human history. But never has it been used more successfully, or destructively, to elect a president of the United States. We have learned, in dramatic fashion, that a demagogue can win the highest office in the United States government. It is my contention that while demagogues can win elections they cannot be effective political leaders using the same tactics. Demagogues can't govern because they must continue to divide the nation to maintain their power. The destructive elements of demagoguery, division, fear, hate, and lies, have corrosive effects on the stability of the nation. Trump has not found a way to heal the divisions caused by his campaign or his first two years in office. His demagoguery on the Mexico wall issue is so vital to him that he cannot compromise with political reality.

This is my second book on the presidency of Donald Trump. The first was *Trump Tsunami: A Historian's Diary of the Trump Campaign and His First Year in Office*, published in 2018. I saw the Trump phenomenon then, and still do, as a massive wave of political destruction and a threat to the stability of our nation. We have never seen anything like this in American history. I have followed his campaign and his time in office with a critical and analytical eye. I am a historian by profession. I try to see Trump in the context of American history and politics. Yet I cannot separate out my personal and emotional reaction to this president, his election, and his time in office.

The election of 2016 is still under investigation. We know that Russia engaged in a massive effort to use social media to influence the campaign. Russian hackers, already named and indicted, were responsible for stealing emails and other files of Hillary Clinton and others connected with the Democratic National Committee. Ongoing investigations have dominated the news throughout Trump's presidency. We still do not know the full extent of the damage done to our electoral process.

Historians usually wait until some dust has settled on the records; until enough time has passed to make better and more objective analyses of historical events. We rely on documentary evidence. The Trump presidency has already resulted in hundreds of books, countless articles, and a massive build-up of resources. Good, solid scholarship will come to play the central role in our understanding of this presidency. This will continue for decades, and perhaps for centuries to come. Those of us living through these times should not have to wait for some distant, final verdict of history. We have a duty to speak out now, even though we are fully aware that all the facts we would like to have to make better judgments are not yet available.

Good books appear each year that reveal important new information on past presidents, and other aspects of our history. We learn new things all the time. In the case of the Trump presidency, it is vital for us to do as much investigation and analysis as we can as events unfold. We need to fully comprehend this election and this presidency. Nothing less is at stake than the survival of the republic.

While there is much to despair, there is also hope. Most of our institutions, most of our government, most of our free press, is responding to and carefully monitoring this presidency. This book ends on a hopeful note that the newly elected 116th Congress will, at last, provide checks and balances to the extreme politics of the president. I do not see the Democratic majority in the House as a panacea to cure all ills. But I do see a House controlled by Democrats to be an important constitutional check on the president. He will learn, for the first time, that Congress is a separate and co-equal branch of government. The Republican majorities in the House and Senate did not challenge Trump sufficiently. The GOP majority was too compliant with Trump's excesses. Now that the House will have a Democratic majority, we should see more push back and more oversight of the executive branch. For the first time the president will come up against the genius of the Founders of this nation, who fully understood that men and women are not angels and that power can corrupt, unless it is checked.

Editorial Note:

A date accompanies the title of each essay. This is the date the essay was written. The date anchors the commentary in a specific moment. Many of the essays were posted to friends on Facebook and a few appeared as op-ed pieces in newspapers. The book unfolds chronologically. I adopted this format to preserve the immediacy of my reaction to events and to news as it happened. I did not go back and change any of the commentary, even when subsequent events might have influenced and changed my judgment of a particular event or action of the president and his administration.

AMERICAN DEMAGOGUE

Should We Expect our Leaders to be Sane?

January 10, 2018

The American Psychiatric Association, a 37,000 member organization, with the consensus of the medical profession and other mental health professionals, agree that professional psychiatrists should not go around making a diagnosis of President Trump without examining him under the strict canons of the profession.

Having said this, let me state that there are not enough mental health professionals in the United States to elect any president of the United States. Presidents are elected by a broad range of citizens and, whether it is a good thing or not, many of us are armchair psychiatrists, and some voters are probably insane. We have little or no medical expertise. We use our eyes and ears, and we read what the president says, watch what he does, and what he tweets, and come to our own conclusions about his mental fitness to serve as president.

We voters are not bound by the canons of the medical profession, although we might certainly learn from them. We are people who decide who we are going to support for both rational and irrational reasons. We vote based on facts, on policies we support, by party label, with emotions such as hope, fear, or hatred, all based on our own intellectual and mental state. We vote for a lot of reasons and sometimes we vote for a single reason. I asked one friend why he voted for Trump and his quick answer was: "Hillary would take my guns away." That was his reason. Maybe he needs to see a psychiatrist too. Maybe the whole country is insane on some issues.

Michael Wolff's *Fire and Fury* paints a disturbing picture of a president that by all common indicators is not acting normally and we should not try to normalize his behavior. And even more troubling, many of the people around the president are not acting normally either. If a thousand psychiatrists examined Trump and declared him sane, I would still make my judgment based on my observations, not as a professional medical person, but as a professional historian who has studied politics for a half century, worked in government as an appointed official of the House of Representatives, met and worked with top government officials from all three branches of government, and based on this kind of personal experience, it is easy to declare that Donald Trump is unfit for office by temperament, by arrogance, by self-absorption, by a total lack of empathy, and for being uninformed about what governance means or how it is done.

Mental health issues have been used against any number of candidates over the years, not from the standpoint of the canons of the medical profession, but from gossip and from popular impressions. Barry Goldwater, in 1964, was portrayed as a loose cannon. He was a fanatic, he was unstable, and he would get us into a nuclear war. Some psychiatrists at the time declared Goldwater unfit, and it is likely they were responding in a partisan, not a professional manner. I have no idea if any psychiatrist ever actually examined Goldwater. After losing the 1964 election, Goldwater was re-elected to the Senate where he served another 20 years as the "Grand Old Man" of the conservative movement, and one of our most distinguished and able senators.

George McGovern's running mate in 1972, Senator Thomas Eagleton, had to withdraw from the Democratic ticket because it became public that he suffered from depression and had been hospitalized at times and had received a form of shock therapy. President Nixon's people made sure the smear went out on Eagleton. This doomed him on the presidential ticket, even though he went on and served with distinction in the Senate for another 15 years. A poll taken in 1972 showed 77% of Americans were not troubled by Senator Eagleton's history with depression.

Look at these two careers, one Republican, one Democrat, both men of long experience in government, players at the highest levels in the political arena, distinguished citizens. Senator Eagleton served in the Navy, was a lawyer, elected at age 31 as attorney general of Missouri, was lieutenant governor, and Senator. After his senate service he taught at Washington University in St. Louis.

Barry Goldwater served in the U.S. Army during World War II and in the Air Force during the Korean Conflict. He rose to the rank of Major General in the Air Force Reserves and had a long distinguished career as Senator from Arizona. Both men knew what public service meant, as civilians, in the military, and in government service.

Now, compare these men and so many other men and women like them in government service to the numbskull in the White House with no prior experience at any level of government, public service, or military experience and tell me that Donald J. Trump is fit for high office whether he suffers from mental illness or not.

If he is not crazy, he sure knows how to act the part every single day of his administration. Inside his White House, by all accounts, it seems more like an asylum than the seat of government. His ignorance of American history and world history and his seeming unwillingness to learn anything, profoundly disable him.

I will take a lesson not from psychiatrists, but from Cicero, who said in 46 B.C. "To be ignorant of what occurred before you were born is to remain always a child." It may not be a clinical diagnosis, but how many people who have observed Trump up close and from far away conclude that he acts like a child? This child-like behavior may not be mental illness, but it is profoundly disturbing in a president of the United States who is 71 years old.

Peaks, Valleys, and the Arc of Justice

January 15, 2018

When I was appointed Historian of the U.S. House of Representatives, the eighty-three-year-old chairman of the Rules Committee, Claude Pepper (D-FL), told me a story he heard from President Franklin D. Roosevelt many years earlier. FDR's school teacher was Endicott Peabody, an Episcopal priest and headmaster at Groton School for Boys. (Later he would preside at the marriage of Eleanor and Franklin).

Peabody told his pupil, young Franklin, that history was a series of peaks and valleys, but if you drew a line along the peaks, it would have an upward trajectory, indicating that history shows that despite downturns and setbacks, we were progressing; civilization was getting better and the United States was moving upward and onward.

Chairman Pepper then told me, that as the new historian, I should keep this in mind and write not only about the peaks of congressional history but also its valleys. It was his way of saying I was not there to whitewash history, but to view it critically. I took his advice in the spirit it was intended and I was always impressed with my encounters with Claude Pepper and his wisdom.

He had seen almost a century of history. He had been a New Deal senator, a supporter of FDR, serving from 1936 to 1951. He lost his Senate seat in a bitter contest in 1950, when he was accused of being a communist, and branded "Red Pepper." Twelve years later he returned to Congress, this time in the House, where he served until his death in 1989. He became one of the great champions of elderly Americans.

Well, Senator Pepper, excuse me if I take a critical look at the theory that history progresses upward, toward betterment, toward improvement. There are peaks and valleys, to be sure. The United States is in a deep valley right now. It is less a valley than it is a bottomless trench, a very deep, unfathomable ditch of despair and confusion, because President Trump and the Republican-controlled Congress is so far out of sync with progress and betterment on any front. They display no humanity and justice only for the favored of society.

If, and when, we come out of this deep ditch, that is devoid of compassion, how high will we reach in a new "peak" before the next downturn? History is too unpredictable to say that things, despite setbacks, eventually get better. But the odds improve dramatically, when good people take action. If we need a revolution it should be about compassion for all. We need more compassion in government and in our daily lives. We must find ways to come together and stop the hate and the division.

Today is Martin Luther King, Jr. Day, and the news media is filled with the annual stories of his life and his martyrdom for the cause of civil rights and human justice. King drew some of his inspiration from men like Mahatma Gandhi, who preached non-violent action to address grievances against government action and misguided policy to improve the lot of mankind. King also liked to quote the abolitionist Theodore Parker, who said, "The arc of the moral universe is long, but it bends towards justice."

This marvelous quotation, which King used to remind people in the civil rights movement that their work was never done, and not to give up hope, has, however, the same flaw as the story of history as a series of peaks and valleys. It assumes a positive inevitability. It assumes that somewhere there is an arc and it is bending in the right direction.

We don't know if the universe is moral. That would be very hard to prove. Most of the world's philosophers for millennia and most of the world's religions assume that goodness will triumph over evil and that justice will prevail over injustice.

The Founders of the United States designed a government to guard against greed and tyranny because they knew men (and women) were not angels. Yet in our two hundred and thirty plus years of constitutional government, we have tended to view government as a given, as something automatic, something that worked by itself like a machine. My late friend, Michael Kammen, wrote a brilliant book almost thirty years ago now, *A Machine that Would Go of Itself*. It was about how Americans viewed their Constitution. Many Americans over two-plus centuries have assumed that once set in motion, the Constitution would keep working forever.

The big theoretical debates over the Constitution center on the idea of the Constitution as an organic document, a living Constitution, that is flexible enough to respond to changing times and circumstances. This view tends to be held by liberals and progressives. The conservatives, on the other hand, think the Constitution is something written in stone, and only the original intent of the men who drafted it has meaning in how we interpret it for our time.

Like literalists in biblical interpretation, the original intent believers, the strict constructionists, tell us the Constitution is a machine, not a living thing. They tell us we cannot give it new meaning beyond the meaning it had in 1787, in a world vastly different from ours.

So, we have stories that talk about the upward progress of history, we have a great and inspiring quotation used by abolitionists and by Martin Luther King, Jr., and we have a Constitution that, like the arc of justice, is something that automatically leads to goodness, someday, perhaps in a galaxy far away, where the gravity is different, and we can see the arc bending.

But the other lesson that comes from people like Franklin D. Roosevelt, Claude Pepper, Martin Luther King, Jr., Mahatma Gandhi, and so many others throughout the world, who worked to bend that mystical arc, is that nothing is automatic. Nothing gets better until we make it better.

You must get into the political arena and fight to make things better. You must vote in every election. You must protest injustice to the best of your ability, in the streets, through donations, by volunteering. You cannot wait for your neighbors to act.

You cannot expect a political party to be automatic about anything. You have to shape the party of your choice. Or try to shape all parties, not just the one you prefer. No theory, no Constitution, no quotation, is enough without active involvement and a vision of where we want to go.

The immediate goal, that would make Martin Luther King, Jr., and most of the people I know feel that the arc was bending toward justice, is to un-elect a Republican Congress that acts to enable a racist president of the United States—a GOP majority that is very close to obstructing a serious investigation of Russia's cyberwar against American Democracy, and the possible collusion in that cyberwar of the president and members of his staff.

"We the People" is the real engine of America that does work when we have a clear vision of what to change and then change it. Will changing the majority party in the House and Senate lead toward getting us out of the deep ditch we are in? Damn right it will.

Consciousness of Guilt

January 17, 2018

Donald Trump is very conscious of his guilt. What remains to be determined is the precise nature of his guilt and how learning of the specifics will determine his ability to stay in office and possibly his ability to remain out of jail. Trump has been guilty of many things over a lengthy career as a con man and flimflam artist.

Some of that guilt is well documented in public records going back to charges that he and his father discriminated against blacks in New York housing, to a more recent proven charge that his Trump University was a complete fraud designed to swindle people out of money. Trump has been involved in constant litigation over the past thirty years, often settling matters with hush money and non-disclosure agreements to keep things out of the public eye.

People who exhibit a consciousness of guilt, no matter how skilled they may be in pulling the wool over the eyes of their victims or in hiding crimes, often exhibit telltale signs that reveal the fact that they are guilty. Police officers have often used consciousness of guilt, explicitly or even unconsciously, when the perpetrator of a crime flees the scene and a chase ensues. Why would an innocent person flee?

The term "consciousness of guilt" has a long history going back to biblical antiquity and extending up to modern court cases. In Proverbs 28:1, as presented in the King James version of the Bible, it says: "The wicked flee when no man pursueth: but the righteous are bold as a lion." If you are guilty, you run and hide, you cover up, you deny guilt. If you are innocent, you stand before your accusers like a lion because you know you are righteous in the eyes of God and the law.

Donald Trump is trying to have it both ways. He said on several occasions that he wants to cooperate with the Mueller investigations. This would be a sign that he had nothing to hide. He said he would appear before Mueller and his investigators. Now that that appearance may be at hand, Trump's lawyers are trying to set the table and limit the president's involvement. While feigning cooperation, Trump has also done everything possible to interfere with the Mueller investigations and even before Mueller was appointed Special Counsel, Trump began the whole "consciousness of guilt" gambit when he fired the Director of the FBI, James Comey, thinking this would end the Russian probe.

Even before Trump fired Comey, he fired Acting Attorney General Sally Yates, when she brought him the news that General Mike Flynn was compromised and could be blackmailed by a foreign power, namely Russia. Remember that Flynn was Trump's hand-picked National Security Advisor. Wouldn't Russia love to have him by the short hairs. What damage he could do to our national security.

Instead of recognizing Sally Yates professionalism and service to her country in this delicate matter, the Trump White House said she had "betrayed" the Department of Justice and she was fired. What could better explain this firing than Trump's consciousness of guilt?

Donald Trump has been obstructing the FBI probes as well as the multiple congressional probes by House and Senate Intelligence Committees and House and Senate Judiciary Committees. The president has been aided and abetted in his obstruction by partisan actions from some of the Republicans on these committees. The most blatant example being House Intelligence Committee Chairman Devin Nunes, (R-CA) whose actions became so bizarre in defense of the president that he was temporarily removed from his chairmanship. There seems to be plenty of consciousness of guilt motivating the president, some of his top aides, and members of the Trump family, all of whom are up to their necks in some very nasty stuff.

There is a term in Washington when scandal is afoot. Everyone involved starts "lawyering up." You may lawyer up to protect your own innocence or you may lawyer up to protect yourself to avoid jail time should it come to that. Having a lawyer in Washington is not a crime. But when people in the Trump administration start lawyering up, you begin to smell a rat.

Go back and look at all the times Donald Trump has said "No collusion," or that the Russian probe is fake news, that it is a ruse, something made up by Democrats. His constant vehement denials of any collusion with Russia is a textbook example of consciousness of guilt.

I never really paid much attention to this term until I started to hear it from some of the Democrats on the committees investigating Russian collusion. This term has been used by Congressman Eric Swalwell (D-CA) who serves on the House Permanent Select Committee on Intelligence, where he and his fellow minority-party Democrats have had to put up with the frustrating antics and obstruction of their Chairman Devin Nunes.

Congressman Swalwell launched his own website to keep the public informed with the kind of information he can talk about without violating the secret investigations of the committee. You can look at it at: https://swalwell.house.gov/russia .

More recently, I heard Ted Lieu (D-CA) talk of Trump's consciousness of guilt on MSNBC, where he was interviewed by Joy Reid. For Congressman Lieu, there were plenty of examples of Trump's actions to hinder, delay, and obstruct the investigations now underway.

Several weeks ago, Trump called House and Senate chairman of the investigative committees and told them to wrap up their work. The president has no business telling Congress to wrap up any investigation, especially those involving members of his own campaign and White House staff, and, of course, the president himself.

One of the earliest and most egregious examples of consciousness of guilt came when Trump fired FBI director Comey. The letter announcing the firing, was filled with denials that Trump was under investigation. In firing Comey, all Trump could talk about was his own innocence. That firing will turn out to be the single best example that President Trump was obstructing justice and covering his own crimes. No court would ever convict anyone on "consciousness of guilt" alone. But it does play a role in some cases.

We expose the real crimes and how they were committed only by painstaking and thorough investigation. But as was the case with Nixon and Watergate, it began with denials, with lies, and with the pretense that the White House was not involved. It escalated to paying hush money to the Watergate burglars, attempts to invoke executive privilege, and eventually to the firing of Special Prosecutor Archibald Cox.

As a final observation, let's go back to one of the original questions asked of Candidate Trump. Why won't you release your income tax returns? Instead of standing like a lion, as the Bible speaks of the innocent, Trump fled like the wicked man in Proverbs.

The first important lie that bears on his crimes, was that he only would release his tax returns after an audit was completed. Once elected president, he changed his tune. Why should he release them now? He is the president. He was elected without showing his returns. There was no legal requirement that he do so. He said only his enemies wanted to see them now. He did not plan to cooperate with his enemies, and he saw enemies all around him.

Some of those who the president may see as enemies, are more likely the champions of the rule of law and the Constitution. And these champions are closing in on the president. They are doing so in the name of law, in the name of justice, in the name of righteousness, in the name of decency and honesty, and to save our republic. We know who the lions are in this story, and we know who has fled.

To Fiddle While Rome Burns

January 19, 2018

The unpopular and tyrannical Roman Emperor Nero, supposedly fiddled while fire ravaged Rome in July of 64 AD, destroying much of the city. Well, it is a piece of fake history. The fire was real. Nero was probably away from Rome at the time, and the fiddle had not yet been invented. But this common saying does have a moral that has lasted for more than two thousand years. The phrase has come to stand for callous, self-absorbed leaders who have no interest in the people, but only in themselves. It stands for leaders who are distracted when serious matters and a crisis threatens the country.

As I write this, the nation is within eleven hours of a government shutdown caused by a completely dysfunctional Congress and a president who changes his mind about legislative matters by the hour. The government is not working. The money to run the government has come in fits and starts with no regular order to appropriations bills. The government runs month to month, day to day, on short term Continuing Resolutions while Congress and the president fiddle away their time in ideological conflicts and posturing for their base supporters.

Governments that are functional do not shut down. Shutting down government, even a so-called "partial shutdown" is simply abhorrent and unconstitutional. There have been a few "technical" short-term shut downs that were more procedural than serious, but longer shutdowns resulting from political failures have become stunts in recent years. Every time it has happened it has harmed the country, wasted money, and embarrassed us before the world. Some shut downs have greatly inconvenienced a lot of Americans going about their daily business. This time a deal has been made to keep the National Parks open, because that shutting the parks has proven very unpopular in the past. The whole idea of a shutdown should be unpopular, but in a climate where so many Americans don't like government to begin with, it seems OK to do it.

Emperor Trump, on the eve of the looming shutdown, has decided to get out of town. He is going to Mar-a-Lago to celebrate his first anniversary in office. We should all stop what we are doing and sing happy anniversary to the president. This is what he expects from the rich toadies and sycophants who will flock to Mar-a-Lago for the occasion. For the modest sum of $100,000 per couple, you can join the president in this gala anniversary fund raiser for his next election. Trump adds a new low to the concept of fiddling while Rome burns.

Trump parties while the government shuts down. And, like Nero and the great fire in Rome, Trump has a scapegoat ready. For Nero it was those nasty Christians who were to blame, and he found new ways to persecute them after the fire. For Trump it is the Democratic Party that is responsible for the shutdown, and Trump will make the Democrats pay for this. After all, with Republicans in control of the House and Senate and the presidency, it must be that nasty minority that is shutting down government.

Perhaps the shutdown will be avoided. Perhaps a last-minute deal will get us through this and on to the next crisis in another few weeks or months, when the next Continuing Resolution will be required to keep the government open. I am sure that Emperor Trump will take full credit if the shutdown is avoided, while denying any responsibility if the shutdown occurs.

Smearing the FBI

January 25, 2018

Senator Joseph McCarthy, Republican of Wisconsin, started his rise to power and infamy with a speech he delivered in Wheeling, West Virginia, on February 9, 1950. He said the struggle in the world was between Christianity and atheistic communism. He told his audience that there was a secret group of communists inside the United States State Department, 57 of them to be precise, who were working to undermine America. McCarthy waved a piece of paper with the names of the traitors on it but never showed it to anyone. In fact, in an advance copy of the speech given to the press, the number of communists in the State Department was 205.

Fast forward to January 24, 2018, and listen to another Republican senator from Wisconsin, Ron Johnson, declare that within the FBI is a secret society working to undermine the Trump administration. What is there in the water in Wisconsin that turns out these conspiracy-minded senators? How does Senator Johnson know this? An informant told him. And the phrase "secret society" was discovered in the emails between FBI Agent Peter Strzok and an FBI lawyer Lisa Page, with whom Strzok was having an affair. Senator Johnson provided no context for the phrase, "secret society," named no members of the secret society, even though news reports indicated the use of that phrase may have been an inside joke between Agent Strzok and his lawyer friend.

Senator Johnson serves as Chairman of the Senate Homeland Security and Government Affairs Committee. He is among the leaders of the hard-right senators and House members who have decided to go after the FBI and the investigation of Special Counsel Mueller. Today Senator Johnson walked back his comments on the secret society because he had no proof and had gone too far yesterday. A backlash was setting in.

But other members of Congress, especially in the House, are sticking by the charge. Fox News spread the word of a secret society and even suggested some names of its members. Rush Limbaugh bellowed like a walrus to his listeners across the land from his "Excellence in Broadcasting" studio, that the secret society was real and that it started as an effort to keep Trump out of the White House. It was

House Member Trey Gowdy, (R-SC) who led numerous investigations against Hillary Clinton, who brought up the secret society idea on Fox News earlier this week.

As speculation increases about how close the Mueller investigation is getting to President Trump, members of the Republican party do not seem to mind going after the FBI. They are ready to smear career FBI agents with impeccable credentials, who were doing magnificent work on behalf of the American people long before Trump became president. Now all these fine agents and leaders of the FBI are being attacked. This is an outrage. It is very close to obstruction of justice. Why are they smearing the FBI for its investigation of Donald Trump and his associates?

You would think Chairman Johnson of the Senate Homeland Security Committee would be more concerned about national defense from "godless communism" rather than worrying about an FBI agent's conduct in private emails when there is no evidence that the agent's personal views affected his work. That agent was removed from the Mueller investigation team immediately after the emails became known. He was not fired. He was not prosecuted for a crime because it is not a crime to act stupidly in private emails, even though he should have known better. He was reassigned.

Even FBI agents have the right to have private opinions, even partisan ones. The difference between a professional and an amateur, or between a nonpartisan and a partisan is that a professional and the nonpartisan can put personal views and private opinions aside and do his or her job faithfully and to the best of their ability. If private opinions affect their work, and bias can be proved, or if the appearance of such opinions might affect their work, or the work of the Mueller investigation, they should be dealt with. In this case they were.

Recently President Trump, who has had a vendetta against a career FBI agent Andrew McCabe, the Deputy Director of the FBI, asked McCabe how he voted in the last election. What business does the president have asking anyone who they voted for? We have secret ballots for a reason. So, our private actions cannot later be held against us by extreme partisans. We can assume that most Americans are Republicans, Democrats, Independents, or maybe Libertarians, or any other minority party. Their party label should have nothing whatsoever to do with their duties in law enforcement, or any other part of government. McCabe's wife, a pediatrician, ran for the Virginia state legislature in 2015 as a Democrat. Trump looks at this information and immediately smells a rat. The wife of the Deputy Director of the FBI is married to a DEMOCRAT! What more proof does one need of a secret society out to get him?

In our poisoned politics, party labels themselves have become politicized. Are we supposed to ask every government employee how they voted in the last election? If they voted for Hillary, should they be suspected of being enemies of the United States, or enemies of our paranoid president? This whole tawdry mess is one more example of how Donald Trump is destroying respect for our institutions and destroying respect for the rule of law. I can only conclude he is trying to destroy law enforcement before it catches up to him with an iron-clad case of high crimes and misdemeanors against the United States.

Why can't the president try to act innocent of wrong-doing for at least 24 hours? He said today that he was frustrated that he could not fight back against the investigation because there was no collusion, no collusion, he repeated it several times. In suggesting he was trying to fight back against the investigation he was admitting that he was trying to impede the investigation. I think he just admitted again that he obstructed justice. The first time was when he fired FBI Director Comey and then said he did so to stop the Russian probe. Given enough time he will indict himself before Mueller does. Today the president tried to play nice again, when he said he welcomed the upcoming interview with the Special Counsel. What he failed to note was he has no choice in the matter. When the Special Counsel does summon the president, he will have to go, because he is not above the law no matter how hard he fights against it.

Don't Turn Away from Watching Trump

January 28, 2018

W e must pay close attention to Trump whether we can stand it or not. This is no time to go soft because we don't like what we see, or think we need a break from it. We must stay informed and on top of his daily actions and keep letting our members of Congress know how we feel about him and the policies of his administration.

Someone asked me recently if I was "biased" in my opinion about Trump. I said, no I am not biased. Bias means to prejudge, to be prejudice. Bias is a word often used to stop conversation. It is one of those ON/OFF words. We dismiss people by saying, "Oh, he's biased."

While I am not biased. I am indeed highly critical of Trump. I have not prejudged him; I have judged him, based on his words, his conduct, and his policies. I am not against Trump for something silly like his label as a Republican. My critique rests on almost 60 years of political study, most of it in nonpartisan professional positions.

Trump is a disaster for this country, not because he is a Republican, not because he is a billionaire, not because he is a TV celebrity, but because he is totally incapable of governing this nation and uniting us. All else flows from this objective fact. If 30% of Americans think he is doing great, this means 70% have various levels of disagreement. But this is not about opinion polls. Any damn fool is entitled to his or her opinion. Opinions mean more when they are backed up by facts, using analyses and critical thinking, and placing them in a political and historical context. This is how I try to approach the Trump phenomenon.

Well-known conservative thinkers and members of the GOP have been every bit as hard on Trump as I have because none of us has never encountered this situation in the entire history of the nation. The Trump presidency is not normal by any objective standard.

I will continue to watch this administration unfold. I will not turn away because my blood pressure goes up, or because I get disgusted with the latest outrage. I will continue to place my critique in as much historical context as I can muster. I do, however, reserve the right to just throw up my hands on occasion and scream out loud. Sometimes this is very good for the soul.

I have become more partisan than at any other time in my 77 years on the planet. I am not used to being partisan, except in the voting booth. Partisan means to be a dedicated supporter of a particular party or a particular cause. What I am partisan about is not simple party affiliation. I believe in a strong two-party system. I want Republicans and Democrats to debate again and work together again.

I am a partisan who is in favor of maintaining the U.S. Constitution and three co-equal branches of government and seeing that this president and the other amateurs he has selected to run the country do not undermine the Constitution or the rule of law.

Watching and critiquing Trump is my cause. I see this as a duty. I don't like what I see President Trump doing. I do not like his daily lies. They are not lies because I say so, they are objectively proven lies. I have not prejudged his ability to be our president. I have judged him to lack that ability based on a full year of his presidency.

I am going to keep watching and writing about him and his administration as long as I can. I will continue to critique the terrible ideological dysfunction in Congress, which only adds to Trump's ineptitude. In my critique I keep asking the president and the Congress: Do Your Jobs.

Those of us who have closely studied American history and government and political science and the Constitution have an obligation to do our jobs too. I am not a member of the American press. I am an American historian. My profession is stepping up to the plate too and we need to do our part. The American press, is starting to do a better job of reporting on Trump and his administration. I have been highly critical of the press for its focus on Trump's tweets, the easy willingness to follow shiny objects and diversions that come out of the White House and the Congress every day. I have also criticized the press for their over-reliance on daily polls, where the polls become breaking news. This is silliness and a diversion of its own. But beneath my critique of the press is my strong and abiding belief in the First Amendment and the vital role of the press to keep watch on government, not just to sell newspapers and advertising, but to save this republic from destruction.

A Gallery Filled with Heroes

January 30, 2018

L est my title for Trump's first State of the Union address seem too harsh and cynical, let me begin by saying I love this event. I love seeing the House chamber filled with members of all three branches and the leaders of our Armed Forces. I loved the times I was on that floor for the State of the Union addresses when I served as House Historian.

The State of the Union address is high political theater and has been since Woodrow Wilson revived the long dormant idea of delivering the speech in person rather than sending it to Congress as a written report. I have studied all the State of Union addresses over the years, both those delivered in person and the many that were sent to Congress in writing. Most of them are not all that memorable, but they are signposts of their times and of the politics and policies of their time. Some are so long and detailed about the intricacies of the executive branch and how it is carrying out its duties, in each agency, that they would bore you to tears. Others have had lofty rhetoric and an inspiring message of unity and purpose.

I have never witnessed one quite like what we saw tonight. Given that President Trump is not a person steeped in our history or familiar with how government works, it was, perhaps, fitting that he put on an emotional showcase of American heroes, an idea begun by Ronald Reagan in 1982, when he acknowledged Lenny Skutnik, a government worker who helped save victims of a plane crash in the icy Potomac just two weeks before the State of the Union Address. Recognizing a hero or two in the gallery has become a feature of these events ever since. It is the one thing that usually gets everyone in the chamber on their feet in applause.

Trump's State of the Union speech was loaded with gallery heroes from the opening salvo of the speech until its end 90 minutes later. More than half the time of the speech was spent on heroes and the extended periods of applause. Since the president had very little to talk about regarding policy or his vision for America, or of finding ways to unite us, we were treated to a Realty Show designed to tug on our heartstrings.

I do not disparage any of the individuals or families that Trump's people arranged to have in the gallery. But in trotting out so many, and spending so much time telling their stories, it revealed that he did not have any substantial policy matters that he could discuss. His pitch was emotional not intellectual. Like the demagogue he is, he put on a people's show.

He began his speech by noting a "new tide of optimism is sweeping over the land" and that he was on an "righteous mission to make America great again for all Americans." I see no optimism. I see no righteous mission. I see uncertainty. I see a badly divided nation with our president as the Divider-in-Chief. I see a nation that wonders if our president could be a crook. I see a president who, with support from zealots in the House, is engaged in a war with the FBI, removing top people involved in the investigation of the president at an alarming rate.

The president did deal with some policy matters, after taking credit for the booming economy with some very misleading "facts." He took credit for creating 2.4 million jobs, even though this is a decline in previous job growth. He said black unemployment was the lowest ever, and so was Hispanic unemployment, but failed to point out that these rates are still twice as high as the overall unemployment figure of 4.1%. At one point he took pride in the 9 trillion dollars in wealth that has been created with the stock market boom. Later in the speech he said we were losing our wealth to other nations. I guess this means we are getting richer and poorer at the same time.

He talked about all the benefits of the new tax bill, which might mean that many working poor and middle-class people will see $1,000 in savings in 2019, as if this would make a significant difference in the lives of most Americans. He did not think to mention what he told his super-rich friends at Mar-a-Lago right after he signed the tax bill, "You just got a lot richer." As Republican strategist Steve Schmidt said in the commentary after the speech, the tax benefits Trump talked about were all "hype," and "67% of Americans do not even have $1,000 in savings."

For a president who does not hold press conferences and talks to the nation via Twitter or through the deceptive mouth of Sarah Huckabee Sanders, this State of the Union speech was one of the longest sustained opportunities to hear the president speak in something more than 144 characters, or to listen to his never-ending campaign speeches. Tonight, he stuck strictly to his script and read it carefully and well from the Teleprompters in the room.

The speech took on a very dark and sinister tone when he talked about immigration. I could feel the words written by the president's chief adviser on immigration, Stephen Miller. Listening to the president I could only conclude that most of the immigrants coming to America are murderers and drug dealers who belong to the MS-13 gang. Trump has not changed his view of immigrants from the first campaign speech, when he called Mexican immigrants rapists and criminals. Four of the gallery heroes were the parents of two young women killed by MS-13 gang members.

Trump offered some hope to the DACA Dreamers but tied this to his $25 billion wall on the Mexican border. Other aspects of his immigration policy would focus on nuclear families rather than allowing whole extended families to immigrate. Nothing he said addressed two of the largest issues regarding immigration facing the entire world, immigrants fleeing political persecution and civil war, and the new kind of immigrant, those dispossessed of their homes and their livelihoods by climate change.

While he praised American veterans, he said nothing about our ongoing wars, other than that we have all but defeated ISIS, which is not true. They have spread to other parts of the world and the places where we have defeated ISIS remain wastelands of destruction.

He said he wanted Americans to stress faith and family not government and the bureaucracy. This divides people from a government that is supposed to serve the people. Trump sees government workers as detrimental to the people. He asked Congress for draconian legislation to allow his cabinet members to fire bureaucrats in droves to improve government. This flies in the face of civil service laws designed to protect career government workers from shifting political winds. Trump is frustrated by the bureaucracy because it follows rules and laws that he thinks do not apply to him or his cabinet members.

He genuflected toward the American flag, not unusual in such speeches, but then took a jab at those sports figures who kneeled in protest during the national anthem. He loves patriots, just not the ones who use their First Amendment right to free speech. Such a jab at American protest disunites us when we desperately need to come together.

He was proud of his record breaking pace of eliminating government regulations, but he gave no specific examples of what regulations he has cut, and what benefits have derived from eliminating specific regulations. He did say his efforts have put an "end to the war on beautiful clean coal." This will play well here in my state of West Virginia, which recent polls have shown is the state with the highest approval of President Trump, the others being North and South Dakota and Wyoming.

The well entrenched and widely-believed myth here in West Virginia, is that Environmental Protection Agency regulations killed coal production. "Clean coal" is itself a misnomer, but widely touted by both political parties in West Virginia. You cannot get elected dog catcher in this state unless you believe coal is coming back. But I am not sure I ever heard "clean" coal called "beautiful" before.

I did not hear a single word about Russia, Russian influence in our elections, or Russian sanctions in the speech. I did not hear that the president was assembling the intelligence agency chiefs to launch new initiatives to stop Russian influence in the 2018 elections. This might have given this speech some substance. But we got nothing, not a single word on this vital topic.

This State of the Union address will not stack up well with the more memorable ones of the past. It was designed to get through a news cycle or two. It was designed to make the president look calm and deliberate, despite the daily chaos in the White House. It may bump him up a few points among his own sagging supporters. It will be a hard speech for historians to read fifty years from now, unless there is video, so they can see the heroes in the gallery, see their real tears, and sense how these good people were used to prop up a failing presidency. Their cathartic experiences tonight and their sense of pride at being saluted by the entire government assembled at their feet, will, I hope, sustain them and be a positive comfort for them. I cannot help but think they were simply guests on Donald Trump's New Reality Show, formerly known as the State of the Union.

The Nunes Memorandum: Innuendo 101

February 2, 2018

The much anticipated and ballyhooed release of the Devin Nunes defense of Donald Trump can be summed up in one word: Innuendo. If you were teaching a class in innuendo, this would be the introductory course. It is totally lacking in substance or legal standing.

Its clear purpose is to smear everyone who gathered information, directly or indirectly, that relates to the Russian probe. It is designed to smear the FBI for bias. It blames Hillary Clinton for funding the so-called "Steele Dossier" that has been eating at Donald Trump since reports of its existence were leaked in late October 2016, in a report published in *Mother Jones*.

It was that dossier, a series of memos that tied Trump and his campaign to Russian activities, that first brought to public attention the possible collusion of the Trump campaign with Russian agents. American intelligence agencies were following these topics long before October 2016. Parts of the dossier have subsequently been established as factually accurate, while other parts remain unproven and highly controversial, including a report of Trump's activities with Russian prostitutes, the most salacious part of the dossier, but, in the end, perhaps not the most damning part. *Buzzfeed* published the entire dossier in January 2017 and it has been the subject of much controversy ever since, resulting in several lawsuits against *Buzzfeed*.

The Nunes Memo, only 3 ½ pages, not counting the cover letter of 1 ½ pages from Donald McGahn, Counsel to the President, spends a page attacking the Steele Dossier and blaming Hillary for it. But anyone who follows these matters in the press can instantly see how highly selective this memo is. It is true that as part of the opposition research conducted by the Democratic National Committee, Clinton campaign funds paid Christopher Steele, a well-respected former British intelligence officer, to look into Trump's connections with Russia. But the original research and the original hiring of Steele were done by conservative Republican Paul Singer who runs the "Washington Free Beacon" website. The Nunes memo leaves out this detail but anyone can Google it and find this information in 30-seconds.

The Nunes Memo gets fairly deep into the issue of how many Foreign Intelligence Surveillance Act (FISA) warrants were used to investigate the activities of Carter Page, a former-Trump adviser with Russian connections. The memo states that the House Intelligence Committee thinks these FISA warrants "represent a troubling breakdown of legal processes established to protect the American people...." But the memo does not prove what is so troubling. These classified warrants are not supposed to be publicly released. While no specific information is released in the memo, we are left with more innuendo that something is foul in the FBI.

FISA warrants come from a judge of the Foreign Intelligence Surveillance Court at the request of intelligence agencies like the FBI. The Nunes memo makes it clear that all the people in the FBI who have caused President Trump trouble are named as being involved in the warrants issued to investigate Carter Page. These include: James Comey, Andrew McCabe, Rod Rosenstein, and Sally Yates. This is pure innuendo because nothing is revealed that suggests the FISA process was abused.

I cannot see where this memo does anything but attempt to soothe the growing anxiety and fear in President Trump that the Mueller investigation is getting so close that they can hear Bob Mueller's footsteps in the hall outside the Oval Office.

This is a smear job with no content that would hold up in any court of law, or even in the court of public opinion. I expect if the Democratic members of the House Intelligence Committee are allowed to release their report, we will see a larger context that will put the Nunes memo in even worse light.

Shame on Chairman Nunes for acting with such partisanship about a matter that is of deep national concern. And shame on Speaker Paul Ryan for letting this go as far as it has. Nunes should be removed immediately from his role as chairman of this committee. The House Intelligence Committee is too important to be squandered on partisan politics.

This committee has every right to conduct oversight of the FBI, the Department of Justice, and all our intelligence gathering agencies, but this oversight should always be conducted to keep America safe, to be a watchdog of abuses in the intelligence community, and to investigate for the purpose of drafting laws that guard against abuse. This memo shows no abuse of power in the FBI, only the suggestion of it for partisan gain.

What Chairman Nunes has done is to ham-handedly try to protect President Trump during a vital, ongoing investigation. In doing so he comes so close to violating the rule of law and engaging in possible obstruction of justice. He clearly has violated all the regular procedures of his own committee. Since Nunes was part of the Trump transition team, maybe he too has something to hide. But this is just innuendo on my part.

The day after the Nunes memo became public, the president tweeted:

Donald J. Trump
@realDonaldTrump

This memo totally vindicates "Trump" in probe. But the Russian Witch Hunt goes on and on. Their was no Collusion and there was no Obstruction (the word now used because, after one year of looking endlessly and finding NOTHING, collusion is dead). This is an American disgrace!

9:40 AM - Feb 3, 2018

Truth, Lasting Values, and the Power of the People

February 5, 2018

On New Year's Eve 2017, former FBI Director James Comey, tweeted to the country, "Here's hoping 2018 brings more ethical leadership, focused on the truth and lasting values...." This message gets at the essential pillar on which good government is built. Director Comey's message was clearly aimed at the lack of ethics and the lack of truth that abound in the current political climate.

More than ever, people across the nation need a broad context to understand the unusual and dangerous political currents that swirl about us. Our political crisis is not something that emerged with the election of Donald J. Trump as President of the United States. Our national political system has suffered from a long series of events that have increased political polarization to the point where Republicans and Democrats are no longer political adversaries, but mortal enemies. When our politics becomes so overheated with hyper-partisanship, truth and the lasting values that the Founders gave us become seriously threatened.

We seem to have lost a common vision of what it means to be an American and what role our government should play in conducting its mission. What is government for? Read the 52-words of the Preamble to the Constitution and ponder their meaning. Look at the government as described in the U.S. Constitution and in our laws and court decisions over more than two centuries. Look at our rich military and civil traditions, and our shared values. We seem adrift from these things.

Can we honestly say that we adhere to what Lincoln said in his first inauguration about our common bonds? With the nation deeply divided, Lincoln appealed to all Americans to recall "The mystic chords of memory, stretching from every battlefield and patriot grave to every living heart and hearthstone all over this broad land, will yet swell the chorus of the Union, when again touched, as surely they will be, by the better angels of our nature."

The better angels of our nature reside not only in our common heritage, but in ethical behavior driven by a clear moral compass that can tell right from wrong. We must be seekers after truth. We must conduct political discourse in an ethical manner. We can argue constantly about how to conduct the policies of the nation. This is what politics is about. But despite our policy differences and our partisanship, we ought to be able to agree on proven facts. There is no such thing as an alternate fact. The nation could fail if we let our political discourse become nothing but a cynical House of Cards.

Since I was the director of a congressional center bearing the name of the late Senator Robert C. Byrd, I am often asked what Senator Byrd would say, and how he would react, to our current political challenges. Alas, he is no longer with us to provide his guidance. But he did leave behind a long history of his personal quest to learn about governance and the enduring values of the Founders. We can still listen to his stirring speeches.

We know from Senator Byrd's book *Losing America*, written long before President Trump was elected, that it is essential for Congress to stand up to reckless and arrogant presidents, no matter who that president might be. Congress was designed to be a check on presidential excesses and abuses of power. Senator Byrd was proud of the fact that he served with eleven U.S. presidents and he always reminded you that the word WITH, was the important word. He did not serve UNDER any president, of either party.

Our political crisis stems from multiple causes that are confusing even to experts who follow government regularly. Everyone I talk to, from both parties, is frustrated and deeply troubled by how far we seem to be from normal behavior from our government in Washington. In the executive branch we have the unprecedented case of a new president that had no prior experience in government when he was elected. Many of the president's cabinet appointments, likewise, have no prior experience in elective office at any level.

In Congress, there has been no "regular order" in how it conducts its business. You will hear experienced legislators from both parties call for "regular order." This means that Congress is supposed to legislate through a committee system and the bills that come out of committee reach the floor of the House and Senate, where they are openly debated and voted up or down.

This process is especially important in the creation and passage of an annual budget which sets the national priorities of how we allocate money to pay for everything from national defense, social security, law enforcement, immigration policy, and all the many things, large and small, that determine how our tax dollars are spent for the benefit of the entire country. We have not had regular order on all the appropriations bill in seven years. In recent years the annual budget of the United States gets passed piecemeal by short-term Continuing Resolutions. As I write this, we may be days away from a second government shutdown in the past two weeks.

We the People have the solemn duty to hold all elected officials to their oaths to defend the U.S. Constitution and if they can't live up to the task we have the power of the vote to correct the situation. While it is very easy to find things to criticize in government, perhaps there is an important part of this critique that we have neglected. Our criticism of what is wrong with government should begin to focus on what is wrong with the citizens of this country.

We citizens have the power to decide what kind of government we want. Do we want a truthful, ethical, responsible, and practical government, or do we like it the way it is? The public needs to arm itself with better information, with knowledge of what government is and should be. We need a free press to inform us about what government is doing.

While we should not have amateurs running the federal government, likewise we cannot have "amateur" citizens either. Citizenship is a birthright, or a right earned through the legal process of becoming a citizen. No other qualifications are necessary to say you are a citizen. But there are duties and responsibilities that go with citizenship. You can be a citizen in name only but this squanders your power. Political activists on the left and the right on the political spectrum go to rallies for their various causes and shout at Congress and the White House to do their jobs. Maybe we should look in the mirror and say the same thing. Citizens have jobs to do to make this country work.

A passive, ill-informed citizenry can easily lead to tyranny. For every activist out there, how many of you know friends, family, and associates, who say to you, "They are all a bunch of crooks and I don't want to bother with any of them." How many of you know people who don't bother to vote? More than 60% of Americans in several polls cannot name the three branches of the federal government. An even higher percentage doesn't know the duties of each branch of government.

James Madison said, "Knowledge will forever govern ignorance, and a people who mean to be their own governors, must arm themselves with the power knowledge gives. A popular government without popular information or the means of acquiring it, is but a prologue to a farce or a tragedy or perhaps both." If we are going to govern ourselves, if we expect to keep our republic and our freedom, we must be engaged citizens.

Un-American Behavior or First Amendment Right?

February 5, 2018

The arrogance of the president was on display again today in a speech he gave in Cincinnati, where he suggested that Democrats who failed to applaud during his State of the Union address were "un-American." The crowd in Cincinnati cheered their approval. Someone in the crowd yelled "treasonous," and the president said, "Yeah, why not? It was treasonous." I guess he thought he was the King going before his subjects when, in reality, he was the head of the executive branch going before the co-equal legislative branch to give a speech.

It is clear he does not know how these events work. The Republicans sat on their hands for eight years of Obama's addresses before Congress and now Democrats sit on their hands for Trump's. This is a long-standing method of quietly demonstrating opposition. I watched these spectacles in person during the administrations of Ronald Reagan, George H. W. Bush, and Bill Clinton. Members of both parties usually rise to their feet in applause when the topic has broad appeal. Last week, during Trump's first such speech, Democrats stood for the president's parade of heroes in the gallery. But they sat in silence the rest of the time, mostly in shock at what they were hearing.

Mr. President, do you think the Supreme Court justices who were in attendance and the Joint Chiefs who were there should stand and applaud your speech? They did the proper thing. They stood when you were introduced and they recognized you for the high office you hold. During the speech, however, they did not applaud. They did not stand. They honored your office, not your political speech. They did their jobs properly. Likewise, the Democrats stood when Trump was introduced as the president, in honor of the office. Then they sat for his speech, while the Republican side of the aisle gave the president dozens of standing ovations.

As partisanship in recent years has increased dramatically, the House chamber has reflected that change. Some Supreme Court justices find it difficult to attend because they do not like being thrust into such a public political spectacle. In 2010 Justice Alito was seen shaking his head and mouthing "not true" when President Obama spoke critically of the flood of money into politics that resulted from the Court's *Citizens United* decision. Justice Alito has not attended one of these events since then.

Only four of the nine justices attended Trump's first State of the Union address. In the television age, the high political theater of the State of the Union address magnifies every gesture of those gathered there. The cameras scan the room for scowls, for those on their cell phones, or even those dozing off. In the early days of televised coverage of these events, when the elderly John McCormack was speaker, we used to joke about how long he would stay awake during the speech. He never failed to doze off.

Trump's elevation of the Democrats behavior in quietly expressing their displeasure with his administration to that of a treasonous, un-American act was an escalation that goes beyond anything said before of either party. Trump sprays acid on our government and its institutions every time he opens his mouth. He corrodes government.

Presidents, when they come before Congress, are there at the invitation of the Congress. Trump cannot go to the Capitol uninvited. This is not a law; it is a long-standing tradition that signals the importance of separate branches of government. Our first president George Washington learned this lesson the hard way. He went to the Senate expecting them to ratify a treaty while he waited. The Senate decided it wanted to deliberate the matter. Washington left in a huff. But he would never have thought to call the Senate's action un-American, and certainly not treasonous. What kind of president talks the way Trump does? A president, of all people, should know the definition of treason and understand its serious consequences.

The President Discovers Due Process

February 13, 2018

The president's lack of moral and legal clarity is evident in his highly-selective application of the concept of due process. He appears to want fairness and due process of law for his friends and associates, and his White House staff, but he doesn't apply the concept to anyone else. And when he ignores important matters like security clearances he jeopardizes national security.

On February 10, the president tweeted:

People's lives are being shattered and destroyed by a mere allegation. Some are true and some are false. Some are old and some are new. There is no recovery for some-one falsely accused - life and career are gone. Is there no such thing any longer as Due Process?

With the removal from office of White House Secretary Rob Portman and Trump speechwriter David Sorenson, over allegations that they abused women, President Trump has continued to defend the men and to call for due process.

The president's hypocrisy is showing again. He certainly was not calling for due process when he shouted to cheering crowds during the campaign that Hillary Clinton should be jailed. "Lock her up!" candidate Trump would yell, "Lock her up!" This chant stretched from the campaign to the White House, with the president still referring to his former adversary as "Crooked Hillary."

Even more disturbing is Trump's long-standing pattern of pre-judging the guilt of those he dislikes, going back to 1989 and the sensational accusations and demands for punishment of the Central Park Five, accused and convicted of a crime of rape and murder that they did not commit. These five teenage African American/Hispanic men served years in jail before they were cleared by DNA evidence. At the time, Trump acted as a self-appointed judge, jury, and executioner, calling for the death penalty. He took out full page ads in New York newspapers demanding justice, his brand of justice.

Trump seems charitable in these matters only to his friends and only to certain white men, like Roger Ailes and Bill O'Reilly, whose sexual transgressions ended their careers recently. The president showed little interest in the career of Democratic Senator Al Franken, who was a thorn in the president's side most of the time. As far as I can tell the president has never urged due process for any of the accusers, including the nineteen women who have charged the president with improper sexual conduct, or the women who spoke out against Judge Roy Moore during his run for the U.S. Senate from Alabama. Trump said emphatically that Roy Moore was innocent because Moore had told him so.

The president, of all people, should recognize that in politics image is as important as reality and often image is the reality. It does not serve the president to have on his staff people who were discovered to be alleged sexual abusers. A "normal" president would fire such a person, once exposed, and not say another word about it. But Trump can't stop tweeting or defending these men before the cameras.

But here is the real problem with the Portman case and other top White House staffers in the Trump administration that goes way beyond that of which they have been accused. It was the due diligence of the FBI in doing background checks on Rob Portman and Jared Kushner and others that revealed serious irregularities that prevented these individuals from obtaining a permanent top security clearance.

The crime that the president does not want to talk about is how such senior positions were filled for so long by people who have failed to be cleared for top security jobs. Why are so many people in the Trump White House working in sensitive jobs at the highest levels of security on temporary clearances that should have expired long ago? This falls to the chief of staff and the legal counsel to explain why Rob Portman could see every piece of highly sensitive information without a final security clearance.

This goes back to the fundamental amateurism of the Trump White House from day one. It goes back before day one. From the time of the election of the president to the day he was sworn in was almost three months. There does not appear to be evidence that Trump expected to win the election. Once he did, he should have had the wheels turning instantly on top staff jobs and starting the security clearance process long before the inauguration on Jan. 20, 2017. This is the job of his transition team. But that team was in a state of flux from the beginning. Nobody seemed to know what to do. And there seemed to be Russians around every corner during the transition.

For these top clearances to still be unsettled for this long a time is clear indication that security concerns were not Trump's top priority, if he considered them at all. He surrounded himself with his own family. Recall the early days of the administration when each news day it seemed Jared Kushner was given a new assignment to fix the American government. Trump has always been afraid of people he does not trust, and he does not trust very many people. Rob Portman was apparently good at his job and was trusted by Trump and Chief-of-Staff John Kelly. Portman's lack of a security clearance was something they brushed aside. In doing so, they may have violated laws designed to protect our national security.

Trump's crocodile tears over the loss of a good man Rob Portman, his false concern with due process for the charges of spousal abuse, is just another shell game, another diversion from what is likely to turn out to be a major breach of national security. How long do we allow incompetent amateurs to play fast and loose with our safety? How long before the president's pleasure with John Kelly is lost and he too is shown the door? Will the president say that John Kelly is a great American and it is a shame he has to go? What will he say when he fires Kelly?

The Siberian Candidate

February 17, 2018

The release of the 36-page indictment of 13 Russian operatives who engaged in criminal acts inside the United States during the 2016 presidential election, got me thinking back to the 1962 movie, "The Manchurian Candidate," based on a 1959 book of the same title by Richard Condon.

In this film, an American soldier, captured during the Korean War, is brainwashed using advanced psychological techniques by Russian and Chinese agents. The brainwashed soldier was sent back to America where he resumed his life. But he was psychologically programmed to be an unwitting communist "sleeper agent." He was so deeply conditioned that when he was shown a playing card, the Queen of Hearts, he was supposed to follow orders, in this case to assassinate the President of the United States so a right-wing McCarthy-like dictator could take over America.

The book and the film came out during the Cold War with the Soviet Union and just a few years after the nation was set on edge by the bullying tactics of the anti-communist crusader Senator Joe McCarthy. Senator McCarthy and his sinister aide, Roy Cohn, went on a witch hunt to find communists in the State Department and other places. McCarthy did not care whose reputation he ruined in his effort to ferret out communists hiding in our government.

And speaking of Roy Cohn, he later became Donald Trump's lawyer and closest confidante, filling the same needs for Trump that he had for Joe McCarthy. When Richard Condon wrote his book, *The Manchurian Candidate*, he said the brainwashed soldier's mother, played by Angela Lansbury in one of the most devilishly sinister roles she ever played, was modeled after Roy Cohn!

McCarthyism added immensely to the anti-communist, anti-Soviet Union hysteria of the mid-to-late 1950s that was even more dramatic because the U.S. and the Soviet Union were engaged at the time in a colossal nuclear arms race.

Anti-communism became a mania in America that affected all aspects of American foreign policy and undermined domestic politics as well. Members of both major political parties in the U.S. could not get elected if they were branded as "soft on communism." This was often shortened to "comsymp" and applied mostly to liberals. To be sympathetic to communists was the kiss of death in politics.

A bit later in our history, presidents of both parties from Dwight Eisenhower through Lyndon Johnson were hellbent on stopping communists in Vietnam from taking over Southeast Asia and eventually spreading to the United States. The anti-communist mania cost the lives of 55,000 Americans and maimed many thousands more, ostensibly to stop the spread of communism.

Fast forward from the 1950s and 1960s to 2018. The Soviet Union is long gone but Russia is still our major adversary in the world at least in terms of military and ideological threats. It is still a communist country, but, ironically, it is run by billionaire oligarchs not unlike a crime syndicate. Russia may adhere to communism, but it runs on the capitalistic corruption of a handful of oil magnates and other monetary czars, all under the watchful eye of the Russian Godfather, Vladimir Putin.

China, our other communist antagonist from the 1950s, was feared not so much for its military threat to the West but for its economic and ideological reach and its vast population and dominance of Asia. China is still communist, but we don't fear it like we did during the Cold War. We can't afford to fear China anymore. The United States owes China more than $1.2 trillion dollars. China has made it possible for the United States to wage all its undeclared and continuous wars without raising taxes to pay for them. It might upset Americans who hate to pay taxes. We don't seem to get upset if our country borrows from a communist country. Each American household owes China more than $10,000. This is what it would take from each family in America to pay off this debt.

In 2018, the President of the United States seems to be in love with Vladimir Putin and he greatly appreciates China. Forget the way it used to be. If we follow the lead of our elected leader, we can all safely be called "comsymps" now and nobody will seem to mind. President Donald J. Trump is very sympathetic with Russia and with Putin—the one world leader he has never criticized.

Just weeks before Trump took the oath of office last year, Max Boot, the Russian-American journalist and historian who is senior fellow at the Council on Foreign Relations, wrote a piece in the *New York*

Times "Donald Trump: A Modern Manchurian Candidate?" [Jan. 11, 2017]. Boot was concerned that Trump had not distanced himself from Vladimir Putin.

Boot wrote, "Mr. Trump himself is doing nothing to dispel suspicions with his hyperbolic attacks and his denials that he has business interests in Russia — when his dealings there go back decades. He accused the intelligence agencies of releasing this 'fake news' to take 'one last shot' at him, and outrageously compared their acts to those of Nazi Germany — as if the Nuremberg Trials were held to punish the leaking of raw intelligence."

The critique that Max Boot laid out more than a year ago is still a key concern. Donald Trump has never found any way to "dispel suspicions" regarding his connections with Russia, going back for many decades, or in more recent times during the presidential campaign and since Trump has been president. Trump has continued to deny, deny, deny any collusion with Russia. But after yesterday's indictment of Russian operatives, he can no longer play down the "meddling" of Russians in the American elections. Yet he still considers them fake, fabricated, and totally unfair to him.

In my book, *Trump Tsunami*, I wrote about how utterly unfathomable it was that Trump, who by nature criticized everything in sight, could not ever say a critical word about Russia or Putin. By the summer of 2017, the American press and most observers and journalists were beginning to connect a lot of the dots that tied Russians to the Trump campaign. We were finding out in public many of the things that U.S. intelligence services had reported before Trump's inauguration and that they knew parts of even earlier.

In August last year I said the Russian connection was an albatross around Trump's neck. I wrote, "The albatross...will continue to rot and drag him down.... If Trump tries to rid himself of this Russian curse by firing Robert Mueller, he will discover that the albatross around his neck will tighten and strangle him. Trump acts as if he knows this already. The curse torments him daily. We are witnessing its corrosive effects."

The release of the Mueller investigation indictment of 13 Russian agents yesterday changes just about everything. It is a very big new piece of this Russian/Trump campaign puzzle. It is not the whole story. Not yet. But it confirms just about everything that has connected the Trump campaign to Russian influence.

It should have silenced the president from claiming this is a witch hunt, but it didn't. The president, following the rulebook he learned from Roy Cohn, doubled down on his denial that there was any collusion with Russia and he said the new Mueller indictment proves there was no collusion. Trump obviously has not read the indictment. Our president sounded just like the Russian Foreign Minister Sergey Lavrov, who said the Mueller indictment was " just blabber." Trump seized on the fact that the Russian meddling in the 2016 election began as early as 2014 and therefore it is Obama's fault.

This new indictment is a bombshell for a lot of reasons. It connects the dots with some of the much-maligned Steele Dossier, and it reveals details that our intelligence community has known for some time.

And it shows how gullible some American citizens can be when they are blinded by their own hyper-partisanship. Some Americans got duped big time by Russians posing as Americans. And all of us on social media probably were exposed to Russian "information warfare" without recognizing it as such. A critic of P.T. Barnum said, "There is a sucker born every minute." Hello suckers!

This new indictment helps educate the American public about the seriousness of the charges that our president has done everything in his power to cover up and to pretend they never happened. I am still studying the full indictment. I am listening to and reading the analysis of this indictment that is dominating the news. I will be watching social media for what other Americans are saying about this indictment. Sometimes big news takes a while before we can fully absorb it.

Presidents Day 2018

February 18, 2018

On the eve of Presidents Day, the current president of the United States, ensconced in his gilded palace in Florida, just 40 miles from the scene of the latest mass school shooting, went on a Twitter rampage that the press is calling a "Twitter Storm."

In this series of 14 strange and often delusional tweets over less than two days, the president damned the FBI for wasting its time on the Russian probe and for dropping the ball and not detecting the shooter at Parkland High School. Earlier, the FBI had admitted that their protocol on detecting potential school shooters was not followed in this case.

Presidents, being the chief law enforcement officers of the United States, are not prone to discuss the specifics of ongoing investigations, and presidents of the United States are not prone to attacking American law enforcement. But Trump is different, and some people seem to like the fact that he talks just like they do. These are apparently the folks who comprise Trump's base. To the base he can do no wrong. The base apparently acts a lot like a religion. You buy into the whole thing and believe it, or you don't.

Trump has been feeling nervous lately, and the tweets are the best evidence of it, in the wake of Robert Mueller's indictment of 13 Russians and three Russian companies for their illegal activities inside the United States. The indictment clearly shows that American election laws and other laws were violated by Russian agents who stole American identities and falsified documents to get visas to enter the United States for the purpose of disrupting the presidential election.

Once Trump was nominated, the plan was to back Trump and work against Hillary Clinton. The money spent on the American campaign by those charged in the indictment was in violation of election laws and their activities constituted fraud. In doing what they did, they engaged in an illegal conspiracy.

These "fake" Americans did interact with Trump campaign officials in several states, but the indictment does not state that this was collusion, per se, because it was unwitting. The Trump campaign people in some of the incidents cited in Florida and Texas, did not know they were being duped by Russians pretending to be Americans for Trump.

This was enough for President Trump to send out Sarah Huckabee Sanders and others to continue the refrain "No collusion." The president himself said the same thing and continued to deny collusion with Russians. According to the president the Russian meddling is something concocted by Hillary Clinton and the Democrats because "They needed an excuse" for losing the election.

One White House spokesman, the Deputy White House Press Secretary, who I had never seen before, a young man named Hogan Gidley, spoke for the president and focused on the fact that the Russians started their plan in 2014, before Trump got into the race, proving it was not about Trump. Mr. Gidley giddily thought his brilliant analysis was proof that Trump was not involved with Russians. Mr. Gidley was a top GOP campaign operative before assuming his current post.

Today, on the eve of Presidents Day, another bomb dropped on the White House and was felt as far away as Mar-a-Lago. Rick Gates, the longtime partner of one-time Trump campaign manager Paul Manafort, is expected to plead guilty to fraud in the next few days according to the *Los Angeles Times*. He had been indicted earlier on counts of conspiracy, money laundering, failure to register as a foreign agent, and for failure to disclose financial statements. This pending plea includes his agreement to testify against Paul Manafort. This case will be about following the money that flowed into the Trump campaign from Russian sources.

Collusion itself is not a crime. Trump knows this. He sticks with "No Collusion" because it is vague and general. Money laundering is a crime. Having your hand-picked campaign chairman allegedly engaging in funneling foreign money into your campaign, is not about collusion, it is about violation of the law.

Rick Gates was caught up in charges that could have sent him to jail for a long time if proven true. When he cops a plea, Mueller can go after a bigger fish, Paul Manafort. The plot thickens again. The walls of the White House seem to be closing in. Time for another Twitter Storm from our leader. Time to send out Sarah Sanders and the whole White House Communications Office. I can't wait to hear what the kid Hogan Gidley has to say on Presidents Day. I do hope the president sends him in front of the cameras again. He is almost as good as Sarah Huckabee Sanders in deflecting reality.

The President's Snakes

February 24, 2018

D uring the presidential campaign Donald Trump would occasionally pull a sheet of paper from his suit coat pocket that contained the lyrics of a 1968 rock and roll song "The Snake," performed by Al Wilson.

When Trump first started using this story it was to warn about the danger of the United States taking in refugees from the war in Syria. Yesterday, the president departed from his prepared remarks at the Conservative Political Action Committee (CPAC) annual meeting at Harbor Place in Maryland to tell the story again. It was obviously a planned departure from the canned Teleprompter speech because Trump had the lyrics with him in his pocket.

Before reading the lyrics, he cautioned the assembly of hardline conservatives that some people liked the story in the lyrics and some people didn't like it, but he didn't care. The horrible people of the press who were covering his speech would have their way with it anyway. He told the audience what he wanted them to be thinking about as he read the lyrics with as much theatrical flare as he could muster. It was about immigration.

The story goes like this: A woman, out walking on a frosty morning, finds a partially frozen snake. She takes pity on the snake, takes it home, feeds it milk and honey and wraps it in a silk blanket, and goes about her business. Later, she discovers to her immense joy that the snake is fully recovered, and it is a beautiful snake. She hugs it to her bosom. The snake, a sinister creature, proceeds to bite the woman who rescued it. As she is dying from the bite, she wonders aloud why, after she was so kind to the snake, that it turned on her. And the snake replies: "'Oh shut up, silly woman,' said the reptile with a grin, 'you knew damn well I was a snake before you took me in.'"

This is a variation on old folk tales in European and African cultures, perhaps best known from the Aesop's Fable "The Farmer and the Viper," but also from the story of the frog who gives a ride to a scorpion to keep it from drowning. Naturally, the scorpion stings the frog, the frog dies, the scorpion drowns, because it was the nature of the scorpion to sting the frog. I am not sure President Trump knows anything about the story's origins. What he does know is how to use it for his own demagogic purposes.

Immigrants are dangerous reptiles. We may think we are being kind to take them in and give them blankets and food and think we are saving them. But you should never bring a snake to your bosom because it will bite you and kill you. Trump completely understands how he wants the moral of the story to go. All his followers need to accept Trump's thesis is to believe that human beings fleeing civil war, economic strife, political persecution, or seeking religious freedom, safe refuge and opportunities for better lives, are nothing but snakes.

Trump's use of this fable is a classic case of xenophobia. He has demonstrated throughout his campaign, and even before, that he is not particularly fond of foreigners coming to the United States unless they meet his strict criteria, which includes exclusion from Muslim countries. Without referring specifically to immigrants from Mexico, he did reiterate at the CPAC meeting yesterday, that other countries "don't send us their best." He did not repeat his campaign charge that Mexicans are rapists and criminals in the CPAC speech, but he did single out Salvadoran gangs in the United States who belong to MS-13. Once he referred to this gang he could not stop himself from going all the way into demagoguery and fear mongering about this gang and their vicious tactics. I am no defender of gangs that commit crimes. When members of such gangs commit crimes, they should face the law and be prosecuted. What we need in any such discussion of gang violence is some perspective and specifics rather than the broad brush that Trump used to suggest that any Salvadoran in the United States is probably a gang member. Trump's wall on the Mexico border would keep out these gangs, he said.

Trump cited specific examples of crimes involving the MS-13 gang, who he described as so vicious they do not use guns. They use knives to hack their victims into little pieces, the president said. He cited an immigrant who drove his car into a group of joggers in New York City killing and maiming more than a dozen people. Trump pointed out that this criminal came to America in a "chain migration" that brought twenty-two members of his family to this country.

Tens of thousands of Americans are dying in an opioid/heroin epidemic, tens of thousands more die in gun violence every year, and

Trump singles out two crimes committed by immigrants to prove that all of them are vicious snakes. And if this wasn't enough, he turned his wrath on Democrats who harbor these criminals in so-called sanctuary cities. It is liberals and Democrats who want to pull the snake to their bosom. It is Democrats who are the kindly lady in the snake story (think Nancy Pelosi) who are so misguided that they don't know the harm they are doing by supporting immigrants.

This is far beyond the textbook definition of xenophobia as a fear of foreigners. It incorporates racism and a concept of racial purity that has no place in the world and no place in American politics. The snake had a "nature" about it. The snake had a genetic predisposition to bite the hand that fed it. Immigrants, the snake-like kind that Trump sees, are not of the right "nature." Their genes are not right. They don't have American genes. Our "American heritage" that he talks about is a white Christian heritage.

Immigrants, unless they are white people from Scandinavia, will poison the American gene pool. Trump is against immigration and wants to deport many who are already here in a last-ditch effort to keep America white. Like St. Patrick, who miraculously drove the snakes out of Ireland, Trump wants to be the one who drives all the snakes out of America. He wants us to believe that certain human beings are not human at all, they are reptiles to be stomped on. And, I am sorry to report, a substantial number of his supporters think this is the right thing to do.

Democrats Collude with the U.S. Government!

February 25, 2018

Perhaps the strangest comment yesterday about the release of the minority report of the House Intelligence Committee came from the committee's chairman, the much beleaguered and controversial Devin Nunes. He and the other Republican members of the committee had earlier issued a 3 ½ page memorandum that accused the FBI of abusing the power of the FISA Court by going after Carter Page, an American close to the Trump campaign with ties to the Russian government.

The memorandum accused the FBI of being in cahoots with the Clinton campaign, which had paid a former British intelligence officer, Christopher Steele, to do opposition research on Donald Trump, which resulted in the controversial and salacious Steele Dossier, the stuff of spy novels. The Nunes memorandum said that the FBI authorized payment to Steele for the Dossier, proving the FBI was pro-Clinton during the campaign.

On Feb. 24, shortly after the release of the Democrats answer to the Nunes memorandum, Chairman Nunes sought immediately to discredit it. He saw the Democrats' report as proof that the Democratic members of his committee are trying to cover up improper actions by the FBI in their investigation of Carter Page. He said of the Democrat response to his memorandum, "It's clear evidence that the Democrats are not only covering this up, but they're also colluding with parts of the government to cover this up." [As reported in the *Washington Post*, Feb. 24, 2018].

All I can say in response to the Nunes statement is that I am sure glad to know that at least one of the major political parties in the United States "colludes" with its own government rather than colluding with Russia. Methinks the word "collude" is overused these days.

The fact that the House Intelligence Committee is so badly divided is, perhaps, the worst aspect of this sordid tale. This is an important committee and its members have usually worked in public harmony, keeping their internal differences within the committee. This committee has oversight of a huge part of the U.S. Intelligence Community, a large and diverse conglomerate of both military and civilian intelligence gathering. This committee's work is, by its very nature, often secret because they deal with secrets. They do conduct public hearings and it is their job to call intelligence agency heads to come before them, under oath, to help inform the public on issues of great national concern and to keep the intelligence agencies accountable to Congress, which they are required to be, by law.

The release yesterday of the report of the Democratic minority on the House Intelligence Committee, titled "Correcting the Record—The Russia Investigations" does clarify certain things. It provides a better context for the dispute between the Republican majority of the House Intelligence Committee, led by the deeply partisan actions of Chairman Nunes and the Democratic minority on that committee led by Ranking Member Adam Schiff (D-CT).

The Democratic report challenges the assertions of the Republicans that the FBI has been engaged in wrong-doing in how the agency handled the court-ordered surveillance of Carter Page, a gadfly character who has been in and out of Russia and in and out of the orbit of the Trump campaign. Page was a target for recruitment of Russian intelligence for several years before the Trump campaign and Page lived in Russia from 2004 to 2007. He was well known to the FBI long before the Trump campaign. But interest in him increased in 2016, when he became a foreign affairs adviser to the Trump campaign, and Page continued to make trips to Russia. While the Republicans assert that it was the dastardly Steele Dossier that caused Carter Page to come under surveillance, the truth is the FBI had been watching Page and his connections with Russia going back to 2013, long before the presidential campaign began. The Steele Dossier had nothing to do with it.

The Nunes memo stated the FBI was authorized to pay Christopher Steele for his work on the Dossier and left it vague, as if the FBI did pay Steele, thus making a connection with the FBI and the Clinton campaign. Hillary is paying Steele and so is the FBI, is the connection Rush Limbaugh made on his radio broadcast of Feb. 9.

The Democratic memo shows that while the FBI was authorized to pay Steele, a known source of reliable information as a Russian expert in other cases, the FBI never paid Steele for his work on the Dossier. But they certainly had paid him for earlier work on other cases. He was a known, reliable resource on Russia.

The Democratic report also addresses the news frenzy surrounding the FBI agent Peter Strzok and his emails with an FBI lawyer Lisa Page, with whom Strzok was romantically involved. The Republicans have blown this into a major scandal showing the bias of the FBI against Trump because of things Strzok and Page said about the president in private emails. Nunes tried to tie Strzok to information presented to the FISA Court to get permission to surveil Carter Page, but neither Strzok nor Lisa Page were involved in the FISA process.

Nunes also accused Strzok and Lisa Page of leaking information to the press, a serious violation, if proven. The Democratic report states that the majority members of the House Intelligence Committee "demonized" these career officials by cherry picking their emails to find bias when, in truth, the emails were typical of what many individuals say in private about public officials. There is no indication that their private comments affected their professional work. But to be safe, Special Prosecutor Mueller removed Strzok from the investigation team and announced this openly and publicly.

It remains a mystery to me why Chairman Devin Nunes is still chairman of his committee. You will recall in March 2017 Nunes ran to the White House supposedly with information about the FBI gathering electronic evidence from a FISA warrant on members of the Trump campaign and possibly Trump himself. It now appears as if it was the White House that provided Nunes with this information and the Chairman willingly acted to release this bombshell to the press.

The FISA warrants are not something for public discussion. Nunes ignored and violated the practice of his own committee. When a firestorm occurred in the press, Nunes did recuse himself from the Russian investigation. But eventually he was back in charge and earlier this year Nunes and the Republican majority released their memo accusing the FBI of colluding with the Clinton campaign. They did this without consulting the minority, a rare move for the Intelligence Committee. It reeked of partisanship. If there were any signs of bias going on, it was coming from the Republican majority of the House Intelligence Committee.

Nunes then did everything in his power to stop the Democrats from rebutting the Nunes memo. His committee voted on a party line vote not to allow the Democrats to rebut the majority memo. But it was eventually released just yesterday after the FBI held it for two weeks and made additional redactions to the document. Earlier, President Trump had refused to release the Democrats' rebuttal.

Chairman Nunes has been a poison pill in this investigation. He has muddied the waters, accused the FBI of bias against President Trump, and for partisan gain he has exposed procedures of the FISA Court and the FISA warrant process involving specific cases related to the Russian investigation that seriously damage his own committee. It also damages the work of the intelligence community, especially the FBI. I can only conclude that Nunes is acting as a stormtrooper in President Trump's attempt to derail the ongoing investigations because they are getting too damn close to the president, and perhaps to others in the Trump campaign, people who were part of the Trump White House, and some who still work there.

It is a shame that both these memos had to see light of day. But they are revealing of the many ways in which the truth can be distorted. They show how half-truths work to mislead as much as outright lies. In my book, *Trump Tsunami*, I speculated that Nunes action to undermine the work of his own committee was done on purpose. He is not seeking to conduct a fair and thorough investigation. Instead of an impartial chairman, Nunes has sided with Trump and is using his committee to impede the investigations of the FBI. What other explanation can there be?

Trade Wars via Dictatorship

March 3, 2018

It is getting harder to judge which of the president's actions are more damaging to the nation. But there is no doubt that his capricious, dictatorial declaration of new tariffs on imported steel and aluminum are right up at the top of everything that is wrong with this president and his administration.

The arbitrary, off-handed way in which the president announced his new tariffs stunned everyone, except, perhaps, Secretary of Commerce Wilbur Ross and Trump's billionaire friend Carl Ichan, who managed to sell off millions of dollars in steel stock in the last two weeks with the final transaction coming one day before Trump's announcement. Special Counsel Robert Mueller may have one more thing to investigate.

Commerce Secretary Wilbur Ross, one of Trump's closest billionaire friends, who, like so many other cabinet members, is totally lacking in previous government service, has been pushing the steel and aluminum tariff idea for some time. Ross seems to have friends in the steel business who will see short term gains in their bottom lines if the new tariff on steel is imposed. Maybe the best explanation is kleptocracy, to cash in before the Trump administration collapses. Carl Icahn was, until recently, one of Trump's advisers on deregulation, but resigned because of potential conflicts of interest.

I don't claim any expertise in American commerce or trade policy. I am sure I will learn more in the weeks ahead from those who do know this field. What I do know, or thought I knew, is how government usually works in fashioning such a major event as a heavy new tariff on essential commodities like steel and aluminum. Whatever knowledge I once had about how government works has changed completely since Trump became president. Everything I learned and observed over the past half-century about government and how it works just flew right out the window.

The president announced his steel and aluminum tariffs without any serious advance study of the complexities of such a move. He did not consult Congress—not the leaders of the House and Senate or the appropriate congressional committees that have jurisdiction in matters of commerce. He did not consult in advance our closest allies and trading partners, Canada and Mexico, or any other of our allies and trading partners who will be affected. He makes insane comments about trade wars being easily winnable and tweeted that trade wars are a good thing. In imposing these stiff tariffs, he flies in the face of conservative orthodoxy for the past forty years that has upheld the idea of free trade as essential to a strong American economy. Trump knows nothing of the history of trade wars that inevitably lead to disaster with nobody winning. The mere announcement of the new tariffs has caused big losses in the stock market.

Yesterday Secretary of Commerce Ross held up a soup can and said the new tariff on steel would only slightly increase the cost of the can, as if it was nothing to worry about. Maybe he should have held up an automobile, or a steel bridge, many of which are in dire need of repair. If an aluminum can of Budweiser goes up a fraction of a penny, who cares? But this one company produces tens of billions of bottles and cans of beer each year. Somebody will pay. That somebody is always the consumer. A piece of Trump's so-called middle-class tax cut just went to pay for your beer cans, not to mention the cost of a new car, which is far more serious. Cars use less steel than they used to, but more aluminum. Either way, the consumer will pay.

I am waiting for Congress to wake up and do its part to check and balance this runaway president, who by all indications has just about come unglued. His White House staff is in full retreat. Even his own family members are falling out of favor. When Trump is cornered, he has a history of lashing out. He is a counterpuncher at his own admission. He is trying to control things with diversionary tactics. He is on the ropes and needs something dramatic to get back in the center of the ring.

Perhaps he sees his arbitrary tariffs as a sign that he is in charge, doing his job. He has always believed he was the smartest person in the room. Why would he trust experts to tell him what to do on something as complex as international trade in major commodities. He sold real estate. He sold the Trump brand. That was his business.

The arbitrary nature of the announcement of the new tariffs just might be the wake-up call that Congress needs. Presidents do not usually engage in tariff matters so directly unless there is a national emergency. What emergency is there that warrants these new tariffs?

All the members of the House and Senate should get out a copy of the U.S. Constitution and turn to Article One, Sec. 8, where it lists the powers of Congress. How clear can it get? This section begins: "The Congress shall have Power To lay and collect Taxes, Duties, Imposts, and Excises, to pay the Debts and provide for the common Defence and General Welfare of the United States..." In that same section of the Constitution it states that among the powers of Congress is the regulation "of Commerce with foreign Nations...." If you look at Article Two of the Constitution, which lays out the powers of the president, you will not find one word about the president's power to arbitrarily impose tariffs. Does anybody look at the Constitution anymore?

Sally Sells Sea Shells in the Seychelles

March 9, 2018

The Russian investigations are getting to be a real tongue twister. It is a gigantic collusion puzzle with complex connections stretching around the world from London, the United Arab Emirates, Russia, and far out into the remote reaches of the tropical Seychelles Islands, 1,400 miles out into the Indian Ocean off the coast of Tanzania. Globetrotting spy James Bond never made it to the Seychelles.

Maybe I should start with a joke to lighten the story. Four guys walk into a bar in the Seychelles on January 11, 2017, just nine days before President Trump's inauguration. One is an American, Erik Prince, founder of the paramilitary company Blackwater, who happens to be the brother of President-elect Trump's nominee to be Secretary of Education, Betsy DeVos. The other is Prince Mohammed Bin Zayed of the Emirates, who, a month earlier, had met with Jared Kushner at Trump Tower. The third man is Kirill Dmitriev, a Russian, who manages a $10 billion fund under the control of Vladimir Putin. The fourth man, George Nader, an operative for the Emirate prince, who also attended meetings at Trump Tower. He was arrested recently by the FBI and is now cooperating with the investigation.

What a nice coincidence that these gentlemen all decided to go this remote spot in the Indian Ocean to get a drink at a bar. It took them all many hours of flying time to go so far for a half hour meeting at a bar. I wonder how long they stayed. Were they on family vacations with the wife and kids and with their beach towels and sandals? Or did they fly half way around the world just to have a drink and then fly home?

Erik Prince says he went to the Seychelles to meet with some former business associates from the Emirates, and while they were at a bar, his business associates introduced him to the Russian. Prince apparently was not expecting to meet a Russian, but he was polite and had a drink with the guy. Prince had a beer with the Russian. He thinks the Russian may have had vodka.

That's it. That's the punch line of the joke about four guys who go into a bar in the Seychelles. This is what Erik Prince told the House Intelligence Committee, while he was under oath. If we believe this meeting took place in one of the most remote regions of the tropical world was a casual coincidence, then the joke is on us.

I am sure someone with a better comedic flair than mine can start out with the line about four guys walking into a bar and make it truly funny. This was funny business, for sure, not that the business they were doing was at all funny.

There are some things that bother me about this because I am not a world traveler like Arab princes, wealthy Americans, and Russian bankers. I would have a dickens of a time figuring out how to get to the Seychelles and deciding which of the 150 islands was best. I think the airlines fly to the island Mahé. Maybe this main island has the best bars. It is not easy to get there. Only a handful of airlines can get you there. Several of them are from Arab countries. If Erik Prince wanted to meet with his friends from the Emirates, why didn't he just fly to Dubai, or Abu Dhabi? If he wanted upscale restaurants and fancy bars and palm trees, they could have met in Palm Jumeirah. This would have saved a lot of airfare for all these gentlemen.

Maybe, just maybe, they were not interested in the quality of the bar at all. Maybe they were more interested in a place where electronic surveillance, FBI agents, or the snooping eyes of spy satellites would be less likely than in the UAE, or just about anywhere else in the world.

There were stories in the press about a December 2016 meeting between Jared Kushner and Russian Ambassador Sergey Kislyak about setting up a back channel for communications between Trump and Putin. Even Ambassador Kislyak seemed surprised at Kushner's audacity in wanting a secret back channel that no one would know about.

Months went by with this story going nowhere because the meeting was seemingly isolated. No particular dots were connected to it. By May 2017, however, stories re-emerged on this subject and again were played down. We were told that many countries have back-channel communications and this is not particularly unusual. Some of the stories suggested that perhaps the inexperienced Jared Kushner was just being sloppy in how he went about developing the back channel.

It seems as if we have been excusing Jared Kushner for his amateurism in government for a long time now. He has made a mess of every assignment his father-in-law has given him. It is too bad Jared wasn't actually at the meeting in the Seychelles because that would have tied the package up with a red ribbon. But it would have been too obvious to send Jared, so Erik Prince went instead, supposedly as a surrogate for President-elect Trump. If Prince was acting as on behalf of Trump, or any other Trump campaign official, then the plot really does thicken into collusion stew, with a dash of conspiracy on the side.

This story has indeed intensified and is now a central piece of the collusion puzzle. It is so important that it has kept the Stormy Daniels sex scandal from dominating the news, although sex scandals usually take precedence over spy stories, or stories of intrigue in remote parts of the world.

When the FBI nabbed George Nader and got him before a grand jury, his story was quite different from that of Erik Prince. The meeting in the Seychelles was set up in advance for the specific purpose of discussing a secret back channel between Trump and Putin. It was not the Emirate prince who incidentally introduced the Russian to Erik Prince. They all knew who would be there. What the Russians wanted, according to Nader, was a lifting of sanctions on Russia and a return to normal trade. Just what Trump wanted out of the deal is not yet clear, other than a secret way to talk to his friend Vladimir.

The big question remains unanswered. If this was nothing more than a diplomatic effort to establish a legitimate back channel communication between Russia and the United States, why, after meetings took place on this earlier in Trump Tower, did these men feel the need to fly to such a remote place to plan for this effort? If it was a legitimate, above board diplomatic mission, why didn't the State Department handle this? Why was it so clandestine? I can only surmise that it was because Trump wanted a truly secret back channel, so he and Putin could speak without our own government knowing about it. No collusion, no collusion, says our president at every opportunity.

A Government of One

March 9, 2018

Donald Trump got the idea that he wanted to meet with North Korea's Kim Jung Un. According to reports from NBC and the *Washington Post*, this idea seemed to come to him while a South Korean national security delegation was in the White House meeting with National Security Adviser H. R. McMaster, Defense Secretary James Mattis, National Intelligence Director Dan Coates, and others.

When Trump found out about the meeting, he interrupted it and told the South Koreans that he wanted to meet with the North Korean leader. The South Koreans alerted Trump to the fact that Kim Jong Un wanted to meet with an American president. Trump was thrilled. He authorized the Korean delegation to speak for him about arranging a meeting in May. Shortly afterwards, Trump stuck his head into the White House press room, where he never goes, and said that a big announcement was coming at 7 PM and for the press to get ready.

Shortly after 7 PM, three Koreans, led by the head of the South Korean National Security Office, Chung Eui-yong, appeared in the parking lot outside the White House before a mass of reporters and cameras, where a brief statement was read about a meeting to be scheduled between the two leaders. The Koreans turned abruptly after reading the statement and re-entered the White House without taking questions. This was like something from an Alice in Wonderland tea party with the Mad Hatter. The American press awaiting an announcement from the President of the United States, in the White House parking lot, with three South Koreans delivering the message.

Pandemonium broke out. What the hell had just happened? Other than a few people around Trump, nobody knew this was in the works because there had been no advance planning. It happened so fast it was like a case of spontaneous combustion. President Trump got a bee in his hairdo and decided a meeting with Rocket Man was just the ticket. The Secretary of State was out of the country and not told in advance. Nobody at the Pentagon knew about this.

None of diplomatic apparatus of government, none of the expertise of the government, none of the national security people, none of our diplomats, and no foreign heads of state knew of this until it happened. No nation in modern history has ever gone into major international negotiations with an adversary power without an agenda and without advance planning.

Trump has no top North Korean experts in his administration, the best one quit just last week. We don't even have an ambassador to South Korea right now. When Trump imposed upon three South Korean officials to speak for him, he ignored his entire government. He acted as a dictator. Imagine sending three South Koreans out into the White House parking lot to spring on the world of a potentially earth-shattering, unprecedented announcement.

No American president has met face to face with the North Korean regime. While it may offer the bold possibility of some success in easing tensions on the Korean peninsula, given President Trump's total lack of knowledge of international diplomacy and nuclear weapons this could be a totally insane proposition. It seems to be merely another Reality TV ploy designed to focus world attention on Donald Trump.

Such a meeting could worsen conditions and exacerbate the dangerous shouting match between two giant egos like Kim Jung Un and Donald Trump. Just why Trump suddenly decided on this meeting with North Korea has everyone speculating. On MSNBC's Morning Joe today, Joe Scarborough suggested Trump did this as a diversion to keep the Stormy Daniels sex scandal out of the news cycle. Morning Joe co-host Mika Brzezinski said the president was the "king of deflection."

Some news analysts are saying this could be simply another wild presidential pronouncement like the time he unilaterally declared that the military would no longer take transgender recruits. It could be like his equally wild and idiotic application of tariffs on steel and aluminum. Since that announcement, Trump has backed down and said Canada and Mexico are temporarily exempt, and that he would be willing to negotiate with other countries that have a problem with these new tariffs.

No one person can run the United States government. It has never been possible and it never will be possible. Who the hell does Trump think he is to even try? This is malfeasance in office, a total dereliction of duty and an insult to every person in the government. It will now be up to the adults in government to find a way to either neutralize this planned visit with North Korea, or to scramble to put the best face on this ugly mess.

In 1994, President Bill Clinton entered into a controversial deal with North Korea to supply them with much needed oil if the North Koreans would cease the development of nuclear weapons. An agreement was reached that was not a treaty, so it did not need Senate ratification. The North Koreans shut down their plutonium operations and we sent them billions of dollars of oil.

Clinton thought this was a good deal to end North Korea's nuclear program. Once President George Bush was in office he reneged on the deal claiming North Korea was cheating, which they were. They had stopped plutonium production but increased enriched uranium production leading to the creation of a few nuclear bombs. North Korea has ignored the Nuclear Non-Proliferation Treaty since that time and has continued its nuclear weapons program and heightened development of ballistic missile delivery systems.

Any negotiations with North Korea would be fraught with peril and given Trump's short attention span, he is not going to be able to negotiate a deal. That will have to be done by experts from both sides, in a series of negotiations that might take years and involve other nations including South Korea, Japan, and China.

As president, Trump could set a positive tone for serious negotiations but so far he has been totally unable to sustain anything but chaos. The only tone he has set with North Korea is to insult their leader and threaten to annihilate them if they extend their ballistic missile program and their nuclear bomb testing.

While writing this essay, I checked the news again late this afternoon and it looks like cooler heads have already prevailed in walking back this May summit meeting between the United States and North Korea. According to reports now coming in, the president still wants to talk but not until there are some concessions from North Korea, which I interpret to mean that there will be no talks any time soon. But who knows, the talks with North Korea may be on again in the next news cycle.

President Trump seems to have been pulled back from the brink of disaster. How long will we have to wait before the next outbreak of presidential chaos? The president is so isolated in the White House and so understaffed that he seems to be bouncing off the walls looking for something presidential to do. He is not serving himself well in this chaos and he is seriously damaging the credibility of the United States. The United States does not deserve a place as the leader of the free world with him in office.

Confronting a Reckless and Arrogant Presidency

March 12, 2018

T he title for this essay needs some explanation. I am sure you thought I was referring to President Trump. I will write about Trump in a minute, but first a word about an earlier president and a senator who fought against him. The title of my entry is taken from the subtitle of a book written by Senator Robert C. Byrd (D-WV) in 2004, called *Losing America*.

Senator Byrd wrote that book as a critique of President George W. Bush and his reckless and arrogant actions that got us into the Iraq War in 2003. Senator Byrd was one of 23 senators who voted against that war, largely on the grounds that we rushed into it without ever debating it in Congress. We know today that the reasons for launching that war were based on lies about weapons of mass destruction that were never there.

A few days ago I took a visitor on a tour of the Robert C. Byrd Center for Congressional History and Education, where we are the custodians of Senator Byrd's extensive collection of papers. In the course of the tour, I picked off the shelf Senator Byrd's personal read-ing copy of *Losing America*. Everything that Senator Byrd read, whether it was the Bible, a book on Roman history, or even his own writing, is filled with underlining in red, and sometimes double underling in red and black. Senator Byrd didn't just read things, he devoured them, often memorizing key passages.

When I opened the book, a card fell out with a printed statement on it. It was not in Senator Byrd's handwriting. This is what it said:

"I AM THE COMMANDER—SEE, I DON'T NEED TO EXPLAIN—I DON'T NEED TO EXPLAIN WHY I SAY THINGS. THAT'S THE INTERESTING THING ABOUT BEING THE PRESIDENT. MAYBE SOMEBODY NEEDS TO EXPLAIN TO ME WHY THEY SAY SOMETHING, BUT I DON'T FEEL LIKE I OWE ANYBODY AN EXPLANATION."

A little research on my part tracked this down. It was from a Bob Woodward interview with President Bush that appeared in the *Washington Post* on Nov. 19, 2002, while the debate on going to war was raging in Washington. It also appeared in Woodward's book *Bush at War*. The statement certainly captures the idea of how an arrogant president might see himself.

This reminds us that Donald Trump is not our first arrogant and reckless president. He is not the first president to think that being president makes him somehow detached from any process to be deliberative, cautious, or balanced. The statement indicates that a president can pretty much do anything he wants without explaining his actions. He leaves it to others to do the explaining.

Presidents who come to this highest of offices with the least of experience are probably the ones who will think this way. It becomes a defense mechanism for their ignorance. It can stop a reporter, a congressperson, or a cabinet officer in his or her tracks if the president feels he owes no explanation for a policy or for what he might say or do.

George W. Bush, unlike his father who was fully qualified by long public service, was pretty much a lightweight when he was elected president and any objective observer could see this. But he had modest paper qualifications and some political experience that far exceeded those of our current president. Trump is a complete novice in the art of governance. Some made fun of George Bush because he said that he was the "Decider." Well, it is true that presidents, as the chief administrator of the federal government, do get to decide a lot. We like to think, however, that decisions are based on the best guidance and the best advice of the best experts in the field.

We like to think that decisions affecting the country and the world are not something that just pop into the president's head and are nothing but gut instincts. We would like to think that a reasonable president, who understood his limited role under the U.S. Constitution, would not ignore Congress, the branch of government with the power of the purse.

We would like to think our presidents would want to explain themselves to the American people, since presidents are accountable to the people. Presidents who unify the country are the ones who can best explain their actions and their policies to the people. Presidents who unify the country are the ones who have respect for government, and our institutions, including the press. President Trump went to

Pennsylvania's 18th District yesterday to campaign for a beleaguered Republican candidate and all he could do was to talk about himself and call Chuck Todd of Meet the Press, a sleepy-eyed son-of-a-bitch.

Trump's idea of being commander is to tweet out about world affairs one minute and insult a critic the next minute. We never know what is coming next. We know the president watches Fox News and then tweets away without explanation. Often his own staff, such as it is, must immediately walk back what the president said to keep Americans, world leaders, or the stock market from over-reacting.

Even worse is the fact that President Trump decides something one minute, and then talks to another person with a different idea, and changes his mind instantly. Trump's ultimate dereliction of duty is his inability to keep his word to anyone. He cannot be trusted to follow through. He has thrown almost half of his White House staff under the bus in his first year in office as they scrambled to make sense of his decisions, or tried to reverse them.

President Trump can't explain why he says things. He may be a decider, but he is not an explainer. He thinks he is the smartest person in any room he enters, yet he is so unable to grasp complexities that he cannot even hold a regular press conference, where for an hour or more he would take tough questions from the press. He can't do that. He doesn't have a grasp of policy. He lacks an understanding of the issues. He fails to grasp the constitutional role he plays. Others must try to fill in the blanks. So far nobody has been able to successfully do that for very long.

In the past week or two we have seen the president flip-flop all over the issue of what to do about guns in the wake of the Parkland, Florida, school tragedy. One day he is for more gun control. He wants to raise the age for gun purchases. The next day he backs away from these plans. He parrots Wayne LaPierre and the NRA with the chant that we should "harden our schools." This means turning schools into armed camps. The NRA's solution to any gun problem is always more guns.

Presidents do have great power. The greatest presidents were humbled by this power and were aware that it needed to be restrained. No person ever to hold this office was perfectly prepared to take the job. But the best of them grew in office and in their ability to administer the executive branch. The greatest presidents were men of their word who did not make 180-degree changes willy-nilly. The greatest presidents shared their power with their staff, with their cabinet officers, and with experts inside and outside of government who were part of the decision-making process on major policy matters. The greatest presidents trusted others and they gave their trust in return. Trump trusts no one. Those who still trust him are living in a fool's paradise.

Bring Back the Idea that All Politics is Local

March 16, 2018

My former boss Speaker Tip O'Neill made famous the statement "all politics is local." People use it even when their meaning is not totally clear. If all politics is local, what, then, is state politics or national politics? When Chris Matthews wrote his book *Hardball*, he described the meaning with a couple of examples from Tip O'Neill's 1982 election for another term in the House from his district in Massachusetts that included Cambridge. His opponent that year was a Republican candidate who funded his campaign largely with money from Texas and Oklahoma oilmen. Tip made political hay out of this outside influence and let everyone know that his opponent was getting his money from faraway places. The outside money didn't sit well with the folks in Tip's district.

House members have to run for office every two years. They must pay attention to the local concerns and keep them uppermost in their campaigns. Tip said the only election he ever lost was for a seat on the Cambridge City Council, where he lost by 160 votes because he took his own neighbors for granted. This is really local, and Tip's advice was to take care of your own backyard first. You cannot get to be a "national" Congressperson, he said, and vote for legislation for the good of the whole country, without first paying attention to the needs and the issues that affect the people in your district, the ones who elect you.

A lot of water has flowed under the bridge of American politics since Tip O'Neill's advice. Elections have changed and not necessarily for the better. Virtually all elections for national office are funded by political action committees (PACs) where it is not certain where the money is coming from. Both political parties help fund local races and they use the "national" money they have to fund local elections, usually with some strings attached. National party committees expect the candidates to stand for certain issues that the national party leaders promote. Elections have become so expensive to run that few candidates can afford to run with money they can personally raise in their districts or states.

In the recent special election in the 18th District of Pennsylvania, the Republican Party spent more than $13 million to elect Rick Saccone, a state representative and supporter of Donald Trump, running against a young, first-time Democratic candidate, Conor Lamb, who spent about $2.5 million. Top Republican officials, including President Trump, stumped the district for the Republican candidate. The Democrat won the election, overcoming a 20-point underdog status in this district that voted heavily in favor of Donald Trump in 2016.

Analysts are saying the secret of Conor Lamb's success was that he ran as a Democrat who was in touch with his district. He stayed local. He was critical of the national face of the Democratic Party, Nancy Pelosi. He kept his own district in mind and enough voters in this Republican stronghold voted for the candidate that had the best local appeal.

Elections have become poll driven, ratings driven, and designed for mass appeal. In the Internet Age, social media seems to turn all local elections into national referendums on big hot-button issues. Cable TV news from MSNBC to FOX turns local politics into national politics for the consumption of a national audience.

The candidates who can stay tuned in to their district voters and not go off chasing rainbows of national interest just might do better this time around. Why should a local candidate for the House of Representatives from either party be more concerned about their support or rejection of Donald Trump than they are about local issues that dominate their districts?

People in both parties seem to be making up their own minds about Donald Trump. By this November we will have had almost two years of his presidency. Trump's administration seems to be falling apart at a rapid rate. While the tendency of Democrats might be to jump on Trump's many faults and ride them to victory in the fall, a better strategy might be to let Trump self-destruct on his own. The best strategy might be to stay clear of the wreckage.

Democrats should focus on the issues (other than Trump) that mean something at home. And Democrats should not be afraid to take independent stands that don't match up completely with the Democratic National Committee or the national faces of the party.

California Democrats just sent a message to the venerable Senator Diane Feinstein that she goes into the primaries without the endorsement of the California party. She may win anyway, because she is still popular and formidable, even at age 85. Likewise, Nancy Pelosi, one of the greatest and best promoters of the Democratic Party for 30 years, has some younger members of the party thinking it is a time for a change in leadership. This is a healthy debate to have. Democrats running for the House should not have to identify themselves with national leaders like Nancy Pelosi, Bernie Sanders, or Elizabeth Warren, to get elected locally.

Democrats should define themselves, not be defined by national faces from states quite different from their own. They can do this and still be good Democrats. If they don't do this, they won't have a chance in red states because voters will think they are voting for Nancy Pelosi or Bernie Sanders when they enter the voting booth. This may work in blue California. It won't work in any red state. Young Colon Lamb has just shown Democrats the way to victory in November. Be local, define yourself, and listen to your constituents. Make Tip O'Neill proud.

What advice do I have for the Republican Party running for the House of Representatives this fall? Do the same thing. Break with the national noise and listen to what is going on at home. If your constituents want you to defend President Trump and his policies, do it. If they would rather hear your ideas for jobs, economic growth, and what it means to have good government and what the Republican Party means to you, not necessarily the current president, then don't defend Trump. Defend Republican values and what they mean to you and what they mean to your constituents.

If both parties would follow this Tip O'Neill formula laid down by a wise old pol of the old school, we could end up with a really good Congress that will make all of us proud.

Stormy Weather

March 17, 2018

One part of me says I really don't care who Donald Trump had sex with in the past or in the present. I believe that even public officials should have the benefit of a private life. Another part of me says the Stormy Daniels case has a lot more to it than just extra-marital sex.

The press and the public did not start prying into the sex lives of current and former presidents or of presidential candidates until the perfect storm that became the Gary Hart saga in 1987. Hart was emerging as a John Kennedy-like candidate, young, talented, and handsome. But his political world came crashing down when the press went after his private life. Hart dared reporters to follow him around to prove he was not having an affair. While no affair was ever proven, his friendship and association with Donna Rice raised the question of infidelity and Hart withdrew from the presidential campaign.

It is safe to say that most modern presidents, and even some of the venerable Founding Fathers, had extra-marital affairs, or affairs considered illicit by the standards of the time. Thomas Jefferson's political enemies exposed his affair with one of his slaves, Sally Hemings. Grover Cleveland, the bachelor governor of New York, fathered a child and this fact became a political scandal of sorts which resulted in the political chant used by his opponent James G. Blaine in 1884: "Ma, Ma, where's my Pa? Gone to the White House Ha, Ha, Ha!" Some anti-Cleveland press stories just before the election alleged that this was a case of rape, which the woman in question, Maria Halpin, also alleged. Whatever the actual circumstances, Cleveland won the election handily and then won again in the election of 1892.

Perhaps only Jimmy Carter, Harry Truman, Barack Obama and one or two others may be free of some extra-marital affairs among recent presidents. Franklin Roosevelt, Lyndon Johnson, John F. Kennedy all had affairs. But while rumors occasionally circulated, the press, the old-fashioned print press, the radio, and the early network TV press usually left this sort of thing alone. A lot of reporters knew about these affairs, but they did not write about them.

There were a lot of good reasons why things changed with Gary Hart and subsequent presidential candidates and presidents since the 1980s. From the mid-twentieth century, right up to the present, we have seen the rise of various movements from women's liberation to the current MeToo movement. The adage that "boys will be boys," is no longer operable. It is a vestige of a past where women were not treated equally. Both law and custom favored men and tolerated their sexual foibles and their exploitation of women. Those days are over, and if they are not, they should be.

Donald Trump and any other man who acts like he does regarding women is not going to get away with it anymore. The social and political winds are shifting rapidly and his exploitation of women including Stormy Daniels can no longer be tolerated or swept under the rug.

A whole generation of American voters has grown up since the checkered history of political investigations of Bill and Hillary Clinton that were backed by rich Republican politicos and their tools in the U.S. Congress. They need to understand what that unceasing effort to bring down a president was like. From the days of Bill Clinton's time as governor of Arkansas and extending all through his presidency and to his eventual impeachment, Bill Clinton, and sometimes Hillary, were subjected to investigations by Congressional committees, special prosecutors, and they suffered various private lawsuits. President Clinton was sued while he was a sitting president by Paula Jones, an Arkansas resident who accused him of sexual discrimination. That case never amounted to much but it was during a deposition in that case that Bill Clinton lied under oath about having sex with Monica Lewinsky.

None of the Congressional investigations, and none of the investigations by special prosecutors found any crimes for which either Bill or Hillary could be indicted. Hillary referred to all the investigations as a right-wing conspiracy to destroy them. She was soundly criticized for saying it in the right-wing media. It may not have been a single right-wing conspiracy against the Clintons, but there is plenty of evidence of well-organized and well-funded attempts to smear them, staring with the "Arkansas Project" of right-wing billionaire Richard Mellon Scaife, who spent millions of dollars smearing the Clintons. On Jerry Falwell's, Old Time Gospel Hour TV show, the

Clintons were accused of a variety of serious crimes including murder, and you could buy the video tape that proved it all from Falwell and from another minister/politician Pat Robertson.

None of this stuck to the Clintons. Prosecutor Ken Starr was all but ready to shut down his investigation when suddenly the Monica Lewinsky story broke. Sex, and lying about it, would lead to the impeachment of the President. Bill Clinton was impeached by the U.S. House of Representatives, but he was not found guilty in his Senate trial. He remained in office and finished his term, but the scandal had seriously damaged his reputation and his sexual escapades sullied the White House. For the first time in history a special prosecutors report to Congress became a runaway best seller full of salacious details of the Clinton/Lewinsky affair.

There are a lot of citizens of this country who do not follow the daily dribble of stories about Russian collusion, money laundering, or the meaning of obstruction of justice and why it is a serious crime. A good portion of this country, perhaps 30 to 40% of American voters, do not seem to be particularly upset by the fact that our president is a chronic liar on all subjects. They say they like him because "he talks like we do."

But I do believe that even Trump's staunchest supporters might begin to focus on the Stormy Daniels case. This is right out of Reality TV, the place from which Donald Trump emerged, and the place where a lot of Americans discovered him on Celebrity Apprentice and still find him to be that same loveable "Your Fired" kind of guy. Some Americans, enamored of Trump the TV star, might discover that Reality TV has no place in the American court system.

So far, a lot of Americans seem to be giving Trump a pass on his alleged affair with a porn movie star. Trump, who said he could shoot someone on 5th Avenue in New York and not get arrested, seems to think that he can have sex with whomever he pleases and its nobody's business. He sees himself as above the law. Having extra-marital sex was not the main issue in the Clinton/Lewinsky affair. It was lying about it while under oath. It was perjury about a sexual affair that led to Clinton's impeachment. How will Trump respond to Stormy Daniels when this gets into a court room? Will he perjure himself?

Will we finally have revealed to us the lengths that Donald Trump has gone to cover up sexual affairs? Trump is already using strong-arm tactics on Stormy Daniels to intimidate her. She may have been physically threatened to keep her mouth shut, as her lawyer alleges. Is this the kind of behavior that we want to see from the President of the United States?

I have no idea if the upcoming interview with Stormy Daniels on CBS's 60 Minutes program will be mostly hype and sensationalism, or if it will reveal how the President of the United States silences women with whom he has had affairs, or women he as sexually mistreated.

The President's lawyers have claimed in the past several days that Stormy Daniels has violated the terms of her non-disclosure agreement and the president's lawyers are seeking $20 million in damages, a ludicrous sum that can only be viewed as pure intimidation. They are engaged in a legal maneuver to get this out of the courts and into the hands of arbitrators, so the case can be kept from public view.

I have always thought that Trump's deep ties with Russia going back many years, was the albatross around his neck, the one thing he would not be able to shake off once the public was informed of this complex web of deceit. Trump now has another albatross around his neck that is weighing him down.

His affair with Stormy Daniels and the lengths he has gone to cover it up could end his presidency every bit as quickly as money-laundering, obstruction of justice, collusion with Russians, and possibly income tax fraud. The careers of Hollywood moguls, TV moguls, members of Congress, and other prominent American celebrities have been ended abruptly in recent months. How is the case of the President of the United States any different? Why should he keep his job while so many others have lost theirs? Nowhere in the U.S. Constitution and nowhere in American law does it say that just because your name is Trump and just because you were elected President of the United States, that you are entitled to be above the law.

Will Special Counsel Robert Mueller be Fired?

March 19, 2018

The mean-spirited, and highly suspicious firing of former Acting FBI Director Andrew McCabe coupled with the unbelievably inappropriate presidential Twitter-storm assault on both McCabe and Special Counsel Robert Mueller, leads me to only one conclusion. Trump plans to fire Mueller very soon and see what happens. The president is famous for saying "We'll see what happens." He is ready to see what happens when he fires Mueller.

So far, the president has not seen much reaction to his public outbursts, except in the media that he already despises, Fox News excepted. His obstructionist smear of the FBI and the Russian investigation seems to be a big snooze on Capitol Hill, where a somnambulistic Congress is so lazy and unresponsive that they can't even muster a yawn of complaint against the president.

The silence of the Congressional lambs is deafening. This silence empowers Trump toward even more irrational behavior. It is the silence of the Republicans, a party so blinded by hyper-partisanship that they have lost all perspective on their role to defend the nation and the Constitution. Under the "leadership" of Paul Ryan in the House and Mitch McConnell in the Senate, the GOP does not have leaders that can rally rank-and-file members toward law and order, the Constitution, or common decency.

The Democratic Party in Congress has no leadership role. It is the minority party. It has no committee chairman, no Speaker, no Senate Majority Leader. It only has moral suasion and public opinion on its side. So far this is not enough to make a difference. If Congress acts to stop Trump from his ongoing obstruction of justice, it will have to come from the sleepwalking GOP.

We have witnessed the collapse of the Permanent Select Committee on House Intelligence, a committee that should be immune from partisanship because it is part of our national security apparatus. It should never be governed by partisanship. But we witnessed the chairman of that committee Devin Nunes and other GOP members bending over backwards to aid and abet a president rather than investigate the case of Russian collusion and related matters.

Over the weekend Congressman Jim Himes (D-CT), a member of the House Intelligence Committee, called on Congress to be prepared to pass a law reinstating the special prosecutor law that would create a prosecutor to continue Mueller's work if he is fired. This special prosecutor, by law, could not be fired by the president. The special prosecutor law expired some time ago and was not renewed. This is why we have a special "counsel" leading the investigation, not a special "prosecutor."

A special counsel can be fired if a president is reckless enough and if Congress is compliant enough. Firing Mueller might also take down Deputy Attorney General Rod Rosenstein, who might resign rather than fire Mueller. I don't think Trump would think twice about this. He has shown no warmth for Rosenstein.

The American people have not been properly informed about the reasons why Andrew McCabe was fired and why it was done in such an underhanded and personally destructive manner. It was the Attorney General who fired McCabe, supposedly on advice from the FBI's Inspector General.

What was Trump's role in this process? He should have no role in the internal business of the FBI or the Justice Department, but we have seen that the president has meddled in these independent entities from day one. He thinks the Justice Department is a bunch of lawyers who work for him, not for the American people.

How did AG Jeff Sessions get back into this when he supposedly recused himself from anything relating to the Russian probe? McCabe was part of that probe. Our Attorney General has been tainted since he misled Congress about his own dealings with Russians.

Special Counsel Mueller has subpoenaed the records of the Trump Organization. The Trump Organization is Donald Trump and his family. Nothing is more important to him than his own world. He will defend his world before he will defend the Constitution. He will protect Trump before he protects the national security of the United States.

Trump is acting like a cornered animal. The face looming before this trapped animal is that of Robert Mueller. Trump will lash out at Mueller. He will try to get away from him by any means necessary.

Most criminals cannot escape the law. But when the President of the United States is the crook, he might think he can banish his accusers by firing them. What has he got to lose? He either goes down fighting and clawing or he comes clean and faces the music. Which do you think Donald Trump will do?

Trump has often described himself as a counter-puncher. His style in the courtroom is to never admit guilt and to bully those who are suing him. When he loses in court, he settles and seeks non-disclosure agreements as part of the settlement to keep things covered up. He learned long ago from his former lawyer, the infamous Roy Cohn, to win by intimidation. His main tool has always been the Big Smear accompanied by a torrent of lies.

We learned only recently that Trump actually got White House staff to sign non-disclosure agreements! This is unprecedented. What kind of president, except one who had plenty to hide, would seek such a extra-legal tool for top employees inside the White House?

Reporting on these non-disclosure agreements revealed that if an employee did disclose something that violated the agreement, the offending employee would have to pay a million dollars to the U.S. Treasury. How can Trump get employees to sign such things? What court is there that would allow such weird agreements to be enforced?

We already have laws that prevent government employees from revealing classified information. This was not sufficient for Trump. He wanted personal loyalty and personal protection. He doesn't trust anyone. Once again it appears he is more concerned with his own hide than he is with the business of the government. Trump will go to any lengths to protect Trump and the Trump family brand.

A Constitutional Crisis in Slow Motion

March 22, 2018

Former White House Counsel John Dean, of Watergate fame, the man who told President Nixon that there was a cancer growing on the White House, said President Trump is engaging in "public obstruction of justice." Stop and think about the word "public." In Watergate, Nixon's crimes were out of sight, they were private, and they were covered up until the investigations finally exposed the actions of Nixon and all the others in the Watergate saga, sending more than three dozen people to jail and ending Nixon's presidency.

What we have in Donald Trump is a criminal operating in full public view. Maybe this is because Trump knows no other way. Maybe he simply cannot hide who he is. Maybe Jared Kushner, for all his so-called business savvy was never meant to operate under the klieg lights of public scrutiny. Trump and his family business enterprises seem to be withering like mushrooms in the hot sun. Too much light is hard on mushrooms and crooks.

Trump's crimes of obstruction were in the open when he fired James Comey and then sat for an interview with Lester Holt and said he fired Comey to end the Russian investigation. That's obstruction! More recently when he fired Andrew McCabe, it was for something he did in relation to the Russian investigations. We have yet to see the FBI Inspector General's report on this to see precisely why McCabe was fired. Add these firings to the president's strongly worded tweets accusing the FBI of being on a witch hunt, and his recent hiring of a lawyer who believes the FBI is part of a vast Deep State conspiracy to get Trump thrown out of office, and a public pattern of obstruction is there for all to see.

Back on February 4, Charles M. Blow, writing in the *New York Times*, described a "Constitutional Crisis in Slow Motion," and he listed a number of things that demonstrated this, including the guilty pleas and the indictments we have seen so far. Mr. Blow minced no words in condemning Trump. He wrote, "Donald Trump will destroy this entire country — its institutions and its safeguards, the rule of law and the customs of civility, the concept of truth and the inviolable nature of valor — to protect his own skin."

The slow motion crisis and the crimes committed right before our eyes began long before President Trump took office. His campaign was populated with a variety of crooks including Paul Manafort and George Papadopoulos. Perhaps the first crooked act was changing the Republican Party platform to eliminate the GOP goal of challenging Vladimir Putin's aggression in the Ukraine. The GOP platform originally called for arming the Ukrainians to help them fight off Russians. Trump, or one of Trump's people, perhaps Paul Manafort who had deep connections in the Ukraine for years, saw to it that the platform was changed to weaken the GOP position, thus favoring Putin. Just how this happened remains a mystery. But it happened. This may be the first example of Russian collusion that will come out of the investigations. It may be the first tangible bit of evidence of the romance between Donald and Vladimir. Trump had to prove something to Putin and this was, perhaps, the first sign that Trump was going play ball with the Russians.

Today, the president's top lawyer in the Mueller investigations, John Dowd, resigned. Just two days ago we learned that Trump had sought the services of a super-star lawyer Theodore B. Olson, only to be turned down. Who is left to defend the president?

A number of distinguished Americans have come out recently with strong statements condemning the president. Former CIA Director John Brennan, who has served this country in various capacities in the CIA for thirty years before becoming director, said of Trump, "You will take your rightful place as a disgraced demagogue in the dustbin of history." Brennan said the president was mean-spirited, lacked integrity, promoted his own interests, and was a failure on many fronts. He also said, what I said in my essay of March 22, that Trump was acting like a "cornered animal."

Retired four-star Army General Barry McCaffrey, one of the most decorated soldiers in American history, said in a tweet on March 16, "Reluctantly I have concluded that President Trump is a serious threat to US national security. He is refusing to protect vital US interests from active Russian attacks. It is apparent that he is for some unknown reason under the sway of Mr Putin." General McCaffrey also expressed outrage that the president's son-in-law, a thirty-year-old with no experience in foreign affairs has been given so much power to represent the United States abroad.

You do not get outstanding citizens like these men to publicly criticize the President of the United States unless we are already in a major crisis. These men have spent their lives serving this country and taking seriously their oath to defend the Constitution. They are men who know the value of being circumspect and dignified in their personal and public conduct. I believe them to be patriots who are speaking truth to power, and also alerting us all that we are in deep trouble with this president.

The time is long past for any serious person of either political party to pretend that Donald Trump will ever get better at being president, or that he will ever be able to extract himself from his unbelievable and unprecedented loyalty to the Russian dictator. And to think that our president would call Putin and congratulate him on his rigged election, when his own national security advisers told him not to do it.

After President Nixon resigned to avoid impeachment, President Ford said "Our long national nightmare is over." We are in a another long national nightmare that seems to be playing out in slow motion, where we cannot move fast enough to stop the constitutional crisis from unfolding before our eyes. How do we get back to normal speed? How do we finally come to the realization that Donald Trump needs to be impeached, indicted, or forced to resign?

How many more indictments will there be? What will happen to Trump's family members who ran Dad's business and were largely out of the glare of public scrutiny that comes to anyone in the White House. Now the full glare is on Jared Kushner in particular. He was allegedly negotiating a half-billion-dollar deal with the United Arab Emirates three months into the Trump presidency. In the midst of all this, the United States changed its policy toward Qatar. Could this have been a quid pro quo for a big loan to the Trump Organization or to Jared Kushner's business? We seem to have turned over the White House to a very sleazy family real estate company, one that is deep in debt, and that has used the White House and the power of the presidency to continue to do private business for personal profit. When will enough of us wake up to what is becoming more obvious with each new revelation, and with each new indictment?

We need to be clear headed about a lot of other things too. We are learning the awful truth about a company called Cambridge Analytica, thanks to a young whistleblower named Christopher Wylie, a pink-haired guy with a nose ring, who just might bring down Cambridge Analytica and possibly Facebook for the way data was gathered and manipulated during the election. Cambridge Analytica is owned by the billionaire Mercer family that backed Steve Bannon's alt-right vision of white nationalism and the growth of the Breitbart News Network. The Mercers were major backers of Trump for president.

Millions of Facebook users have had their data used for targeted political messaging and other nefarious purposes, including bots that flooded social media with pro-Trump and anti-Hillary messages. We are learning that some of the standard phrases that became common in the campaign, like "Drain the Swamp," the "Deep State," and "Build the Wall," were found to have mass appeal and resonance, and who hasn't used these words in one fashion or another?

All of us who use Facebook and Twitter, and other social media, helped create the propaganda that was used to influence the 2016 election. This new social media that we love so much and that we use so often takes all our likes and dislikes, all the data we create with each keystroke and sells it to the highest bidder. This data can be used for legitimate advertising or it can be used for propaganda, and it can analyze each of us right down to our own zip code and our own Internet address. This new tool, used by Russians who bought "advertising," gave us Donald Trump.

My Friend George Will

March 25, 2018

I met George Will once, briefly, at a Washington party, many years ago. But I have been reading his columns in the *Washington Post* for what seems like a lifetime, going back to the mid-1970s. My politics has always been on the liberal side of the spectrum and his on the conservative side. But I read him to help round out my understanding of the conservative movement and conservative thought. I followed William F. Buckley too, because as much as that man could infuriate me, it was the kind of feeling that I relished. It kept my intellectual juices flowing.

My uneasy and often uncomfortable feeling when reading conservative thinkers was a healthy emotion. You cannot pretend to go into the arena of political thought with only your own ideas and your own prejudices. You grow mentally only when challenged—only when pushed out of your comfort zone. This does not mean that you abandon your own core values, it means, if you are lucky, that you can respect the ideas of those with whom you disagree and learn from them.

George Will's columns always got under my skin in one way or another. Sometimes I would throw down the paper and say to myself, or to my wife if she was in the room, that George Will was, as usual, full of shit again today. But I always went back to him because he has a great ability to cut to the chase. I liked him because he did not suffer fools gladly, even if some of the fools were my favorite politicians or thinkers. He writes with the insights of a serious critical thinker in a world were critical thinking is often considered dangerous.

With the rise of Donald Trump, Will's columns have surprised me because I find they reflect my own thinking about this populist demagogue. My critical writing about our inept president often pale before the things Will is writing. I say to my wife, "Be sure to read George Will today," as we pass around sections of the *Washington Post*.

Will has not abandoned conservatism. His core principles remain rock solid. But the so-called conservatism that is on display in Congress and in our new president has no resemblance to the principled, foundational views of American conservatism that Will has championed for so long. He has joined a lot of Democrats and Republicans in saying the GOP controlled government we have right now in no way resembles the Republican Party he once knew, and in no way resembles most of the tenets of conservatism.

After Donald Trump made disparaging and racist comments about an American judge of Mexican ancestry in the summer of 2016, George Will formally left the Republican Party and changed his registration to unaffiliated. Trump, upon hearing the news, tweeted that Will was "one of the most overrated pundits...."

I was inspired to write this after reading Will's piece in today's *Washington Post* because it was particularly good analysis of the new danger about to enter the White House, John Bolton, soon to be President Trump's National Security Adviser. This piece is a gem on many levels. I highly recommend it.

Will begins, "Because John Bolton is five things President Trump is not—intelligent, educated, principled, articulate, and experienced—and because of Bolton's West Wing proximity to a president responsive to the most recent thought he has heard.... Bolton will soon be the second-most dangerous American."

Will sees the latest shake-up in the White House staff as marking the end of a delusion that many have had about the Trump administration, that if we just got some sensible adults to surround our childish president, he could be "cocooned within layers of adult supervision." That bubble has burst. The president now has an all-Fox News team surrounding him on TV and in person in the West Wing.

One single question in Will's column particularly grabbed my attention. The question, and his answer to it, is a brilliant insight, perfectly stated: "How can the president square his convictions with Bolton's? Let's say this one more time: Trump. Has. No. Convictions."

In Defense of Post Offices and Post Roads
March 30, 2018

President Trump tweeted yesterday another attack on Amazon and Jeff Bezos that demonstrates once again his ignorance of American history. What he said, however, was well-calculated red meat for the many places in America with hollowed-out economies and ghost-town business districts.

Here is what the president said in his tweet on Thursday:

"I have stated my concerns with Amazon long before the Election. Unlike others, they pay little or no taxes to state & local governments, use our Postal System as their Delivery Boy (causing tremendous loss to the U.S.), and are putting many thousands of retailers out of business!"

This is one of his better propaganda tweets. Compared to the 37,000-plus times he has tweeted since going on Twitter, this one has the surface appearance of near "normal" behavior—not that having a president who makes pronouncements and fires his staff by Twitter is anything near normal.

Fact checkers have already pointed out that contrary to the president's tweet; Amazon does pay state and local taxes. Maybe Trump remembers the early days of Amazon, and other Internet retailers, when they were out-of-state businesses that were not required to collect local and state taxes. The tax issue changed a number of years ago. But Trump gets more raw emotion from his rant if he lies about it. Facts can be downright boring.

Trump's second point, that Amazon's massive use of the U.S. Postal Service is causing tremendous losses to the U.S. is laughable on the surface but even more intriguing when we look at the role of the U.S. Post Office in American history.

I have studied many petitions that Americans wrote to Congress in the early years of the republic, and most of them were from what we would call today small business owners. The two things that the petitions mentioned frequently was the need to develop post offices and "post roads" (roads designed for regular mail routes), and the other was to build lighthouses to make commercial traffic by sailing ships safer along the East Coast.

Take a look at Article 1, Sec. 8 of the U. S. Constitution, the part that describes the powers of Congress. There is a whole separate line that states one power of Congress is: "To Establish Post Offices and post Roads."

Early American businesses wanted a "delivery boy" as Trump put it. Today we take post offices and post roads for granted. We don't call our vast Interstate Highway system "post roads" anymore. But we still need goods to be delivered.

If President Trump thinks the U.S. Postal Service is going down the tubes because of Amazon's extensive use of the service, he should understand his own role in the process. Perhaps the president doesn't realize who controls the postal service. Go to its website and you will find: "The USPS is often mistaken for a government-owned corporation (e.g., Amtrak) because it operates much like a business. It is, however, an 'establishment of the executive branch of the Government of the United States', (39 U.S.C. § 201) as it is controlled by Presidential appointees and the Postmaster General."

Breaking News! As I was writing this essay, the president tweeted again this morning (March 30). This time he got specific and said:

"Why is the United States Post Office, which is losing many billions of dollars a year, while charging Amazon and others so little to deliver their packages, making Amazon richer and the Post Office dumber and poorer? Should be charging MUCH MORE!"

This tweet caused Amazon stock to drop almost two points in today's trading (as I write this). I am sure the professional leadership team at the USPS, from the Postmaster General on down, did not need to learn via Twitter that the president doesn't think Amazon is charged enough, even though they are charged the same rate as all other large bulk shippers. Who gets hurt when postal rates go up? It is always the consumer, because Amazon and every other business would pass the shipping costs on to the customer.

In his Thursday tweet, the president said that Amazon is putting "many thousands of retailers out of business." To blame one company, albeit a really big one, for retail business bankruptcies is another of Trump's partly true/partly false statements that make the best kind of propaganda for receptive ears.

We can all see cities and towns across America where once flourishing business districts and shopping centers are now ghost towns. Something happened to cause this decline, but what was it?

To blame this on Amazon is to ignore history. Certainly the Internet has transformed the way we do business. Electronic communications is our new "post road." Email and social media have drastically altered the use of first class mail, which once played a larger role in post office income.

But look at what really caused the demise of thousands of retail businesses long before Amazon was born in 1994, just twenty-four years ago. Much larger economic forces have been at work for a long time, going back to the end of World War II, that have drastically altered the cities and towns of America and hollowed so many of them out into sad places of decay and killed off tens of thousands of retail businesses.

The causes of loss of retail businesses and blight we see in cities and towns across America include: the decline of heavy industries as those industries went overseas; the expansion of new energy sources that caused coal mining to decline; the near death of the American auto industry as foreign competition emerged in the 1960s; the development of the shopping mall, which turned many "Main Streets" across America into empty storefronts; the rise of big box stores and mass retailers, especially Walmart; and eventually, in the last two dozen years, the rise of Internet retailing.

And there is one other big cause that is too big to discuss right now, but that I must mention. We have allowed so many parts of our country to decay because we would rather fight wars across the globe for some regime change that never occurs the way we want it to. Our cities and towns and our small businesses have declined because we fight never-ending foreign wars.

I saw all these signs of blight and neglect happen in my lifetime, in my own hometown of Harvey, Illinois, an industrial suburb 20 miles south of Chicago's Loop. I can see it today on the the main streets of Martinsburg, West Virginia, where I now reside. I see it everywhere I travel in this country.

Trump taps all the anguish we all can see. This is the part of his success that liberals cannot see as well as they should. People voted for Trump because they had nothing to lose. Trump won't fix any of this, but he will use the anger, the frustration, to increase his own power.

The president singles out Amazon because he does not like the politics of Jeff Bezos, especially the *Washington Post*, which Bezos owns. The *Post* is a huge thorn in the president's side, as it should be. "Democracy Dies in Darkness" is on the masthead of the *Post*, and Trump thinks the *Post* is out to get him. So why not bully the newspaper's owner? It is what this president does. Taking on Amazon is just another way to take on the free press.

Our First Solipsist President

April 4, 2018

S olipsism is the idea that only the self exists. Anything external to the self is not real. Only your own mind is real. Everything else is dream-like and lacking in substance and meaning. A solipsist cannot verify anything outside his or her own mind. We have in Donald Trump our first solipsist president.

Some observers, including a few in his own cabinet, have criticized the president for being a moron and an idiot. Others have called him insane, paranoid, schizophrenic, self-centered, egoistic, a Mad Hatter, a Looney Toon, a buffoon, and an arrogant bully who lacks any feeling for others. Some have called him both venal and senile. Many of his critics see him as being devoid of compassion, empathy, ethics, and morality. And then there is the compulsive, constant, everyday lying, not to mention his racism and misogyny.

I propose that our president's critics need to look at the overriding problem. He suffers from a terrible malady. He is a classic solipsist who thinks only He is real, only He is sane, only He can fix things, and only He is smart enough to run the entire government of the United States by Himself because nothing else can be proven to be real. Everything is a figment of his imagination.

In his mind Donald Trump is Reality. The rest of us are part of his dream world. We are a frustrating TV show to him. When he was running his own business, he could function fairly well and when things got out of hand, he had lawyers. But he is President of the United States now. Large realities outside his own mind are competing for his attention. He can no longer just change the channel if he doesn't like what he sees.

A celebrity Reality TV show host, our president is more comfortable in his own mind when he controls what he sees. He has adopted Fox News as part of his reality and therefore he does not believe what he hears from people in his own administration or on other TV channels. Everything goes in and out of reality for him, depending on the latest stimuli. He has moved Fox News people off the TV and into the Oval Office to make that part of his mind more real. Fox News is President Trump's therapist.

If he likes a message offered to him, he may ingest it into his mind where it becomes temporarily real, real enough for him to act on it. This lasts until the next message he ingests into his solitary mind takes precedence over the previous one. In the mind of a solipsist, reality depends on what the solipsist is thinking about at the moment.

A solipsist can encompass the outward symptoms of a variety of mental illnesses. It explains his lack of empathy. If the president is indeed a solipsist, it explains a lot about the arbitrary nature of his actions, his unilateral approach to foreign affairs, his many contradictory statements, and his incessant lying. A solipsist cannot lie. Only external voices can be liars. Whatever a solipsist thinks must be true because there is no other reality that can challenge the one in Trump's brain.

Trump's reality includes a trade war that will fix our trade imbalance. He doesn't study this issue. He doesn't consult experts; he doesn't negotiate with our trading partners. Why would he need to? If the idea is in his head, it is real and true. So, he unilaterally starts a trade war. Trump says repeatedly "We will see what happens." This is the perfect statement of a solipsist. "We," meaning him, will discover the results of his actions only after he has decided what he will do.

If the mind of Trump wants to militarize the border with Mexico all he has to do is tell the military to do it. His reality takes precedence over American law and practice on how the military is used inside the United States. He still struggles with his own mind over having Mexico pay for the wall. He cannot understand why this reality is so hard to accept when it is clear in his mind.

If Trump likes Putin it is OK. It is a reality in his head. Only his view matters, not the troublesome newspapers or the unreal Congress. Certainly not the Special Counsel, a recurring nightmare for the president.

When we dream, sometimes the dream can seem very real. Sometimes we know we are dreaming but we can't wake up. We only awake just before the monster grabs us, or just before we go over the cliff. In the mind of a solipsist it becomes a daily struggle to keep all the outside dreams at bay.

Solipsists are the loneliest kind of human being. They may want to wake up. They may want to find a larger reality. Watch Donald Trump and you will see an unhappy man who only shows some happiness when he is talking about himself and listening to people cheer him. This is a reality he likes. This reality is focused on him. When he is cheered he is having a pleasant dream.

I do not think the 25th Amendment to the U.S. Constitution, that describes the process of relieving the president of his duties because he is "unable to discharge the powers and duties of his office," includes a diagnosis of solipsism. We will never impeach a president for being a solipsist. But we might impeach, or even indict, a president for the actions of a solipsist who cannot tell right from wrong.

A solipsist like Trump might think he could shoot someone in broad daylight on Fifth Avenue and not be arrested. But there just might be another reality out there called the Law. Only the Law might be able to awaken this solipsist from his dream world and save this country from its latest, and most troubling nightmare.

Sarah Huckabee Sanders Needs a Civics Lesson
April 7, 2018

At her April 6, 2018, White House Press Briefing, the president's spokesperson was asked a question about the process the White House goes through when the president makes a policy announcement and then the White House staff, or others in government agencies, must walk back the president's statements.

The examples cited were the president's sudden announcement that he wanted to pull American troops out of Syria and that he called for sending U.S. soldiers to the Mexico border. Shortly thereafter the president announced that our troops would stay in Syria, and that the National Guard, not regular U.S. Army troops would be sent to the border with Mexico. Someone must have whispered to him that the American military is not supposed to be deployed as a police force inside the United States. That law was passed in 1878, when Rutherford B. Hayes was president.

Ms. Sanders said that anyone who didn't understand how the president works doesn't "understand how civics works." She went on to explain that the president is the only one elected who can make such announcements, and when he makes announcements it is up to the White House to implement them.

She said this is exactly what the American people want him to do. I wish she would quit confusing "the American people" with Trump's political base. A lot of Americans do not want the president to be a dictator operating on whimsy.

Dear Sarah: You are the one who needs a civics lesson. Your description of how the president acts and how he issues policy announcements described the method most often employed by autocratic leaders and dictators. Donald Trump decrees, the government acts, is not the way our government is supposed to work.

The president is not the only official in government who is a policy maker. It does seem as if the president has difficulty with any policy announced by a cabinet officer. Trump lords over his cabinet to the point of rendering them useless figureheads, not partners in governance. Presidents are supposed to consult their cabinet, the Joint Chiefs, leaders in Congress, and even outside experts before making policy. Historically, major policy decisions are often explained to the American people in advance, via press conferences, appearances before joint meetings of Congress, and direct addresses to the American people. What we get from President Trump is a sudden tweet, where a whole policy is reduced to one or two tweets, often with misspelled words, and often when no one in the White House, no one in the State Department, no one in Congress, and no one at the Pentagon has been alerted in advance.

Sarah Huckabee Sanders thinks this is the normal way of doing business with this president. She thinks he is the only one empowered to do what he does. What she described is a one-man-band, a lone wolf, a solitary Decider, who seems to enjoy keeping the entire government off balance and scrambling to make sense of what the president does.

We have never had a president who has tried to rule by decree without consulting anyone else in advance, except, perhaps, the people at Fox News who he listens to and often acts based on what's on TV each morning. Apparently his "research" on an issue might include a long phone call with Sean Hannity.

President Trump does not trust very many people, and this is one of his most serious flaws as a leader. He has made the most powerful office in the world into a travesty of confusing and contradictory edicts. One day we are pulling out of Syria. The next day we are staying. China is a bad trading partner. Trump decides to punish them. Nobody seemed to see this coming. Who did he consult before launching a trade war? Even the numbers he cites to show how unfair China trade is, are off by almost $200 billion dollars.

No civics book ever published has ever said that the President of the United States has the power to make policy without a deliberative process that extends beyond the president's personal whims. And the best civics lesson of all, for Sarah and her boss, the president, would be to read the Constitution. Read it to understand checks and balances, to understand that the power of the purse resides in Congress, and that Congress is a partner in policy making.

The agencies of the executive branch and the military have vast tools to collect and analyze economic data and intelligence, and all the kinds of information government needs to function properly. Some agencies like the Justice Department, are designed to be independent of presidential meddling. But nobody ever told Donald Trump.

Trump supporters seem to like Trump's style of governance. Some have said that what he is doing is "draining the swamp." His supporter's like his brash disregard of government bureaucracy because they often describe bureaucrats as pencil pushers, makers of red tape, and slavish enforcers of stupid regulations. Add cynicism about government to the list of reasons people voted for Trump.

I see government workers as public servants who perform a wide variety of essential functions. I worked with a lot of them and I saw their dedication, their honesty, their ethical standards, and the pride they have in their jobs. Civilian and military alike, government workers in all agencies are the only glue holding this government together right now. Maybe the whole country needs a civics lesson about the value of good government and how to achieve it.

House Speakers Who Failed

April 12, 2018

Paul Ryan will not seek re-election. The speculation about this is over. He never liked the job and it never fit him well. As the former House Historian who worked with three Speakers, I hereby dub him: The Reluctant Speaker. He was reluctant to take the job. He was reluctant to challenge members of his own party in the so-called Freedom Caucus. He was reluctant to cooperate across the aisle. And he was very reluctant to challenge our demagogue president. Furthermore, he has been reluctant to use his constitutional office to help set the national agenda. He was never able to get the House to work using the regular order of business. He bears a good deal of the blame for the terrible dysfunction in the House during his tenure.

I described Ryan as the "reluctant speaker" on April 11 in a short post to Facebook friends. This morning I was pleasantly surprised to hear David Ignatius of the *Washington Post* say on MSNBC's Morning Joe, that he saw Ryan as "The Reluctant Speaker!" Remember who said it first! I was glad to see that my characterization was similar in content and exactly the same in title, as David Ignatius, whom I admire as a keen analyst.

Last night, however, also on MSNBC, Lawrence O'Donnell took a much harder line with Speaker Ryan calling him the Worst Speaker Ever. I thought he was way off base on this one.

The all-time worst speaker ever, hands down, is Newt Gingrich. Note: full disclosure, it was Newt Gingrich who fired me from my position as Historian of the U.S. House of Representatives in 1995. But I don't think he was the worst speaker because he fired me, some 23 years ago. He is the worst because his gigantic ego led him to believe he was leading a revolution. He rose to power by demonizing the House of Representatives as a swamp and also as a whorehouse. One of his books "A House of Ill-Repute" had a cover that replaced the Statue of Freedom on top of the Capitol dome with a red light. Yet it was Newt who was among the most unethical of members. As he amassed power, he told rank and file members to go home and raise money and only come back for votes. Newt would be ready to tell the Republican members how to vote. He would set the agenda.

While Gingrich is a lot smarter than our current president, Newt suffered then, and still does, from delusions of grandeur. He thought then, and still thinks, that he is a transformational world-class leader, ready to take America, and the world, to the next level. He described himself this way. There is documentary evidence. Newt taught courses where GOP candidates learned how to treat their Democratic opponents as enemies. Gingrich was then, and still is, a major contributor to extreme polarized politics.

Gingrich spent his energy trying to reform the House to suit his own ego. He acted as if he was a Prime Minister rather than a Speaker. He thought he could use the speakership to rival the president in power and he thought his speakership could launch him into the presidency. He once asked me to recommend a biography of James K. Polk that he could read. Newt knew that Polk was the only speaker ever to get elected as president. I guess he was looking for a role model on how a speaker gets to the White House.

Gingrich's own brash style kept the House leadership in chaos and Newt's relentless efforts to bring down President Bill Clinton backfired in the off-year congressional elections of November 1997. Instead of picking up seats, the Republicans lost five. This may seem like a small number but they expected to pick up more than 40, and they expected a super-majority of 60 in the Senate. The party out of the White House had not lost seats in an off-year election since 1822! Newt had to take the blame. He was also beset by scandals and ethics charges. The House GOP became disillusioned with his leadership, and his failure to win seats in 1998 led to his ouster from leadership and his resignation in 1999.

But like a bad penny, Newt kept turning up to muddy the political waters and ingratiate himself with Republicans in power. He helped elect several Tea Party members in 2010. He started running for president in 2011, but that was a flop. He befriended Donald Trump and wrote a book flattering Trump that got the endorsement of Fox News' Sean Hannity, who declared it to be "Inspiring and informative—I highly recommend it."

And finally, just last night, almost two decades after he left the speakership in disgrace, there was Newt on Fox News, participating in Sean Hannity's vile program that purported to reveal the sinister nature of the deep state Robert Mueller Crime Family. It was not even close to being a news program. It was a smear campaign, a piece of blatant propaganda orchestrated by Fox News to undermine Special Counsel Mueller. President Trump had tweeted to the world that this show was an important one that everyone should watch. Trump loves Sean Hannity.

On that Fox News show last night, Newt Gingrich, the worst speaker in American history, said about the FBI raid on Trump's lawyer: "We're supposed to have the rule of law. It ain't the rule of law when they kick in your door at 3:00 in the morning and you're faced with armed men and you have had no reason to be told you're going to have that kind of treatment. That's Stalin. That's the Gestapo in Germany. That shouldn't be the American FBI."

Gingrich has always been a bomb-thrower, an ego-centric politician who thinks that he and he alone, can transform the United States and the world. Only the worst speaker in American history would, in the name of defending the rule of law, state that Robert Mueller and his investigation resembled the likes of Joseph Stalin's ruthless dictatorship, or the fascist police state of Adolf Hitler. Newt cannot stop smearing America if he thinks it can advance his interests. I guess he wants badly to get into the Trump White House along with all the other misfits that are populating the place these days.

The Chaos before the Storm

April 26, 2018

In my book *Trump Tsunami*, the diary entry for December 6, 2017, raised the question "Can we survive President Trump's last big legal battle?" At that time General Michael Flynn had just pleaded guilty to lying to the FBI about meetings with Russian officials. This guilty plea took the Mueller investigations inside the White House for the first time. I speculated that Trump might try to pardon members of his own family; that he would act irrationally and do anything to keep the walls from closing in on him.

Now, in the waning days of April 2018, the president finds himself in an even smaller White House, where the walls have closed in to the point that he has become more unhinged than ever. We have seen the growing "Fire and Fury," of Michael Wolff's book about the chaos inside the White House getting worse. With each passing day, and with each revelation of the president's legal jeopardy, he retreats even further into his own world.

He wanted to get rid of the head of the Veterans Administration, David Shulkin, so he fired him and announced a replacement, his personal physician Rear Admiral Ronny Jackson. Shulkin claims he was fired but the White House maintained Shulkin resigned. Whatever the case, the president picked a guy he liked who had no experience running a large agency. Subsequently we learned of allegations about Admiral Jackson's drinking problem, being cavalier with the dispensing of prescription drugs, and for being a difficult person to work with. This morning the president withdrew Jackson's name from consideration. One more person thrown under the bus.

President Trump created this problem and contributed to the public ridicule of Admiral Jackson by not properly vetting a candidate for a very important government job. Trump blames Democrats on the Hill, especially Congressman Jon Tester of Montana, and vows that Tester will be punished at the polls. Trump denigrated the confirmation process by saying Jackson should not have to "be abused by a bunch of politicians."

The walls closed in even tighter on the president yesterday when the president's lawyer-fixer-dealmaker Michael Cohen pleaded the Fifth

Amendment in the Stormy Daniels case. This morning on Fox News the president was irate and needed to talk to his Fox Friends about both the Jackson withdrawal and Cohen's pleading the Fifth. The president turned to a television program to vent his spleen about the unfairness he sees all around him. The president told Fox and Friends that the Cohen plea had nothing to do with him.

Numerous video tapes surfaced from the Trump campaign where Trump suggested that only criminals, only the mob, pleads the Fifth. Does he think is own lawyer is a mobster? He told Fox News that Cohen only did a tiny fraction of his legal work. Then he blurted out that among that legal work was the Stormy Daniels case. Earlier, he had denied any connection with the case. He had just told his Fox Friends that Cohen's plea had nothing to do with him. The president is so unhinged that he practically indicts himself every time he tweets or goes on Fox News.

No wonder his lawyers tell him never to speak to Special Counsel Mueller. Trump is incapable of saving himself. He would perjure himself in the first five minutes of any interview with Robert Mueller and his investigators. Trump simply cannot stop lying about everything. Yet, the president's newest lawyer, Rudy Giuliani, seems to want to get the president to speak to Mueller.

The question of pardons has come up again. Will the president try to pardon Michael Cohen? Will the offer of a pardon keep Cohen from flipping over to the prosecution and "ratting out" the president? The president has pardoned three people so far, seemingly to test his powers and to anger Democrats. His first pardon of the controversial Arizona Sheriff Joe Arpaio, threw raw meat to his base. His pardon of Scooter Libby, former adviser to Vice President Dick Cheney, for lying and leaking classified information apparently came out of the blue and according to several reports gave the president a "thrill."

Last month Trump pardoned a Navy sailor, Kristian Saucier, who had taken photographs of classified parts of a nuclear sub and was sentenced to a year in jail. Trump made political hay out of this case during the campaign by saying this sailor got locked up, but Hillary never got locked up for her sloppy email practice. Recently Sylvester Stallone suggested to the president that the black boxer Jack Johnson should be pardoned posthumously for his crimes of more than a century ago. Trump seems to like the idea.

In these pardons the president did not use the Justice Department's Office of Pardons to help him with his decisions. This office has been around since the 1840s, and before that the Secretary of State and the Attorney General gave advice to presidents about clemency and pardons. Trump makes up his own mind. He doesn't like others telling him what to do, even experts, especially experts. The Office of Pardons has examined more than 180 petitions for pardons and clemency since Trump became president and he has not acted on any of them.

It is the Cohen case that is driving the president's frenzied behavior. Cohen is the key that unlocks all of Trump's secrets, most immediately the Stormy Daniels case, but also potential campaign finance violations, bank fraud, and other serious matters. The president made the ludicrous suggestion that he should be the one to examine the Cohen documents now in the hands of New York prosecutors to see what can or cannot be used in court. Trump's hiring of Rudy Giuliani to negotiate with Special Counsel Mueller seems a last-ditch effort to gain control of a runaway situation. At least a dozen major lawyers have refused to represent the president in the Mueller investigations.

If the president fires any more officials at the Justice Department or the FBI, it should be the trigger to begin hearings on his impeachment. If he tries to pardon Michael Cohen, this too should trigger impeachment proceedings. It would at most times in our history, but we have a GOP-controlled Congress that seems willing to aid and abet the president in his attempts to cover up crimes. How long can the Congress stand by with our legal institutions threatened?

A Reflection on James Comey

April 29, 2018

At this moment, everyone who follows American politics is trying to understand the role of fired FBI Director James Comey in this giant mess we are living through. I just finished his book, *A Higher Loyalty: Truth, Lies, and Leadership,* and wanted to record some of my observations about him and the maelstrom that swirls around him. This is not going to be a book review or an attempt to retrace the dramatic events that have unfolded since the Trump campaign or since the president fired Comey. This will be a reflection on some of the things I have been thinking about in relation to this central figure in the Trump investigations.

Senator Susan Collins (R-ME) recently said on Meet the Press that Comey should not have written his book. She characterized Comey's release of his notes of his meetings with Trump to be leaks. She said he did not follow Justice Department protocol when he thrust himself into the election process. And she concluded that he should not have published his book in the middle of an investigation.

This was a polite and measured response from a serious Republican senator, but it encompasses the main talking points against Comey. Others, including the President of the United States, are not as polished in their critique as was Senator Collins. At a pep rally last night in Michigan the president railed against Comey for being a liar, a leaker, and someone who should be in jail. He said he did the country a favor by firing him.

Frank Luntz, who does focus groups about as well as anyone in the business, gathered a group of Republicans and Democrats, gave them sophisticated button pads to record their feelings, and had them watch George Stephanopoulos's first interview with Comey following the publication of his book. In the end, Democrats believed Comey, tended to forgive him for missteps he made, and found him truthful, while the Republicans saw Comey as an arrogant liar who was untrustworthy and was cashing in with his book.

But there were some surprises from the Luntz focus group. Neither the Republicans nor the Democrats thought Trump should have fired Comey. And neither group wants to see the president impeached, because they see impeachment as "harmful" to the political life of the nation.

We are as polarized about James Comey as we are about all our politics. It is not surprising that when it comes to Comey vs Trump, most people retreat to their own political tribe for answers. I am not going to pretend that I am any different. Nobody has a clear idea yet of how this is going to play out. Only the passage of time will determine a more balanced view of Comey.

But maybe all we need to know about him is in front of us now. I think it is. I am in the camp that thinks James Comey is an honorable man who made some costly mistakes of judgment. Unlike Hillary Clinton, however, I am not going to blame Comey's awkward and terribly untimely statements about her email during the campaign as the main cause that Hillary was defeated. It was a crucial factor. But not the only one.

Comey's mistakes were not crimes. But his mistakes get magnified with hindsight and they keep coming up not in the context of a balanced view of him, but in an environment filled with propaganda, and filled with the daily frothing and tweeting of President Trump. In this milieu, Comey doesn't have a chance, no matter how many talk-show appearances and book-talks he might make.

When I first learned that he was writing a book, I too thought it was too soon. It never crossed my mind that he was doing it to cash in, although a 57-year-old man just thrown out of the best job of his life, and suddenly unemployed, just might be thinking about monetary matters. The reason I thought it was too soon was because I had some preconceived notions of what the book might be. It is not a kiss-and-tell book. He reveals nothing new about Trump or the investigations. He does not leak anything that is not in the public domain already. The book is not sensational in the same way that Michael Wolff's book, *Fire and Fury*, describes in great detail the chaos in the White House.

Comey's book is an argument in favor of the rule of law. It is an argument for respect for our governmental institutions which are under daily assault by the president. It is an argument that ethical behavior and a moral compass are essential elements for our elected officials and for our entire society. He argues that leaders cannot systematically lie to the American people. It is never too soon to write about subjects like these.

I believe Comey felt that to remain silent when the president was not remaining silent changed the rules. His critics say he should not have written a book until the investigations are over. Well, how about telling the President of the United States to shut up until the investigations are over? The president attacks the FBI every day. He attacks Comey every day. Is there a higher ground that says you should stay aloof and silent while the president plays by a separate set of rules?

Comey describes in his book about being bullied when he was a child. The best way to deal with a bully is to stand up, not shut up. Comey has become the president's punching bag. Comey is punching back with a story of dedication to the law and the importance of ethical behavior. I know which side I am on in this fight.

When Comey states President Trump is "morally unfit to be president," I heartily concur. It is why I felt compelled to start systematically writing my thoughts about this president almost two years ago. I could not stay silent. Trump is not a normal president. He is not, as his followers claim, a president who is draining the swamp and shaking up the Washington Establishment. He is destroying the government and the U. S. Constitution because he knows no other way to act. He acts to defend himself at any cost.

Comey, a prosecutor of major crime figures, described the president as projecting that same style that crime bosses do. Everything must be about them and for them. Crime bosses demand personal loyalty. The first thing Trump asked of Comey was that he be personally loyal to him. But as the title of Comey's book suggests, a president and all officers of the government must have a "higher loyalty" to the Constitution, to the rule of law, and to the American people. You cannot be loyal to the people of this nation if you lie to them day in and day out about things large and small.

When I was growing up in Harvey, Illinois, south of Chicago, I heard stories about the mobster Al Capone, who was still a folk hero to some people in the 1940s and 50s. Capone operated on the South Side, in places close to where I grew up. Everyone knew Capone broke the law, that he was a crime boss, but if they weren't personally hurt by his actions, they often liked the guy.

Capone ran booze during Prohibition. How could you fault that? I heard stories about how kind Capone could be to the down-and-out poor during the Depression. He started a soup kitchen to feed the needy. He gave out turkeys at Thanksgiving. I had an uncle who borrowed money from the mob on the South Side. People said, what the mob did was none of their business and if you stayed out of Capone's business he wouldn't hurt you.

I have nagging thoughts that some Americans have already made Trump into a mobster-like folk hero. He is an anti-government guy who talks and thinks the way a lot of Americans do. Some Americans admire the way Trump bullies the government. They like his swagger. They like his gaudy displays of wealth. They liked the image of Trump from the "The Apprentice." People will overlook a lot of faults if you give them a turkey at Thanksgiving or a small tax cut at Christmas time.

Trump's crude comments have appeal to some Americans who are impatient with the kind of careful diplomatic language used in government to avoid offending anyone. Our politics has become a form of entertainment for some. It is like the TV series "House of Cards," only real. Some Americans flock to Trump's rallies for the same reason they go to a circus, to see the celebrity in the tent and hear him say outrageous things. At his rally in Michigan yesterday the president took full credit for ending the Korean War and the crowd immediately yelled for him to get the Nobel Peace Prize. Who set that one up?

If Comey comes across to some as a stuffed shirt who recoils at the thought of a man like Trump in the White House, then I count myself as a stuffed shirt too and I am honored to join him in this view. We need to speak out against the president's crudeness, his lies, and his moral incompetence. As Comey says, no president should be shouting to lock up any American citizen. Who is he to unilaterally act as judge, jury, and executioner?

Trump is unfit by temperament or experience to lead this nation and we see examples of it every day. His White House staff is in shambles, his cabinet is composed of kleptocrats who are so arrogant that they think public service has no rules other than to help them and their friends make money and fly first class at taxpayer expense. How is this any different than the mobsters that Comey used to prosecute?

Comey, when asked by George Stephanopoulos, if Trump should be impeached gave a most interesting answer. Comey described it as an answer some would find strange. He said, "I hope not because I think impeaching and removing Donald Trump from office would let the American people off the hook and have something happen indirectly that I believe they're duty bound to do directly. People in this country need to stand up and go to the voting booth and vote their values."

I liked this answer because it put the burden back where it belonged on the American people. It was the American electorate at the ballot box that gave us Donald Trump. Many voters, including me, were shocked at the time, but the whole nation accepted the results and Trump was sworn in because we all honored the electoral process, even if more than half of the voters didn't like the outcome.

It would be best if the American people, at the ballot box in 2018 and again in 2020 would reject Trump and Trump candidates for election to Congress. This would be the cleanest, most straightforward way to send a signal to the president, the nation, and the world, that Trump's days are numbered and that the ship of state is not sinking.

An impeachment may still be in the offing depending on the results of the Mueller investigations, or depending on future unconstitutional acts by President Trump, such as firing any more officials at the Justice Department or the FBI. An impeachment in a polarized political climate might contribute mightily to further polarization and stress. But under some circumstances, we should not be afraid to impeach the president and face the consequences, which, as James Comey says, were of our own making in the last election. We can look for scapegoats all we want. We all need to take responsibility at the ballot box and get ourselves off the hook the right way.

Authentic People, Thinkers, and Experts

May 6, 2018

I spent a good part of this rainy Sunday in May reading the newspaper, some magazines, and a book. The subjects of today's reading seemed unconnected at first. But as I pondered them, I discovered connections that got me thinking about important but often hidden aspects of the Donald Trump phenomenon.

David Von Drehle, writing on Senator John McCain in the *Washington Post*, turns to the Bible to ask a question from the Book of James, "What is your life? For you are a mist that appears for a little time and then vanishes." (4:14). To Von Drehle, the essence of McCain's life can be distilled from his act of honor and sacrifice when he was a prisoner of war.

McCain was no ordinary prisoner; his father and grandfather were both admirals, and his father was in command of operations in Vietnam at the time. McCain's captors offered to release him, but McCain refused to exercise his privileged status and would not abandon his fellow prisoners.

This single act of honor, for which McCain was tortured during his years of captivity, was a defining moment that answered the biblical question: what is your life? In McCain's case, a life of honor defined by a singular act of courage and character, which set a tone of honor that carried him through his entire life.

Von Drehle, turns to another life, to Donald Trump, who early in his campaign said of John McCain that he didn't like people who got captured. How, when we look at the life of Donald Trump, do we answer the question in the Book of James, what is your life? Von Drehle sees fame in Trump's life but not honor, and he concludes "that reality is not a TV show; that fame is mist but honor granite; that heroes don't need fixers on retainer."

Later today, I was browsing in a thick book by Kevin Young, with the intriguing title: *Bunk: The Rise of Hoaxes, Humbug, Plagiarists, Phonies, Post-Facts, and Fake News.* This is a fascinating history of all the fakery that is embedded in American culture and in our politics, personified by the master-entertainer of fakery, P.T. Barnum.

Kevin Young started writing this book years before the rise of Donald Trump, but his observations on Trump in the last chapter of his book certainly show that Trump fits into a long line of American con men, fakers, liars, and flimflam artists. One line in Young's book, set off as a single paragraph, struck me as the best single-sentence critique of what is wrong with Trump and Trumpism that I have read to date:

"What Trump really heralds is a time when there are no more experts."

We have seen ample evidence in Trump's cabinet picks and in many of his appointments to top executive agency jobs, that he picks friends, cronies, people he likes, or acquaintances of people he likes, to take top positions without concern for their level of expertise. He gave top jobs to members of his own family who, like the president, had no experience whatsoever in government service.

Trump brought a string of fellow billionaires with him because, like most Americans, Trump too believes the myth that government is best run by people who have proven themselves in the business world. Governing the nation is not the same as running a business, but this is a difficult thing for many Americans, including Trump, to understand. Government is supposed to serve and protect the people. Business is supposed to serve and protect the stockholders.

Trump is uncomfortable around experts. The president's briefings, that come from experts, must be boiled down to a page or two, because Trump gets jittery around too much information. He has said on numerous occasions that he trusts his own instincts. He can decide from his gut. He doesn't need experts.

Expertise is dangerous to those who live by lies and fakery. Experts are people who know how to engage in critical thinking. It is their job, whatever their area of expertise, to find facts, to verify them, to weigh their merit, to put facts into a context, to pay attention to the chronology of when things happened and their relationship to other things that are happening.

Experts are people who can separate facts from fakery and lies. Trump has good reason to fear experts. Among the experts he fears the most are the men and women of the FBI and the Justice Department, whose job it is to ferret out criminals and con artists who use lies and deceit to cover their tracks.

Trump has existed his whole life in a fake world of his own design, where he set out to brand himself as a bold, brash, raconteur billionaire and celebrity. Never in the history of bunk and fakery in America has a con man succeeded as well as Donald Trump. He has risen to the top of political power and celebrity status based not on honor, character, or expertise, but merely on the illusion of success itself.

During his campaign Trump promulgated the myth that many Americans already believed, that successful people are smarter, better, and more talented than those with less success. Americans believe that successful business people who are also world-class celebrities are the epitome what America is all about. Such people exist on the highest rung of the evolutionary ladder.

In the last campaign, American voters, mad at politicians and presuming that politics is not a worthy or noble profession, turned to a businessman to make America run like a Fortune 500 company. In doing so, voters went all the way and picked a fake businessman who built his empire on image and fraud rather than the reality of the bottom-line. Trump's actual personality was hidden while his fake personality was enhanced to celebrityhood by a TV reality show. A lot of Americans watched Trump, the TV actor, and came to admire the fake tycoon he portrayed.

There is a famous American quotation "There is a sucker born every minute," that has been attributed to many people, including P.T. Barnum. Whoever it was that said it first, it is a universal statement of the gullibility of humans. Even when we know something is fake, we are drawn to it like circus goers used to be drawn to the bearded lady and the two-headed calf.

What will it take in the United States in 2018 to break the spell of the most successful Fake President in the history of the nation? When will we come to realize that we need experts and thinkers in our government and in governments around the world? We desperately need people who can help solve big problems. There are thinkers, experts, honest men and women in all areas of American life who should be encouraged to serve their country. We cannot survive for long on a shell game of promises to make things great. We cannot survive for long with incompetence at the highest levels of the executive branch.

When will we come to realize that authenticity, honor, and character, are the qualities that make real heroes, real leaders, and real American citizens?

Lie Number 3,001

May 7, 2018

Numerous reports have placed the number of lies and misinformation that have been uttered or tweeted by President Trump to be 3,000. Today, add one more to the list. This morning the president tweeted that the "Witch Hunt" against him is being orchestrated by 13 Democrats, who he does not name.

I am sure that if we searched all through the FBI and the Justice Department and into the States Attorneys offices in Southern New York and in Virginia, that we would probably find 13 Democrats, not necessarily leading the "Witch Hunt," but playing some part in the various investigations. In conducting this search we would also find plenty of Republicans.

In order to make this a partisan Witch Hunt, Trump has to ignore all the judges and prosecutors appointed by Republican presidents, or the fact that Robert Mueller is a registered Republican, and that Rod Rosenstein's political affiliation might be Republican. He was, after all, appointed to his current position as Deputy Attorney General by Donald Trump and was confirmed by a Republican-controlled Senate by the incredibly bipartisan vote of 94-6.

Once again Trump lies to inflame partisanship in the nation and keep the country divided as we head into the November election cycle. But the bigger lie he is telling is that all the people in law enforcement, and all public servants, regardless of their political affiliations or no affiliations at all, are seen as conducting their professional responsibilities and duties as partisans rather than professionals. This is an insult to every public servant who does his or her duty faithfully, and whose party label does not come into play. Trump insults every faithful and loyal public servant by reducing them to party labels, and presuming they act first and foremost out of party loyalty.

Trump cannot grasp the idea that the Rule of Law and an Oath to Defend the Constitution are far more important than a party label. But wait! Maybe he does know this. Maybe Trump's lie about who is after him is really just his latest attempt to hoodwink the American people in an election year. Maybe what he is really saying, and wishing, is that the American people get the message that in order to stop this Witch Hunt against the poor, innocent, Donald, that only Republicans should be elected in the fall. He is crying out to his base: Save Me from the Dastardly Democrats.

I really hope the American people, Republicans and Democrats alike can see through Lie 3,001, and recognize that justice in America does not come from partisan politics. It comes from a Higher Loyalty (to use the title of James Comey's book), a loyalty to the Constitution, to country, and to our finest traditions of fairness and justice, that have never been the exclusive province of either political party. Can we not, at last, agree that Republicans, Democrats, Independents, and persons with no party affiliation, are all, first and foremost, fellow citizens?

Donald Trump in the Bible

May 13, 2018

Politics, religion, foreign relations, and international diplomacy, all were stressed to the breaking point today by the official ceremony transferring the U.S. Embassy to Jerusalem. Every aspect of this event, the result of President Trump's unilateral decision to move the embassy when no previous president going back to Harry Truman would do it, has stirred controversy. It is a victory for Israeli President Benjamin Netanyahu; it is a popular decision in Israel.

Moving the embassy from Tel Aviv to Jerusalem has divided American Jews. But the move has strong appeal based on literal biblical interpretation for most American evangelicals. Overall, Trump's decision has exacerbated our political divisions at home and inflamed Palestine. We can no longer be an arbiter between Israel and Palestine. We took Israel's side. Being an ally of Israel has always been the position of the United States, but now any diplomatic subtlety that we had to keep a door open, at least a crack, to the U.S. acting as an arbiter of peace in that region is gone.

Today we saw the divisions of Trump's decision in sharp contrast. While the high and mighty of American and Israeli politics met with ceremonial pomp in Jerusalem, Palestinians from the crowded confines of the Gaza Strip marched in protest to the wire fence separating them from Israel, where, as I write this, more than 40 have been shot dead, and thousands injured. Israeli President Netanyahu, in the secure surroundings of what will become the American Embassy, praised the Israeli Army for defending their country at the border. The audience roared its approval.

Trump said during his campaign that he would recognize Jerusalem as the capital of Israel. Jared Kushner, speaking for President Trump at the embassy ceremony said "When President Trump makes a promise, he keeps it." But at what cost at home and abroad?

President Trump, in executing this decision, decided to go all the way with his own base. He sent a controversial Southern Baptist megachurch minister, Robert Jeffress, to speak at the ceremony. Trump showed, once more, how insensitive he could be to everyone except his base. On the eve of the ceremony, Mitt Romney, running for the Senate from Utah, expressed his opposition in a tweet: "Robert Jeffress says 'you can't be saved by being a Jew,' and 'Mormonism is a heresy from the pit of hell.' He's said the same about Islam. Such a religious bigot should not be giving the prayer that opens the United States Embassy in Jerusalem."

It was Robert Jeffress who prayed for Trump at his inauguration, during a private dinner, when he compared Trump to Nehemiah the biblical builder who was ordered by God to build a wall around Jerusalem to keep out its enemies. Jeffress said, "You see, God is NOT against building walls."

At the Jerusalem ceremony today, Jeffress once again put Trump on the side of God for fulfilling the 3,000 year old biblical prophecy that Jerusalem would be the capital of Israel. When Jeffress concluded his prayer, he did so in the name of Jesus Christ. A lukewarm smattering of applause broke out.

You can see why Trump likes this preacher, whose radio program is broadcast on 1,200 stations, reaching evangelicals across America. Mitt Romney's criticism of Trump for sending this man to represent the United States is accurate enough, but left out the fact that Jeffress has also said the Catholic Church is pagan and corrupt and is an instrument of Satan. He has also said on numerous occasions what is surely music to Trump's ears that all Clinton supporters were going to hell too.

Jeffress got on the program because Trump wanted him there. Jeffress wraps Trump in the Bible and claims he is fulfilling prophecy. This is enough for Trump. Trump obviously never noticed that the guy is a first-class bigot who has condemned damn near everyone to hell, including all Jews! Only an insensitive, self-absorbed man like Trump would send a preacher like this to Israel. Once again it is about Trump, not Israel or the Jewish people.

Trump sent another evangelical preacher too, who gave the benediction at the embassy ceremony. This was John Hagee, leader of Christians United for Israel, who some years ago called Hitler an instrument of God for forcing Jews back to Israel. Of all the fine clergy in America, is this the best we can do to represent the United States, in Israel of all places? This was a presidential decision to send these men. Nobody else at the White House seems to know how it happened. Today White House spokesman Raj Shah had to say the White House doesn't endorse the idea that all Jews are going to hell.

The world will little note nor long remember who President Trump sent to speak at the opening of the American embassy in Jerusalem. Unfolding world events of greater import will push this ceremony into a footnote of history. Jared and Ivanka looked sharp and immaculately dressed, sitting there near President Netanyahu, and not far from American casino magnate and mega-Trump supporter Sheldon Adelson, all listening to an American preacher who thinks everyone from every other religion in the world but his and everyone from the Democratic Party is going to burn in hell.

While I spend my eternity burning in hell for voting for Hillary Clinton, I will have plenty of time to contemplate Donald Trump and Robert Jeffress, sitting smugly in heaven at the right hand of God. There must be a word in our language that is stronger than bigotry. But for now it will do.

Save the Mueller Investigations

May 17, 2018

President Donald Trump cannot stop complaining that the Mueller investigation is the Greatest Witch Hunt in American History. Count this as one of his greatest lies. The Mueller investigation is the single most important investigation of high crimes and misdemeanors in American history.

It is also the first investigation into a new kind of deadly serious cyberwarfare representing one of the most dangerous threats to democracy and the stability of the United States government in modern times. There can be no time limit on matters this vital to the very survival of the United States of America and American democracy and independence. Russian agents and operatives infiltrated the American election process and infiltrated the Trump campaign and continue to influence the actions of Donald Trump since he became president. What could be more serious?

There is a strong likelihood that these foreign agents and hackers were aided and abetted by citizens of the United States, including officials of the Trump campaign, some of whom have already pled guilty, with others under indictment. What could be more ludicrous that putting such a monumental series of investigations in an artificial time frame, as if one year is long enough? When we hear the president, his lawyers, the vice-president, and GOP members of Congress, and damn near everyone on Fox News saying, "time to wrap this up," it should be time to wonder what they have to hide and why they are in such a hurry to subvert a legitimate and absolutely vital investigation.

Politics and political posturing should have nothing to do with investigations conducted by the United States Department of Justice, the FBI, or investigations in any jurisdiction at the local, state, or federal level. We are either a nation of laws, or we are a nation of sheep being led to the slaughter. Trump is constantly scheming to obstruct justice.

Time-wise, how do the Mueller investigations stack up with other major investigations in recent American history? Congress conducted labor racketeering investigations from 1957 to 1961, which resulted in 141 Teamsters' Union officials accused of dishonest dealings. Teamster president Dave Beck pleaded the Fifth Amendment

140 times, but information turned up by the investigation led to his resignation and later he was convicted and jailed.

The Watergate investigations of 1973-74, stemmed from a break-in of Democratic National Committee headquarters on June 17, 1972. By September that year, Bob Woodward and Carl Bernstein of the *Washington Post* revealed that Attorney General John Mitchell had a slush fund for gathering political intelligence against Nixon's opponents, the start of a complex money trail. President Nixon was not connected to this yet, and he was re-elected as president in 1972. In early 1973 Nixon top aides G. Gordon Liddy and James W. McCord were found guilty of conspiracy, burglary, and wiretapping.

More than a year later, the Nixon White House refused to turn over tape recordings to investigators. In October 1973, Nixon fired Special Prosecutor Archibald Cox, causing the Attorney General and the Deputy Attorney General to resign. Getting rid of top Justice Department officials did not stop the investigation. Dragging things out, Nixon eventually released extensive edited transcripts of the White House tapes.

This was not enough. The Supreme Court required Nixon to turn over the actual tape recordings of 64 specific tapes on July 24, 1974. Three days later the House Judiciary Committee passed articles of impeachment. Less than two weeks later, Nixon resigned rather than face impeachment. Those of us who lived through this thought it would never end. But it did, on its own complex time schedule.

In the case of the Iran-Contra investigation, this began as Congressional hearings conducted in 1987, to get to the bottom of illegal acts of the Reagan Administration, which clandestinely sold missiles to Iran in exchange for hostages held in Lebanon, with the money from the missile sales funneled illegally to help rebels fighting against the Sandinista government in Nicaragua.

This illegal activity actually began in 1981 with President Reagan's secret authorization to help the contra rebels in their attempt to overthrow the government of Nicaragua. Reagan's attempt to help the contras was banned by law in 1983, but continued anyway. The Congressional hearings implicated Reagan officials in crimes, but no "smoking gun" was found connecting the president to the illegalities.

The investigations of Iran Contra involved two other investigations besides the Congressional hearings, the independent Tower Commission and a special prosecutor Lawrence Welch. The special prosecutor did not issue his final report until six years after the Congressional hearings of 1987.

By 1993, the statute of limitations had run out on some crimes, others indicted and convicted had their convictions overturned on appeal, and the final six top Reagan officials were pardoned by incoming President George H.W. Bush. This investigation lasted more than six years and cost $36 million.

President Bill Clinton was investigated more than any president in history and was impeached by the House of Representatives but not convicted by the Senate. The subjects of the investigations began with activities related to the Whitewater Land Company in Arkansas, even before Clinton was elected president.

Once in office, Clinton faced investigations from House and Senate committees related to firing seven employees of the White House Travel Office, the death of deputy White House Council Vince Foster, who committed suicide. Some members of Congress thought he was murdered. Video tapes circulated by right-wing groups claimed the Clintons were guilty of several murders. Several congressional committees and two special prosecutors concluded Vince Foster committed suicide. But even to this day you can find websites devoted to Foster's death as a deep Clinton conspiracy.

In 1994 Robert Fiske was appointed special prosecutor for the Whitewater investigation and was replaced 8 months later by Ken Starr. The House Banking Committee and the Fiske investigations found no wrongdoing in Whitewater. The Starr investigations found no crimes, until the sex scandal with Monica Lewinsky broke in 1998.

Starr got permission to expand his investigation into the sex scandal, and eventually the president lied under oath to a grand jury about having sex with Lewinsky, thus committing perjury. The House, in the hands of Republicans since 1995, quickly impeached the president.

The Republican Congress spent more than $80 million investigating Bill Clinton, and the special prosecutor's three-year investigation cost more than $30 million more. In the end the U.S. Senate decided that lying about a sexual affair was not sufficient constitutional grounds to remove a president from office.

Most of the major investigations in American history took a year or two to complete, while others, noted above, took much longer. While politicians and their partisan supporters talk about the time and money involved, we need to keep our eyes on the prize of justice being done. We should demand that criminals are prosecuted and that the innocent are exonerated. For the vital safety of the nation and in the strongest interests of national security we cannot stop an investigation that addresses the possibility of major crimes being perpetrated at the highest levels of our government.

Given the relatively short time of the Mueller investigation, the results have been remarkably productive so far, with four guilty pleas and numerous indictments of Americans and Russians, with more to come. Each day brings new revelations of serious crimes. While Trump denies "collusion" on a daily basis, I am not even interested in that word, which is vague and has little legal meaning.

I am sure Robert Mueller and his investigators are not looking for "collusion" unless it is specifically tied to crimes like conspiracy, money-laundering, wire fraud, bank fraud, income tax evasion, campaign finance violations, illegally acting as a foreign agent, treason, and the much misunderstood but very important factor of violation of the Constitution's emoluments clause, something the Framers of the Constitution included to prevent the corruption of American officials if they were allowed to accept anything of value from a foreign power.

I will end with one troubling example of the emoluments clause. We learned recently that Trump's support of the Chinese phone company ZTE "coincidentally" corresponded to an announcement that the Chinese government was putting $500 million into an Indonesian theme park with ties to the Trump Organization. Earlier, China had given potentially lucrative patents to products sold by Ivanka Trump in her business and by Donald Trump through the Trump Organization. All the shady dealings and corrupt bargains Trump had before his election as president, followed him right into the White House and right into a massive collision with the law and our system of justice. No wonder Trump was as shocked as the rest of us when he won the election.

If money for an Indonesian theme park with Trump Organization interests is more important to the president than the national security of the United States, we need to remove him from office. He just may be the first major international crime boss ever to occupy the White House.

The Never-Ending Assault on Justice

May 21, 2018

The cornered animal that is our president, is getting more manic every day. He is trying to goad Deputy Attorney General Rod Rosenstein into resigning. Trump is very close to blowing up the American justice system just to save his own hide and that of his family. Damage to the rule of law is becoming so severe that this president has become the biggest single threat to the security and well-being of the nation.

The history books will forget most of President Trump's tweets, but they will not forget his ongoing war with the FBI and the Justice Department. His demand that the Justice Department investigate an unsubstantiated charge that someone from the FBI infiltrated the Trump Campaign to politically undermine Trump is the latest egregious assault on the Constitution and the law.

If Rosenstein is forced out of office, the president will quickly find a way to fire Robert Mueller. Trump may have been told that this much tampering with American justice backfired badly on President Nixon, forcing him to resign before facing impeachment. But Trump does not respond to historical evidence. He knows about the powers of his office, but he does not know about the limits of that power. He does not have absolute power over anything. He thinks he has absolute power over everything. He may, however, have enough power to seriously derail the ongoing investigations until after the November elections.

What should be obvious to every American is that it is dead wrong and most likely illegal for Trump to try to stop an investigation about him and his own campaign. What does obstruction of justice mean? It means trying to interfere or stop a legitimate investigation into wrongdoing. Trump is pointing fingers at those investigating him and calling them corrupt. Even though this investigation is being conducted by mostly Republicans, with Republican-appointed judges issuing FISA warrants, Trump wants us to believe that this is a Democratic Party inspired Witch Hunt.

Rod Rosenstein is playing a dangerous cat and mouse game with Trump. Rather than telling the president he has no grounds to call for an investigation of the investigators, Rosenstein authorized the Department of Justice's Inspector General to look into the matter. This is a stalling tactic. But it is also a concession to Trump and this is very troublesome. When you concede to a bully, the bully wins.

Trump's allegations have no basis in fact. He says what he does to smear the FBI and the Mueller investigations. He wants the Mueller report to be so corrupted by Trump's lies and diversions that by the time it comes out it will have been completely smeared in advance. This is how a criminal would attack those prosecuting him.

Going back to day one of the campaign, Trump and his campaign people were told that if foreigners approached the campaign, they were required by law to notify the FBI. Trump's campaign had Russians falling out of the trees, to paraphrase Congressman Eric Swalwell of the House Intelligence Committee. Yet nobody on the Trump campaign ever contacted the FBI.

Donald Trump, Jr. held at least two meetings with foreigners including Russians and from Arab countries, at Trump Tower in New York, yet he never reported this to the FBI. These meetings were one floor down from Trump's offices. Yet Don Jr. and Jared Kushner claim they never told Trump about these meetings. This is beyond belief. You will recall that Trump put together an excuse for the Russian meeting at Trump Tower by saying the subject of that meeting was adoption of Russian orphans. Did Trump expect anyone to belief that whopper?

We all need to hang tough and hope the Justice Department and the FBI do too. We cannot allow Trump's unparalleled assault on the law, the free press, and on our national security, to succeed. He is being aided and abetted by some GOP members of Congress and this is something we must carefully watch. We all know about Devin Nunes, who completely scuttled the House Intelligence Committee investigation, but there are others, especially Mark Meadows (R-NC) and Jim Jordan (R-Ohio) who are keeping congressional pressure on the FBI that goes beyond the role of normal oversight.

Amateur Autocrat

May 24, 2018

The much-ballyhooed summit meeting between President Trump and Kim Jong Un of North Korea was unilaterally and arbitrarily scuttled today in a one-page letter from a petulant president who gave as his excuse the fact that North Korea said nasty things about Vice President Pence, calling the vice-president a "political dummy." To earn this insult, Pence had made comparisons with our strategy to stop North Korean nukes using methods like those used years earlier with Muammar Gaddafi in Libya.

Gaddafi was subsequently overthrown and murdered in 2011. This is not the kind of thing Pence should have been talking about weeks before the summit was to take place. But it does reveal with strong documentary evidence how amateurish and childish our president can be when confronted with childish insults from Kim Jong Un. Someone should remind Trump of the adage, sticks and stones may break my bones, but names will never hurt me. He was hurt, or feigned being hurt, by a verbal insult. If he is that thin-skinned, how could he possibly negotiate a complex agreement to denuclearize North Korea?

Trump's withdrawal came as a complete surprise to our State Department and to our allies in South Korea and Japan. President Moon of South Korea was just here in the United States two days ago. Why wasn't he told of Trump's sudden change of heart? I can only conclude that Trump decided this on his own, on the spur of the moment. It is a monumental foreign policy blunder.

After cancelling the summit, and scolding North Korea for insulting the vice president, Trump lapsed into the kind of boilerplate language often found in business letters. He told the North Korean leader "If you change your mind having to do with this most important summit, please do not hesitate to call me or write."

One thing is very clear. This summit was not going to be conducted according to diplomatic protocol, where the deliverable results for both sides are worked out in lengthy negotiations held at lower levels of government, using experts in diplomacy and in nuclear weaponry. Trump believes his own branding that he is a great negotiator who knows how to close a deal. But what he has demonstrated time and again is that he is a complete amateur in governance and diplomacy. He cannot share power with other high-level government officials, like the Secretary of State. He does not trust anyone sufficiently to share power. The result of his mistrust is that he shrinks the great wealth of resources and expertise in this country down to one terribly flawed man.

This news was startling enough today, but we also learned that Jared Kushner has finally been granted a top-secret clearance. This is another example of Trump the autocrat at work. It is also a clear sign of how deep the nepotism of the Trump family goes. Presidents have the ultimate authority to classify or declassify government secrets. This system relies on the president using good judgment, paying attention to the national security of the country and protecting our intelligence-gathering agencies and the men and women of the clandestine services. It seems the president has brushed aside all considerations of national security to give his son-in-law access to the nation's secrets. What kind of pressure did the president bring to bear on the review process that allowed an amateur like Kushner to get this clearance?

The news came fast and furious today on yet another front. The heads of our intelligence agencies are meeting with the president at the White House today. There are two meetings scheduled. The first is with two Republicans. A second meeting will include the same Republicans and Democrats will be added to the mix. The purpose of these meetings is to go over President Trump's charges, now referred to as "Spygate" by the president, to look at evidence that the FBI may have "infiltrated" the Trump campaign for political purposes. The president has been using his big megaphone to hype this issue and demand an investigation without offering a shred of evidence of wrongdoing on the part of the FBI. Yet Trump is calling this bigger than Watergate.

The fact that he would call in the intelligence agency heads to meet only with Republicans was an outrage of its own. Trump, in calling for an investigation of the investigators for being political, could only see "transparency" in sharing information with Republicans in Congress. No Democrats need apply. Trump completely politicized the process, and then, with a straight face, said he was doing so because transparency is so important.

Congressional Democrats would have none of this. It will be interesting to see how much muscle inside Congress was used so Democrats could be included. Trump's attempt to get information from the intelligence agencies without sharing that same information with Democrats could be construed as another example of obstruction of justice. But it is clearly a political ploy that has no place in any investigation. Calling in intelligence services to give information only to one political party is a serious assault on the independence of these agencies. It undermines the veracity of our intelligence services. Come to think of it, isn't this exactly what Trump wants to happen to the FBI and the Department of Justice? Isn't it his goal to smear the agencies that are investigating his campaign and aspects of his presidency? Isn't it his goal to question the procedures of our clandestine services?

Trump may be a complete failure as a president and as an autocrat. But he is no amateur when it comes to fighting to save his own hide. He has been doing this his whole life. In more than 3,500 lawsuits, many of them using the sleaziest lawyer of them all, the late Roy Cohn, Trump has been a total professional at protecting his own interests.

When he became president, he could no longer hide in his New York underworld of intimidation, bullying, threats of lawsuits, bribes, and making deals under the table. The culture of the White House is not the same as the culture of Trump Tower. The struggle facing us is for enough Americans to understand the difference.

It is not OK for Trump to pretend he is draining some swamp when he is the swamp. Trump sees the "Swamp" as every person or agency of government that is threatening him. I see the "Swamp" as President Trump and his corrupt administration.

Donald Trump did not invent corruption in high places. He did not invent nepotism, obstruction of justice, conspiracy, and fraud. He did not invent lying. But he has taken these things to levels not seen in modern America since the corruption and scandals of the Reconstruction Era, 150 years ago. Our great challenge is to end the corruption that Trump brought with him into the executive branch of the United States government. The only way to do this that will have enduring value to the future success of American government is for law and order to prevail.

Impeachment Requires Public Sentiment

May 28, 2018

R udy Giuliani, President Trump's carnival-barker-TV-lawyer, said that his strategy and that of the president is to constantly attack the Russian investigation and related matters in a conscious effort to influence public opinion. The issue, according to Giuliani, has come down to impeachment or no impeachment. Trump thinks he can stop impeachment if he convinces enough Americans that he is being unfairly investigated. Giuliani admitted that the "Spygate" controversy is a public relations stunt in anticipation of Trump being impeached. The president, without any evidence, accused the FBI of planting a spy in his campaign for political purposes. Now that this has been proven to be a hoax, what's next?

Charles Danner writing in the *New Yorker* on May 27, reported that Giuliani said, "And so our jury is — as it should be — the American people. And the American people, yes, are ... Republicans, largely, independents, pretty substantially, and even some Democrats now question the legitimacy of [the Mueller investigation]." Rudy Giuliani may want to believe that the American people question the investigation, and some do, but the investigation has not been completed. No one has seen a report from the Mueller investigations. All we have seen is the steady results of parts of the investigations that have key Trump campaign people pleading guilty, while others are under indictment.

Trump expects to be impeached (or possibly indicted) and when that day comes he wants to be able to say that it is all a plot by evil people, especially Democrats, and the Liberal Press, and the FBI, where there are supposedly 13 Democrats in the deep, deep bowels of the FBI Building who are pulling the strings to end Trump's presidency. When that moment comes when he is charged, Trump expects the American people to rise and save him from an impeachment, and if he is impeached to spread enough doubt and put enough public pressure on the Senate that two-thirds of the Senate will not convict him.

Trump would like nothing better than to be impeached and then escape conviction, like Bill Clinton. It would make him unbearable.

He would brag about his innocence. All his lies would be vindicated. He would feel untouchable by the law for the remainder of his term of office.

Trump said something to Leslie Stahl of CBS in a private conversation back in 2016 that should cause any decent American to worry. In what he said to Stahl, you can see that Trump's thousands of lies and his relentless assault on the press are all part of the same strategy that Giuliani just revealed. In a conversation with PBS's Judy Woodruff at the recent Deadline Club Awards, Stahl shared her 2016 encounter with Trump in his Trump Tower office when she asked him why he attacked the press so much. "I said, you know that is getting tired, why are you doing this? You're doing it over and over and it's boring. ... He said, 'You know why I do it? I do it to discredit you all and demean you all, so when you write negative stories about me no one will believe you.' He said that. So put that in your head for a minute."

Giuliani has been like a cuckoo clock lately when discussing the president's willingness to be interviewed by the Mueller investigators. He pops out and says it would not be a good idea for the president to allow an interview because Mueller would try to get the president in a perjury trap. Then, the very next day, he pops out of his cuckoo clock again to announce it would be just fine for Mueller to interview the president. Which is it? Giuliani wants to pretend the president has nothing to hide, that he is innocent, so an interview would be OK.

Giuliani has worried openly that the president and Mueller may have "a different truth." I guess Truth and Facts are relative things when you are trying to hide from the law. What should the American public believe? —Mueller's documented evidence backed up by timelines, corroborated by other witnesses, based on bank transactions, tax filings, and other facts, or are we supposed to believe Donald Trump's One "Fact"—his One "Truth" that Mueller's facts are not really facts.

Giuliani is right about one thing and he was not the first to say it. Abraham Lincoln said, "With public sentiment, nothing can fail. Without it, nothing can succeed." A president cannot move an agenda without the backing of the people. Without public support members of the House of Representatives are not likely to act to impeach the president. They have the constitutional power to impeach a president, but they are not likely to exercise that power without public support. Public sentiment is important to create an environment that is conducive to impeachment.

Right now, the Republican "base" does not want an impeachment. Republicans dominate the House. Democrats can clamor for impeachment all they want. There will be no impeachment for at least seven more months. If the House has a Democratic Party majority after the 2018 elections, the likelihood of impeachment goes up.

The only way the Republican-controlled House would impeach Trump is if the Mueller report is so devastating that the public will demand it, or unless Trump, in the next seven months, does something so egregious that it would cry out for action. Trump's firing of James Comey was sufficient grounds on its own to launch an impeachment inquiry for obstruction of justice. But the American public was so far behind the curve of understanding the severity of that firing that it never reached critical mass. Public sentiment takes time to develop and with a president using the power of his office to constantly undermine his critics, it makes it harder for the public to find consensus on what to do about our runaway crook in the White House.

Trump will continue to find ways to escalate his assault on the Justice Department and the FBI, and he will continue to undermine the American press. If the legal system of the United States is left in a smoldering heap in the next year or two and only Donald Trump stands over the ashes left from his unmerciful assault on Truth, he will see this as vindication. It will be the moment that the United States becomes a banana republic of criminal oligarchs.

Here is the most frightening thing of all. A considerable number of Americans seem willing to see the United States descend into petty dictatorship, hoping that the dictator will deliver them what they want when democracy hasn't. Lincoln thought public sentiment was a public good. He assumed the wisdom of the American people would bend toward good outcomes. He said in one debate with Stephen Douglas that it would be public sentiment that ended slavery.

Lincoln was a great, wise, and compassionate president and I hesitate to be critical of his view of public sentiment. But slavery was not ended by public sentiment. It was public sentiment that led to secession and Civil War. It was 700,000 dead on both sides; it was the utter defeat of the Confederacy, that changed public sentiment. And even in defeat, the Confederate "base" continued to fight the Lost Cause. Their descendants are still with us, still defending Confederate statues and longing for the Antebellum South. They tend to support Donald Trump. What will it take this time for public sentiment to rid the nation of a corrupt and racist president?

Trump Declares He is Above the Law

June 3, 2018

On June 2, the *New York Times* published a leaked 20-page memo that President Trump's lawyers sent to Special Counsel Robert Mueller last January. The *Times* highlighted sections of the memo that get to the heart of what Trump's lawyers hoped to convey to Robert Mueller. It is fascinating, essential reading, a key document in the unfolding saga the president's efforts to block the investigations of the Trump campaign's incredible coziness with Russian agents. If the day comes when Trump acts on the arguments presented in this memo, it will be a coup d'état.

The memo reveals how chaotic things are in the White House and have been for many months. The helter-skelter legal reasoning in this document reminded me very much of the last days of Watergate when a lot of people in the Nixon administration were trying to figure out ways to avoid perjuring themselves and found out it was a hopeless exercise. None of their stories jived. Their lies and their cover-ups had gotten so convoluted that there was no way they could defend themselves.

This memo, written by Jay Sekulow, who has been the longest-serving Trump lawyer, should be a wake-up call to all Americans that the White House is engaged in an effort to completely undermine the rule of law. The memo argues that the president is above the law, that he is the physical embodiment of American Justice, and that he is not answerable to mere Special Counsels.

Trump's legal team is going so far beyond what Nixon's lawyers could propose, that Trump's lawyers have turned American Law upside-down. We have seen President Trump act as if he is above the law. He acts unilaterally. He violates the norms of the office with impunity. He fires the head of the FBI and then lies about why he did it. We have seen in videotape evidence where Trump and his lawyers say one thing on a Monday and the opposite on Tuesday.

We have seen his contradictory tweets and his outrageous statements made at his never-ending campaign rallies. We have also seen recently how the president has sent forth as his TV-defender, the pathetic Rudy Giuliani, whose job it is to sell the idea that Trump has the power to end the Mueller investigation tomorrow, but maybe he won't—but maybe he will. But we have never seen the full thinking of Trump's lawyer's and how desperate they are until the revelation of the memo that Jay Sekulow sent to Mueller six months ago.

If Trump considers using the extreme justification for his unbridled power to determine what the law is and how it applies to him and his administration, American government as we have known it for 230 years will be out the window, swept away by a maniac in the White House and his enablers in Congress and among the American people.

I am tired of pundits talking about what Trump might do that would create a "constitutional crisis." We are in a constitutional crisis now. In fact, we are in multiple constitutional crises because of the president's inability to govern the nation. The pundits never explain how these multiple crises get fixed. The only solution, it seems, is that the president's actions could lead to impeachment.

If the president and his lawyers try to implement the extreme arguments in the Sekulow memo, by firing Mueller, by stopping the investigation altogether, by firing the Attorney General, by keeping Trump from testifying before Mueller or a grand jury, or by putting the president above the law, the courts, the Congress, and above the American people, then the term "constitutional crisis" will be shown to be a hollow and empty phrase, a toothless tiger. It will represent the overthrow of justice by a crazed dictator who is so hellbent on saving himself from his crimes that he would destroy the United States of America.

In the meantime, we sleepwalk toward our own destruction while we watch all this unfold as if it is nothing but a reality show starring Donald Trump. In Donald Trump's script, the Mueller investigation will be so undermined by the time a report appears, that Trump will laugh it off and move on to the next outrage.

Trump cannot pull off this coup d'état by himself. He needs enablers. We need to put pressure on Congress to act immediately, not necessarily toward impeachment but by passing a new law. Several have already been drafted. Congress has the power to protect the Mueller investigation, but it has not acted to do so. Congress needs to send a much clearer signal to President Trump that if he fires Mueller while the president himself is a subject of the investigation, then this too will become an article of impeachment.

Football and Patriotism

June 6, 2018

In the final reckoning of the Trump Administration, whenever that day comes, the president's flap with the Philadelphia Eagles will probably not make the history books. There will be too many other egregious circumstances and events to report than this minor episode along the path of our Pretended-Patriot-in-Chief. But it does offer a lesson about patriotism.

The president, in high dudgeon and with much childishness, called off a planned visit to the White House by the Super Bowl champions, the Philadelphia Eagles, when he discovered that the whole team was not planning to come. He accused the team, and the entire National Football League, of lacking patriotism.

The president said of the Eagles team, "They disagree with their president because he insists that they proudly stand for the national anthem, hand on heart, in honor of the great men and women of our military and the people of our country." Nobody on the Eagles team took a knee during the playing of the national anthem during the 2017 season, but this distinction was lost on Donald Trump.

As a substitute for the Eagles' visit, the president ordered the U.S. Army Chorus and the U.S. Marine Corps Band, to appear on the White House lawn with a small gathering that was supposed to be Eagles' fans but looked like bureaucrats in suits hastily assembled for the occasion.

The band, instead, played the Star-Spangled Banner. Trump spoke briefly and could not pass up the opportunity to praise himself and his administration saying, according to the *Washington Post*, that the United States "has never done better than it's doing right now. Never. We have record numbers at every outpost." Then the band and chorus rendered "America the Beautiful," with Trump, hand on heart, attempting to sing along, but it is not clear he knew the words. His mouth did not sync with the lyrics and mostly he just nodded along, according to the *Post*. The whole ceremony lasted 6 minutes and was interrupted once by a kneeling heckler who was booed by the assembled crowd.

The press accounts of this incident, and other incidents where Trump has questioned the patriotism of the NFL, other individuals, and organizations often cite a famous quotation from the 18th Century. It is from James Boswell's *The Life of Samuel Johnson* (1791), where Boswell quotes Johnson as saying "Patriotism is the last refuge of the scoundrel." Supposedly Johnson said this in April 1775, but to what he was specifically referring was not recorded. It is a marvelous insight nonetheless and has been used since that time to denote those who want to call attention to themselves, or to criticize others, by "wrapping themselves in the flag," as we would say in the 21st Century.

Accusing others of lacking patriotism has been a standard ploy of demagogues and dictators throughout history. It is akin to calling someone a traitor. It vanquishes enemies and it can be used to control populations. According to Trump, you can be a disloyal American for not putting your hand over your heart when the national anthem is played. He even suggested that people kneeling during the national anthem or failing to put hand over heart, should leave the country. By Trump's standard, you are certainly disloyal if you exercise your First Amendment rights to express grievances with the government during the playing of the national anthem.

There is another quotation from the 18th Century that has long been a favorite of mine. This one was recorded by James Madison during the debates over the nature of democracy during the Federal Convention of 1787, where Massachusetts delegate Elbridge Gerry said: "The evils we experience flow from the excess of democracy. The people do not want virtue, but are the dupes of pretended patriots. In Massts. it had been fully confirmed by experience that they are daily misled into the most baneful measures and opinions by the false reports circulated by designing men, and which no one on the spot can refute."

Donald Trump is the latest in a long line of "pretended patriots" who uses patriotism not for pride of country and time-honored tradition that unites the American people, but as a weapon to smite his enemies. And this president sees enemies all around him. They are inside his executive branch, in Congress, and in the National Football League. His enemies certainly include everyone who is a member of the Democratic Party and the American press in general and the Washington Press Corps in particular. He is even at war with his own hand-picked Attorney General. And then there is the Deep State conspiracy theory, where 13 unnamed Democrats are pulling the strings of the Special Counsel's investigations.

Who is left that is loyal to the president and can be considered as Patriotic Americans? Apparently the only loyal Americans are those in the president's "base." This base is hard to define but does consist of a sizable part of the Republican Party that is often religiously or racially motivated. It also includes a large number of Americans who generally vote for single issues no matter what else is before the country. These include those who vote for gun rights above all else, the absolute banning of all abortions above all else, tax cuts above all else, coal above all other forms of energy, and a good selection of Americans who believe that government itself is the problem and that Washington is nothing but a swamp.

The Trump base also includes a pretty good cross section of billionaires and other rich people who like the idea that 1% of America has it all and they want to keep it that way. Trump appeals to the American version of oligarchy, individuals and corporations who are used to controlling politics with their vast wealth. And his base includes a wide swath of dispossessed Americans who have been marginalized by the rapidly changing nature of the world's economy and by changing energy sources, and increased use of robots instead of people. This is a lot of Americans. Trump thinks it is a sufficient number to maintain control of power and to keep Congress at bay.

Patriotism is so much deeper than its symbols, the flag, a hand over the heart, or a salute, not that these things don't have their place. I write this on June 6, the 74th anniversary of D-Day, when the big push to liberate Europe from Nazi tyranny took place. Think of the sacrifice and patriotism of that event, where 160,000 members of the allied forces stormed the French coast, facing withering fire from enemy guns.

On the tenth anniversary of D-Day, Dwight D. Eisenhower was president of the United States. He had been the Supreme Allied Commander who led that massive invasion. What did Ike do that day to show his patriotism? He issued a 300-word statement commending the cooperation and skill of all the personnel involved from many nations. He spent that day quietly out of the limelight, at his Camp David retreat. It was not about him.

This is the kind of quiet patriotism I have seen from many Americans, both civilian and military. It is true patriotism. It is about public service. It is about love of country. It is about recognizing that there are things larger than self-interest. It is about unity and national purpose. It is about toleration of our differences. It is what Abraham Lincoln called "The mystic chords of memory, stretching from every battle-field, and patriot grave, to every living heart and hearth-stone, all over this broad land, will yet swell the chorus of the Union, when again touched, as surely they will be, by the better angels of our nature." Patriotism is what we do when we honor the better angels of our nature, not the worst tendencies of would-be dictators.

Imagine that Donald Trump, or a character like him, a self-serving demagogue, was running for president in 1954, on the tenth anniversary of D-Day. What would this Donald Trump say to attack his opponent? He would say "Dwight Eisenhower is no patriot. He has turned his back on those who sacrificed on D-Day. He won't even go to Normandy to honor our dead. He is playing golf at Camp David on this sacred day! All he could come up with was 300 words, probably written by someone else. Salute the Flag. Put your hand over your heart and vote for ME, because I will go to Normandy and honor the sacred memory of those who died for America." This, ladies and gentlemen, is how a pretended patriot would do it. Pretended patriots have no shame. Since Trump is no patriot and does not know what patriotism is, he can only pretend by putting his hand over his heart, by passing out miniature American flags, and puffing his chest.

Love is a Many-Splendored Thing

June 14, 2018

T he title to this essay does not suggest what it is about until you know what was running through my head as I watched the Reality Show Special called the Summit between our president and the dictator of North Korea. The song, from the 1955 movie of the same name, came to mind as I watched Kim and Donald shaking hands. I supplied my own lyrics:

> Love is a many-splendored thing
> In the Singapore mist
> Two Liars kissed
> And the world stood still…

While it is obviously better for the United States to be negotiating and acting nice with our adversaries, this was not a negotiation, it was a photo-op. It was ad hoc, unilateral diplomacy with no back up by serious professionals, with no real plan, no agreement on what "denuclearization" means, and with a phony signing ceremony, where the 200-word document the two leaders signed was hollow and vacuous. It was a Mock Summit. The signing ceremony came first, and the negotiations haven't happened yet. It was an Upside-Down Summit.

Trump relishes his upside-down style of governance because he is doing it his way. He has convinced himself that 230 years of learning how to govern under the American Constitution means nothing to him. The Pseudo-Summit gave Trump another 24-hour news cycle, while it gave Kim Jung Un precious recognition on the world stage, something North Korea has sought for decades. There was the president, ignoring human rights issues, laying hands on and praising the world's most repressive dictator. When reporters questioned the president on Kim's murderous regime, the president just said that Kim was a "tough leader." He expressed no concern for any concept of morality. He said other leaders have killed people too. Which is true, but such a brush off shows the president's lack of interest in human rights.

What was this summit for? World peace? Trump said as much in his tweet. He said we could all sleep easy now that there is no threat of nuclear war with North Korea. Yet not one thing was accomplished that benefitted the United States, and, if anything we lost big time, because Trump, completely off the cuff, and with no input from the Pentagon, or South Korea, said we would stop annual joint military maneuvers with South Korea, because, of all things, they were too expensive. This was not in the 200 word Nothing Burger Document they signed. It was something Trump threw in later—giving away more of our clout in that part of the world and getting nothing for it except weakening our national security.

Earlier negotiations with North Korea going back more than 20 years, have clearly shown that North Korea has never lived up to prior agreements. This time around there is nothing to live up to. It may lead to future negotiations, and if so, this will be something to pursue, because it is always good policy to keep the doors of diplomacy open. The alternative might be war.

How can any country in the world negotiate in good faith with the United States while Donald Trump is president? The only pattern in foreign relations that has emerged is that he thrills at meeting dictators and has no problem singing their praises. While he is praising dictators, he delights at trashing our long-standing allies. As Trump flew off to Singapore he had to trash the leader of Canada, of all people. Having just meet with the G7, our strongest allies, he refused to sign their joint communique because he was mad at Prime Minister Justin Trudeau. This is not acceptable behavior. It makes the world less safe, it is a major embarrassment to the United States, and our reputation as a world leader, has gone down the toilet.

In 1938, British Prime Minister Neville Chamberlain tried one more time to negotiate with Hitler. He returned with a signed non-aggression pact with Germany, Italy, and France. He declared a message of "peace in our times." Hitler agreed in September of 1938 not to go to war with Great Britain. A year later Hitler invaded Czechoslovakia and the world was engulfed in war, and shortly after that, Hitler started bombing England. Chamberlain's failure has become a stark lesson used especially by war hawks, to say you can never appease an enemy and that appeasement is weak diplomacy.

By this standard, President Trump appeased North Korea. He told us we could sleep well, knowing nuclear war has been averted. For how long? Until his next temper tantrum against Kim? Until he turns on Kim the way he turned on Canada?

John F. Kennedy, in his student days, wrote a thesis "Why England Slept," which was highly critical of Chamberlain for his appeasement with Hitler. Later as president, he said we had to negotiate not just for peace in our time, but peace for all time. This is hard to do but it has one great virtue as an idea. It suggests that leaders need to think beyond their own party, beyond their own tenure in power, and always look for ways to be building a better world.

Trump simply does not understand this. His day trading, transactional style, his concern with his own image on TV each 24-hours, makes him the exact opposite of a visionary and the exact opposite of a builder of a better world. His style of Fake Summitry is the exact opposite of a serious negotiator who understands that diplomacy is a never-ending process of constantly mending relationships with nations, both friend and foe.

Trump has cast his lot with trade wars with our allies and sucking up to dictators in China, Russia, and North Korea. His racism and fear of foreigners is palpable, and the world sees this. Our friends in the world are embarrassed for us. How many times have you heard stories, or perhaps experienced them personally, where you were asked by friends or acquaintances from other countries to explain how the United States could elect a man like Trump.

Do the numbers. The world has a population of more than 7.5 billion. The United States has a population of 327 million. The United States represents about 5% of the world's population, but we have 25% of the world's wealth. Can we be so arrogant to think that we can dictate to the world? Can we be so arrogant to think that the world-wide markets we need to keep our standing as one of the richest nations on Earth, can be dictated by whimsy by a half-baked real-estate mogul?

Can we be governed by a TV personality who watches TV all day and has no experience in governing, no knowledge of world history, and no knowledge of economics or diplomacy? Can we entrust him to keep our position in the world, all by himself, with all his phobias and prejudices? Can we entrust this president, who starts trade wars at the drop of hat one day, and changes them the next day, with keeping the peace, at home or abroad?

Declining Ethics in Government

June 15, 2018

Sixty years ago there was a nasty scandal at the White House that brought down President Eisenhower's powerful chief-of-staff, Sherman Adams. It is instructive to look back at what happened then and to compare it with what is happening now.

Sherman Adams was an upstanding citizen, a Dartmouth graduate and ex-Marine, who served as governor of New Hampshire before joining Eisenhower's presidential campaign. Adams was an old line Republican, a descendant of Henry Adams, of the distinguished Adams family of Massachusetts, that earlier had given us two U.S. presidents and some Revolutionary War heroes, not to mention that famous hop-grower Samuel Adams.

By all accounts Sherman Adams was the most powerful man in the White House after the President. Eisenhower, in good military fashion, ran a tight White House operation during his presidency. Nobody got to him unless they had gone through Adams first. When Eisenhower had a heart attack while in office, a team of White House appointees headed by Adams, literally ran the country.

But Adams career came abruptly to an end as a result of him accepting a gift from a friend. Someone he had known for ten years, a man named Bernard Goldfine, a Massachusetts millionaire in the textile business. Goldfine gave Adams a vicuna topcoat. A vicuna is a small camel-like animal that lives in the Andes and produces the softest and most expensive wool in the world. When the scandal broke in 1958, a men's vicuna topcoat would sell for $400.

Adams' defenders said the fact that Goldfine owned woolen mills, the coat probably cost him $69, but whatever the cost, it was a gift from a man who liked to spend money on politicians in Washington. Golfine had a shady reputation and was later convicted of income tax violation and went to jail. Washington columnist Jack Anderson broke the story on the vicuna coat and a congressional committee investigated the matter.

Everybody seemed to see this as influence pedaling and even though Adams protested that there was never a quid pro quo for the coat. He never did political favors for Goldfine. It mattered not; he was trapped in a scandal that blew up in the press. President Eisenhower praised Adams as a fine and honest public servant, but it did not matter. Sherman Adams had to go.

Eisenhower didn't have the stomach to fire him so the head of the Republican National Committee did it. Adams returned to New Hampshire and went into the business of running a successful ski lodge. He was never charged with a crime. He received no punishment other than being fired for accepting an expensive gift.

This was not a case of violating the emoluments clause of the Constitution, it was a matter related to the law, to the United States Code that prohibits government employees from accepting anything of value under a list of specific circumstances. In Sherman Adams case, there was the appearance of favoritism and this was enough to oust him. It seems so minor by today's lack of standards. Maybe this indicates how far we have slipped in our governmental ethics. Maybe it indicates how little the public knows about how government employees are supposed to conduct themselves, be they at the top or in the rank-and-file of government service, where the rules and the laws are equally applicable.

We learned recently that President Trump's daughter Ivanka, and her husband Jared Kushner, both high level White House employees, earned from their personal business interests last year at least $82 million. The government financial reporting forms that reveal this, have a range in which you report income, so you do not have to list a specific amount. It could be $100 million for all we know. The president himself has made millions of dollars from the Trump International Hotel in DC, which he leases from the government. He had that lease before he was president, but I wonder how and by what convoluted logic he was able to keep that lease after he became president. He wines and dines foreign leaders there and when they pay their expensive hotel bills, part of it goes to Trump.

Then there is the matter of the emoluments clause of the Constitution, which prohibits any gift or money or title of nobility, to be given to any government official or employee, without the consent of Congress. Ivanka Trump has received numerous patents from China for the products she sells there. This is clearly an emolument. She is receiving something of value from a foreign government. It is something clearly prohibited in the Constitution. Even worse, some of these patents seem curiously to follow in the wake of President Trump's favorable pronouncements on policy matters related to the Chinese phone company.

The Republican-controlled Congress does not have the backbone to investigate these matters. The Trump family has not received permission from Congress to receive gifts from foreign governments. Yet it is clear they are receiving enough money, or favors worth millions, from a whole variety of foreign business interests and foreign leaders.

If the head of the Chinese government gave Ivanka Trump a vicuna coat, she would model it proudly before the cameras and think nothing of it. Such a coat today might cost $20,000 or more. But for the Trumps this is chump change. It is nothing to get excited about. How could anyone be corrupted by a coat worth a mere $20,000?

Then there is the case of Scott Pruitt, the chief kleptocrat among Trump's cabinet. He seems to relish flying around the world in first class seats, receiving gifts large and small, and spending taxpayer money on fancy fountain pens and using his high office and the time of his own employees to find his wife a job, and the list goes on. Donald Trump likes Scott Pruitt and will not fire him. He sees no reason to fire him. What has he done wrong? What has Pruitt done that the Trump family has not done many times over?

God bless you Sherman Adams. I hope your soul is resting in peace. I hope you are warmed in heaven by a vicuna blanket. Please, if you can, come back and be chief-of-staff in another Republican White House, in a time so far away from your time, in an America that has fallen so far in ethics and morality that gifts like the one given to you do not even register as scandal-worthy.

Kidnapper-in-Chief

June 19, 2018

The totally unnecessary human disaster occurring on the border with Mexico shows the complete lack of empathy and decency in our president and the attorney general. The policy of the Trump Administration, as articulated by the attorney general, is to separate children of all ages from parents or from adults who accompanied them across our border with Mexico.

No distinction seems to be made between those who are seeking to become immigrants to the United States, or those who are seeking asylum. Defenders of Trump's Border Fiasco say it is Congress's fault for not giving them enough judges to handle the situation. It is Congress's fault for not fixing the laws. And most of all, according to Trump, it is the Democrats who are to blame, even though Democrats are not in power in any branch of government.

Trump should have thought of the negative consequences of his new policy before launching this draconian plan, but he never thinks about anything in advance. And it is clear that he wanted this policy to be draconian. He likes draconian.

I realize that calling our president our Kidnapper-in-Chief would not stand up in court. I am not suggesting we add this to a list of articles of impeachment. Kidnapping is a complex thing that is defined differently in state law and federal law depending on the nature of the crime. The common definition of kidnapping is: take (someone) away illegally by force, typically to obtain a ransom. Synonyms: abduct, carry off, capture, seize, snatch, or take hostage.

Since it is a policy of the president and the attorney general it might not be an illegal snatching of children, but it is dead wrong and without an ounce of human compassion. It is designed to be a harsh policy because Trump and the attorney general think snatching children is a deterrent to coming to America!

It is immoral kidnapping. It is snatching and carrying off children by force using armed border agents. It is a national outrage that we treat any human being this way. Where are the family values this country is supposed to stand for? "Family values" used to be the rallying cry of the Republican Party. Where are the religious organizations, that do missionary work all around the world, but can't seem to have a position on what is happening at our own border?

The shear audacity of those defending this policy defies all logic and decency. The kids, we are told, will be placed in foster care and be just fine. Is it the policy of the United States to make orphans of children who have parents?

We hear excuses that say rounding up kids and placing them in prison-like conditions is good for them. We hear excuses on top of excuses. The children are being fed. They are being taken care of. They are not in prison, but some are in rooms made of chain-link fence. Laura Ingraham of Fox News likened the experience to summer camp! So far three governors have refused to send National Guard troops to the border because the National Guard should not be a part of this dreadful business.

As in so many other misconceived policies of this president, everyone who comes in contact with this mess is corrupted and compromised. The Secretary of Homeland Security, Kirstjen Nielsen, showed how utterly clueless she was in one of the most disastrous press conferences ever held by a cabinet officer.

The men and women who patrol our borders have a thankless task and an overwhelming one under the best of circumstances. None of these government workers should be put in the position of aiding and abetting the kidnapping of children.

The immigration laws of the United States have been broken for a long time and this larger, longstanding issue can be laid at the feet of both political parties and a Congress that has been dysfunctional for almost a decade. We cannot find a solution because we have lost sight of the fact that America is a land of immigrants. Trump describes the people coming across the southern border as murderers, rapists, and gang members. We call them aliens as if they were an invading species from another planet.

We will not solve our immigration problem; we will not get better laws governing immigration until we quit demonizing the people seeking a better life and those fleeing from the anarchy and lawlessness of their home countries. The movement of human beings seeking a better life or fleeing war and famine is a global one that will only get more challenging in the years ahead. Climate change will cause populations to move. It is doing so right now. Water shortages will increase worldwide in the coming decades. Places that support life and cultures now will be deserts or under water in decades ahead. Population is increasing at a rapid rate. The whole world needs a better solution to moving populations.

Walls are not the answer. Trump wants America to be a gated community for white Christians. He only cares about the Christians because quite a few evangelicals support him. So they will be inside the gate. Muslims, Mexicans, people from other Latin American nations, Africans, need not apply. This is not the solution for a better world. It is a formula for global warfare.

In the meantime, while we work through this complex immigration policy in the years ahead, one thing is crystal clear. Stop kidnapping children to punish their parents for seeking asylum or a brighter future. President Trump and Attorney General Sessions, and that little White House sneak Stephen Miller, who probably wrote this policy, have you, at last, no shame? Have you, at last, not a single ounce of human decency?

Good Citizens at Work

I spent two very interesting days in DC attending briefings and participating in the roll out of a new initiative of the No Labels Organization on changing the rules of the House of Representatives to allow bipartisan bills to get to the floor for a vote. The No Labels Organization is dedicated to finding ways to end the dysfunction and extreme partisanship that plagues Congress. One of the exciting projects of No Labels is their fostering role in encouraging members from both parties to create a new caucus of House Republicans and Democrats called the "Problem Solvers Caucus." There are 48 members in the caucus right now, 24 Democrats and 24 Republicans. They have been working together for almost two years. It is a most impressive group and I met about half the caucus over the two days of the meetings.

But before I say any more about the Problem Solvers, let me tell you a story. One of the key speakers at our meetings was Dick Gephardt, who served in the House from Missouri for 24 years, was House Majority Leader during half the time I served as House Historian, and he also ran for president in 1988 and 2004. I always admired him as one of the finest public servants I ever met. It was so good to see him again. He and I are the same age, born a week apart in 1941.

Dick told the group of about 100 persons at a Kennedy Center dinner that he had been in politics for more than 40 years, having gotten his start as a precinct captain in St. Louis, Missouri in 1966. At my table, as we did a round of introductions, when my turn came I added a little twist based on what Gephardt had told us. I said, "I have been following politics two years longer than Dick Gephardt, since I got my start as a deputy precinct captain in Illinois in 1964! The Congressman seated next to me, Republican Lloyd Smucker of Pennsylvania, said "I was born in 1964!" We all got a laugh out of that. And it reminded me of how long I have been engaging in one way or another in the political process.

Gephardt told a story of being in Russia not long after the collapse of the Soviet Union, meeting with Boris Yeltsin, the new president of the Russian Federation. Dick asked one of Yeltsin's top advisers "What is it your country needs the most." Gephardt expected it would be something to do with the economy or perhaps national security, but the reply was, "We need citizens. We don't have citizens." The Soviet Union had subjects who, in the Soviet hierarchy, could do all right if they towed the party line, if they were good communists, if they didn't rock the boat or challenge the authoritarian state. But with the Soviet Union gone, the Russian people would have to do things for themselves that the government had done before. They had to find ways to empower themselves and become citizens.

I could not help but think, as Gephardt told his Russian story, that this country too needs citizens—and we need them badly. Far too many of us have taken our responsibilities as citizens for granted. We might as well be in an authoritarian state, where we let the government tell us what to do rather than us telling the government what we want it to do.

Our politics is badly broken right now because so many of us have learned to demonize the other party. Or we have succumbed to numbing propaganda that says government is the problem. So many of us are so mad at the "system" that instead of rolling up our sleeves and trying to change it, we opt out. We give government the finger. We fail to vote. Or we vote to hurt the other side, the side we have learned to hate. The side we have forgotten is just as American as the side we think is American—which is whatever side we are on.

If we are going to be active, responsible, citizens we must find a way to talk to one another again. To get out of our echo chambers, to think about our political opponents not as enemies but people with different ideas. The No Labels Organization is working to make this happen. Put labels aside, sit down together, and try like hell to solve problems. The people I was with in DC a few days ago, were Republicans, Democrats, and Independents. The folks who support No Labels with donations, are Republicans, Democrats, and Independents. They see the bigger picture that our worst problem is our dysfunctional government, where party ideology and the need to get elected with the help of extreme voters in our primary elections, and the need to constantly raise money to get re-elected have all combined to make a total disaster.

We must turn it around. It has not always been this way. We must restore a functioning government. Citizens can do this at the polls. Elected officials can work to make changes in how Congress conducts its business. The majority party cannot completely ignore the minority party. We need the whole House to work its will, not just the majority.

This does not mean that the majority party should not be in control. But it needs to be fair. It needs to let the votes of all members count. The Hastert Rule (named for former Republican Speaker, Dennis Hastert), stated that no bill can come to the floor of the House for a vote unless it can be passed with Republican votes alone. This rule says, in effect, that no Democrats count. This bad rule disenfranchises all the congressional districts in the United States that voted for Democrats.

But it is even worse than this. A small group of fanatics in the House, the Freedom Caucus, tries to control the agenda of the entire Republican Party and with the Hastert Rule in effect they can push their extreme positions, or block any bills they don't like. Mark Meadows of the Freedom Caucus even used a "motion to vacate the chair" to challenge Speaker Boehner's leadership. It is a motion that hasn't been used more than 100 years. Since the motion was sent to committee and not voted on immediately, Boehner was not directly threatened with the loss of his speakership.

But it wasn't long afterwards that Boehner resigned. Paul Ryan succeeded him and Ryan too, will resign at the end of the year, another Speaker who was unable to challenge the uncompromising hotheads in the Freedom Caucus. The House Rules Committee which determines the procedure that will govern debate on any bill, is composed of 9 Republicans and 4 Democrats. The Republican Party alone controls how bills are debated and whether any amendments can be offered and debated.

Only when enough House members of both parties can decide to step up and do the job they were elected to do, which is to solve problems for the American people, will we be able to end the dysfunction. We need a functioning Congress, with two strong parties, to check an even greater dysfunction in the executive branch.

Those Democrats who are wishing and praying for a Blue Wave in November to stop the tyranny of the GOP in the House, may find that they will be sorely disappointed this fall. Right now, the serious pollsters do not see a Blue Wave, or a Red Wave that Donald Trump talks about. They see the Democrats gaining seats but maybe a few short of taking control of the chamber. The Republicans are likely to lose seats, but maybe not enough to lose the majority. But if they do lose the majority, it may be by only a few seats. So whichever party wins, it will be faced with the same problems of how to forge a workable majority to pass bills. Each new House, elected every two years, must elect a speaker and adopt a set of rules under which it will operate. The Problem Solvers Caucus is hoping to push whomever the next speaker is to have the will to agree that bipartisan legislation is a positive thing for the country and for restoring function to the House.

What impressed me the most in my two days of participation with the No Labels Organization and with the House members in the Problem Solvers Caucus, and the dedicated donors who have given to both parties in the past, was that all the conversations were about finding solutions. Nobody was wringing their hands and complaining about the idiot in the White House, or the fools in the Freedom Caucus. These were adults. I sensed they knew that their time would be wasted if all they did was lambaste the obvious faults. They already knew the faults in our government. They were looking for solutions.

These two days were so refreshing to me because I saw on display the very best of American politics coming from citizens and elected officials from both parties. American culture and American politics has always had a practical side. Americans are pragmatists. We solve problems. Now we must see if good old-fashioned roll-up-your-sleeves and go to work is still how we define good citizens and good elected officials. Anybody got any better ideas? I am listening. Because just like everyone else I met on this trip to DC, I do not claim to have all the answers, maybe not any of them. I need help. We all do.

If you want to learn more about the No Labels Organization, please Google them and see what they are up to. I liked what I saw. I joined No Labels as a member. I like their level-headed approach to good citizenship.

The Strzok Inquisition

July 12, 2018

It was 45 years ago this summer, while on vacation at the Outer Banks of North Carolina, that I spent a whole day watching the Watergate hearings on TV rather than playing on the sunny beach. Fast forward 45 years and here I am at the ocean again, this time in South Carolina, spending the whole day watching two House committees, the Government Oversight and Judiciary Committees grill FBI agent Peter Strzok for eight hours, mostly about Hillary Clinton's emails and the infamous Anthony Weiner Laptop.

But today's hearing was clearly a broader attempt on the part of the GOP majority to smear Agent Strzok for bias in the Russian investigations, to scold him for his personal conduct for writing private texts that were critical of Donald Trump, and for having an affair with an FBI attorney, even though he is a married man. The not-so-hidden agenda of the majority party was to undermine the integrity and impartiality of the Robert Mueller investigation, using Agent Strzok as Exhibit A.

I don't think there is a person in the United States that is so perfect that they could not be smeared, insulted, and demeaned by a congressional committee using McCarthy-era smear techniques. Such was the case today. Peter Strozk had just enough flaws to give the GOP the opportunity to exploit him all day long. But Strzok turned out to have Moxie. He was not about to be brow beaten and assailed. He stood up to the GOP bullies and was buoyed up by the minority Democrats who kept calling the hearing a travesty.

During the McCarty era in the 1950s, Senator Joe McCarthy and his sidekick lawyer Roy Cohn (the same Cohn who would years later become Trump's personal lawyer) used to hold secret hearings to test how a witness would hold up under their wilting questions. If they found a witness who was strong-willed and stood up to them, they would seldom call such witnesses to testify in public hearings. When they found people who were more easily intimidated, for whatever reason, these would be be bullied in public. The McCarthy secret hearings were sealed for 50 years, but my friend Don Ritchie in the Senate Historical Office edited these for publication in 2003. The five volumes are fascinating reading, involving 500 witnesses.

The GOP, under the leadership of committee chairmen Trey Gowdy (R-SC) and Bob Goodlatte (R-VA), went right to the McCarthy playbook. They held 11 hours of secret hearings with Strozk and created a transcript, which was not made public. Today, the GOP used the transcript selectively to make them seem as though they had all the answers they needed and had already concluded that Strozk was a biased, anti-Trump agent who was removed from the investigation by Robert Mueller because of his bias.

The Republicans under-estimated Strzok's aggressive public defense of his lack bias. He never wilted. He had the stamina for the day. Most of all, his knowledge of events gave him the power to tell members when they were wrong. Members don't like to be told they are wrong. In his opening statement, Trey Gowdy wanted to hold Strzok in contempt, right off the bat. This was an obvious ploy designed to put fear in him. But he did not flinch. He was able to explain time and again the difference between personal political opinions, which everyone has, and the ability of a professional person not to be swayed by political considerations.

The GOP inquisitors tried all day to redefine bias to prove Strzok was guilty of it. They parsed his many private text messages, many to FBI lawyer Lisa Page, with whom he was sexually involved, to try to show that Strzok and therefore the entire FBI was out to stop Trump. Agent Strzok kept placing his comments back into their context. Usually he was stopped before he could complete his statement.

There is no doubt that this was a "show trial" designed to put discrediting clips from the hearing on Fox News to convince the Trump base that the FBI is out to get him and that the FBI is flawed and biased just like Agent Strzok. Soon the GOP will go to the smear one more time when they bring FBI lawyer Lisa Page in to testify. Maybe the GOP feels they can bully the woman who was having an affair.

I am sure the video of this hearing is being edited as I write this to fit the Fox News crowd and the MSNBC crowd. MSNBC will have interviews with Democrats. Fox will have interviews with Republicans. Fox will conclude Agent Strzok and his boss Mueller are suspect, and the investigation should stop. MSNBC will report this as a show trial for the Trump base.

This was a pathetic display of the hyper-partisanship that has divided the country so badly. This hearing turned up nothing new. It was a sham investigation of Hillary Clinton disguised as an assault on the Robert Mueller investigation. Every GOP member who questioned Agent Strzok seemed oblivious about the convictions and the indictments that have come from the Mueller investigations. The Democrats on the committees mentioned this fact on several occasions.

President Trump's campaign chairman is currently in jail and is about to go to trial on multiple criminal charges. Is this the time to say Mueller should stop investigating? Why? What is the GOP afraid of? If they think Trump is innocent, they should be happy to see the investigation continue to exonerate the president. If, however, they think Trump is guilty of crimes, then their actions today and in past hearings and investigations from congressional Republicans, come very close to being obstruction of justice. They are stalling and undermining the rule of law. This is extremely serious. At best, the House GOP is abusing its power to investigate. At worst, the Republican Party is obstructing justice. In doing so they put party before country. They are doing nothing to find ways to stop more Russian influence in the elections coming up this fall.

Whatever personal flaws and shortcomings Agent Peter Strzok has, and he certainly admitted that his personal emails and texts were inappropriate and problematic once they became public, and he admitted readily that his personal affair has hurt his family, he should not be allowed to be made a scapegoat or an excuse to destroy the FBI in order to save a president. If President Trump is not a crook, he sure was surrounded by a bunch of them. Maybe, like Nixon, Trump will become an unindicted co-conspirator. Like Nixon, Trump will not have to be indicted for crimes to be declared a criminal. If he becomes an unindicted co-conspirator, we should demand that Congress impeach him.

Donald Trump is Not on Team America

July 17, 2018

President Trump's presidency fell completely apart this week. The world is aghast at the number of unforced errors he was able to make in just one week of visits to Great Britain, Scotland, and Helsinki, Finland.

These errors follow closely on the heels of another week of grisly performances at the G-7 Summit, where he insulted all our strongest allies and then conducted a bizarre private meeting with one of the world's worst dictators, welcoming Kim Jong Un as an equal head of state, followed by the signing of a worthless piece of paper about de-nuclearization of North Korea amidst much fanfare and ballyhoo.

I have been searching for an explanation for this utter failure of Donald Trump to be able to function as President of the United States. Everyone has a theory. Everyone has a string of adjectives to define Trump including idiot and moron, to name those that came from his own cabinet.

Republicans, trying hard to stay loyal to Trump, are beside themselves after the meeting with Russian President Putin, when President Trump fawned over Putin and expressed that Putin was " extremely strong and forceful" in denying any interference in our 2016 elections. The president trashed the American government that he heads in front of the Russian autocrat for all the world to see. No president in American history has ever done this.

Trump then uttered the sentence heard 'round the world that he would have no reason to believe Putin meddled in our elections. Today, in a hastily called news conference, Trump gave his supporters a feeble way to save face by correcting himself. He meant to say he "wouldn't" have any reason to doubt that Russia was behind the cyber attacks on our elections,

The world can relax again. It was all just a slip of the tongue. Trump now believes the intelligence agencies of the United States rather than Putin, the former KGB agent, who was trained to undermine America. As commentator Sam Stein said on MSNBC tonight,

Trump read his message of correction as if he was in front of the cameras as the subject of a hostage video. The man does not like to be told what to say.

Here is my theory of what is wrong with President Trump. I am going to use a sports analogy.

When all is said and done about Trump's failures in his role as president, the biggest single problem is that he is totally incapable of being a team player. He does not listen to his cabinet and agency heads. He does not listen to any criticism from any other part of government. He fights opposition at every turn. He cannot take criticism. He tries hard to appeal to 40% of his team, while ignoring the majority of equally talented team members.

He simply does not understand that running the United States is the greatest of all team sports. It is a team composed of three branches of government. He sets himself up as the only coach. He doesn't listen to his assistant coaches. Congress and the Federal Court System are not assistant coaches. They are co-equal coaches. Trump has to be the one and only Head Coach.

This Team America is composed of a government that has more than 5 million Americans in civilian and military service (including 600,000 postal workers). Those who wear the uniforms of our military services are willing to lay down their lives on the orders of the Head Coach. They are highly trained and dedicated defenders of the United States who took an oath to be loyal to the team and all the things Team America stands for. There are just 1.2 million Americans on active duty right now, who defend us all.

Team America has a contract. It is called the United States Constitution. Team America also has rules. Just like every sport has rules and referees and umpires. We have laws we agree to follow. If you are loyal to Team America, you are loyal to the Constitution and you are loyal to the Rule of Law. These things are even more important than the current Head Coach. Every team member knows that coaches come and go. But the Team endures.

Team America has 327 million citizens. We are so successful as a nation of opportunity that people from all over the world want to join Team America. And this team has benefited greatly and has been made stronger and has been enriched by team members from all over the globe.

This had been true from the very beginning of the United States, when all who would call themselves Americans, were immigrants. I went to a minor league baseball game in South Carolina recently and the team included members from Mexico, Venezuela, Dominican Republic, Curacao, and other countries. They all wore the same uniform. They all worked as a team. I have no idea if they were liberals or conservatives. It didn't matter to the team or to the fans.

And the important thing to remember about citizens is that all of us are coaches too. The Head Coach works for us. We keep him as Head Coach if Team America is living up to its promise and if he is living up to his oath of office.

Think of all the kinds of teams, both in sport, in community service and volunteering, in churches, in business and industry, in entertainment, in journalism, in schools and universities, in police and fire protection, in local and state governments from coast to coast who are part of Team America.

A team like this needs a lot of coaches and a lot of assistant coaches. One coach cannot manage it, no matter how brilliant or gifted that coach might be. Successful presidents share their power and in doing so expand it. Trump shrinks the entire government down to the size of one man and makes us weak.

What we saw at the Helsinki Summit with Russian President Vladimir Putin was a case where our Coach was bested and badly beaten by the Coach of one of our greatest adversaries in the world. It was an embarrassing and humiliating defeat. We were never really in the game. We did not come to play. We lost because our Coach went into the game with no clear idea of what the game plan was. He was told by his assistant coaches, the Secretary of State and the heads of our intelligence services what to look out for and how to prepare. But Trump simply cannot be a team player. He could not bother to read his briefing papers. He wings it every time.

Russia's economy is about the size of that of New York State. It is not one of our major trading partners. It is an autocracy, a country that survives on selling fossil fuels to Europe and other places. It is dangerous because it has so many nuclear weapons inherited from the old Soviet Union and because it has a clear game plan to enhance its power by destabilizing western democracies in Europe and in North America.

Putin survives by running a sophisticated military and police state in cahoots with business oligarchs and crime syndicates. Putin is a Major League player who had no trouble twisting our Little League rookie president around his finger and then handing Trump a soccer ball for his trouble.

Trump's experience in governance began with his election to the highest office in the country. He has not practiced learning what this means. You might win a few games without practicing. But ask any athlete in any sport about the discipline and training necessary to play at the top of your game. The same is true of governing a nation. It is not a job for amateurs. All presidents find the job overwhelming. Some are better at building teams to help them through the arduous task of governing. Lincoln used a team of rivals, so he could hear both sides before deciding what to do.

Team America desperately needs a new Head Coach. A Coach that knows Team America is in the Major Leagues. To stay in the majors requires practice, dedication, vision, hard work, and building team spirit (not tearing it down). Most of all, a great coach always thinks first of the team, all of them. In this case, the team includes the United States and our partners and allies in the world. If the coach is in it only for his own glory, (or only to save his own skin from possible wrong-doing) then Team America will fail to achieve greatness again. Great coaches make their teams great, not themselves.

President Trump as Commander Queeg

July 19, 2018

President Trump is a lot like the character in the fictional novel *The Caine Mutiny*, the 1951 Pulitzer Prize winning book about the commander of a World War II destroyer who was incompetent at running his ship, displayed disturbing mental quirks, was extremely paranoid, and drove his crew to hate him. The crew lost confidence in their commander, became disloyal, and eventually mutinied against him and took over the ship during a typhoon at sea, when the commander proved incapable of acting to save his own vessel.

President Donald John Trump, our Commander in Chief, is acting more each day like Lt. Commander Philip Francis Queeg, from the Caine Mutiny. He is incapable of acting to save the ship of state. He thinks He is the ship of state. He acts to protect his own interests and the interests of his family.

Commander Queeg became so obsessed with looking for a lost key supposedly stolen by a crew member and trying to find out who ate his strawberries from the ship's mess, that he could not even think of his duties as commander. Trump's obsession is not about who ate the strawberries, it is about Robert Mueller.

What to do about a runaway president who is openly colluding with the president of the Russian Federation right before our eyes and obstructing justice in broad daylight practically every day, has become a more urgent discussion since the horrendous performance of President Trump at the Helsinki Summit with Vladimir Putin.

It was a summit that was not a real summit. It merely appeared to be one. It was a secret meeting between Trump and Putin with no other persons in the room except translators. The secret meeting was followed by a press conference in which the President of the United States criticized the failings of the United States intelligence agencies while finding little to complain about when it came to the Russian cyber-war on western democracies including Russia's dramatic and profound interference with our presidential election in 2016.

What about a mutiny? Are parts of our government who know what is really going on behind the scenes ready to engage in a mild form of mutiny against the President of the United States? Can there be a "mild" form of mutiny?

I do not talk about mutiny lightly. I am not calling for a mutiny of any kind. Even the word is repugnant to me as an assault to regular order of our nation and its laws. But let's explore the idea, just to add another option on the table. I sense that mutiny, perhaps best put as growing opposition to Trump's unwillingness to accept the Mueller investigation, is causing some government officials, and former officials, to take their public opposition to the next level.

In the Caine Mutiny, the fictional tale, the crew takes over the USS Caine and the lieutenant who ordered the captain relieved of his duty was brought before a court martial on the charge of mutiny. The dramatic part of the book, the movies that have been made, and even the successful play of the Caine Mutiny Court Martial, left no doubt that anyone engaged in a mutiny better be ready to face the consequences.

It was the trial, it was Commander Queeg on the witness stand, that revealed his flawed character, his paranoia, his self-absorption, and his disregard for the duties of his command. The mutiny was a serious violation of military law. The trial absolved the mutineers once the judges saw Queeg as what George Will recently said of Trump, "This sad, embarrassing, wreck of a man."

President Trump has never been a normal president. We attributed some of his behavior to his amateur status. He never governed anything, and his first office is the highest office in the land.

It is worse than him just being an amateur with no learning curve. He is hostile to his own government and most of its institutions. He is hostile to the press which, like Hitler—yes, just like Hitler—calls the American Press liars and purveyors of Fake News. Hitler called German journalists the "Lügenpresse" (the Lying Press). Trump even attacked the American press during the Helsinki meeting, refusing to call on some reporters he did not like, and letting a worldwide audience see his performance.

We have two governments in the United States right now. They are at war with one another. First, there is the Government of One, the president, the would-be dictator, who is supported, most of the time, by Republicans in Congress who think about party ideology and their own power before they think about their country. Trump has a few true believers working for him in the White House who prop up Trump and often lead him.

And then there is the rest of the government consisting of hundreds of thousands of loyal Americans, Republicans, Democrats, Independents, black and white, gay and straight, religious and non-religious, male and female, in a variety of highly professional and skilled jobs that keep this nation functioning and protect us from our enemies at home and abroad. The biggest part of this is the military, which is doing its job of protecting us regardless of what is going on inside the White House. But what would the military do if our Queeg-like commander ordered them to do something terribly wrong?

I have full faith and confidence in this vast part of the federal government. It is what is keeping us together. Parts of our government are doing their best to repair the damage from the wrecking ball that is our president. Our strong institutions, our strong military, though weakened and undermined by Trump's assaults, are still up to the job. But the assaults keep coming.

Some things, large and small, are not on the public radar, at least not yet. Until the flap over the private meeting in Helsinki with no other staff present, most Americans had no idea of the role of official White House stenographers who are in the room to record presidential conversations so there is a check on what is said; so that conversations can be verified. It is also the law. Conversations need to be preserved as part of the Presidential Records Act, passed in the wake of the Watergate fiasco. What secrets of ours might the president have told Putin in Helsinki? What private deals did they arrange?

Instead of a private back-channel with Putin, Trump used a highly public summit to engage in private back-channel talk with no one to tell what was said except an American translator, who is now under terrific pressure to reveal what was said. The only two persons in that meeting, other than the innocent translators, are world-class professional liars. How will we ever know what was said?

Perhaps there is a silent form of mutiny already underway in the form of leaks and disclosuers usually kept out of public scrutiny. Maybe there are those in government who think their duty to the country requires the public have more information to understand what our president is doing.

Think back to the secret aid that Associate FBI Director Mark Felt ("Deep Throat") gave to *Washington Post* reporters Woodward and Bernstein that helped to unravel the Watergate scandal and led eventually to the resignation of President Nixon.

Governments sometimes need to rely on leaks even though no one likes to admit what a useful tool they are. If classified information is leaked, that is a crime. But then the question becomes, what is the meaning of classified and who classified it? When is holding a secret more damaging that releasing it?

Reporting in today's *New York Times* by David E. Sanger and Matthew Rosenberg states that Donald Trump was fully briefed on January 6, 2017, with highly classified documents about Vladimir Putin's direct orders to launch a cyberattack on the U.S. elections. This was two weeks before Trump's inauguration. Trump saw the evidence, yet he has been strangely reluctant to believe it, and has spent his entire presidency so far playing it down and attacking the investigations into the cyberattack.

The *New York Times* reporting did not name sources, although the information had to come from some of the intelligence officials in the room at Trump Tower, when the president-elect was briefed. This hardly qualifies as a mutiny, or as a revelation of classified material, but it is a step beyond what intelligence agencies usually do.

Trump may have seen some of the actual evidence that appeared in the recent indictment of the 12 Russian government operatives who did the deed. To explain the indictments, the Mueller team had to go into remarkable detail about how the evidence against the Russians was gathered. It required that techniques for electronic intelligence gathering, usually keep secret, had to be revealed. We had to give up some secrets to explain things to courts of law and to the public. If this is leaking, it is sophisticated, quite effective, and absolutely necessary. It may be the mild form of mutiny we desperately need.

Trump in the Long View of History and Civilization

July 26, 2018

Throughout human history people in every culture have been told what to believe and what not to believe. Whole civilizations have been built on elaborate belief systems. There have been countless gods that humans have believed in, until they were believed in no more.

The president went before the Veterans of Foreign Wars convention on July 26 and told the conventioneers and the nation that "What you are seeing and reading is not what's happening." The President of the United States wants us to doubt the reporting of the American press and the indictments that have come so far from the Mueller investigations. Trump wants us to suspend our belief in anything that is happening in American politics. We are supposed to trust him to tell us what to believe, even when the clear majority of Americans know that our president is a chronic liar.

H. L. Mencken, the great American journalist and observer of the human condition, once published a long list of forgotten gods to remind us of the ephemeral nature of religious beliefs as well as the passing of kings, queens, emperors, and shoguns, once thought to derive their powers from a deity, or because they were believed to be deities themselves. Some observers have noted that Trump is developing a cult-like following. No one thinks he is a god, but a surprising number of Americans seem to have god-like faith in him. Cults come and go and I think of such things when I want to imagine the passing into oblivion of Donald Trump.

Humans engage in illusionary practices on so many levels that it is often hard to discover what is real. We firmly declare our most closely held illusions to be reality, even when the visage of Jesus appears on a piece of toast. We are easily fooled, by others, and by ourselves. In 2016 enough of us believed in Donald Trump to elect the first outright demagogue and practitioner of fraud in the history of presidential elections.

In modern politics as well as in the politics of ancient and extinct civilizations, image has often substituted for reality to sway the masses, to start wars (or end them), to create alliances and define enemies, and to set priorities of how civilizations are organized and how the commerce of any civilization is distributed.

Trump has spent a lifetime advertising himself and creating an image, a brand, of who he is and how wonderfully successful and rich he is. More than 60 million Americans liked this image. Some of them said that he seemed authentic, real, and not just another phony politician with empty promises. He was a businessman. Businessmen are good for business. Businessmen are better executives than politicians, many of us believed.

Those that are possessed of land, power, and goods, create illusionary justifications for why others should be dispossessed of their share of the wealth. Often the dispossession is predicated on the fact that individuals or groups are not of the right religion, or the right social class, the right nationality, the right race, the right sex, or that they fail to speak the right language.

In 2016, enough American voters decided to cast their ballots for a billionaire TV personality who promised them jobs, a tough policy on immigration, and plenty of dog whistles about insuring that the white race would continue to rule America.

There is no way we can completely get away from our illusion-making and our constant defining and re-defining of reality. History is the story of how this illusion-making plays out at different times over many centuries and eons of the human experience. The United States may be exceptional in some ways in its historical context, but history also shows that we are totally unexceptional in all the same ways that past civilizations have been when it comes to who controls power.

Donald Trump has put our darkest, least exceptional characteristics in the spotlight of world history. Not only are most Americans aghast because of his election and his subsequent performance in office, but so is the rest of the world. Our allies around the globe are embarrassed for us. They are confused. They have their own demons to deal with, but now they see that the United States is just another country with lots of power that is floundering badly without decent leadership and no moral authority.

We create governments and devise rules designed for stability and even for happiness among the people. "We hold these truths to be self-evident, that all Men are created equal, that they are endowed by their Creator with certain unalienable Rights, and among these are Life, Liberty, and the Pursuit of Happiness," wrote Thomas Jefferson in a world filled with serfs, slaves, kings, emperors, and shoguns. Jefferson offered a fresh belief that all the people, not just the rulers, deserved something better. Americans still like to believe this.

In the United States we have something called the "American Credo," our system of beliefs that is often based on the Bill of Rights, the U.S. Constitution, and the Rule of Law. But there is no one American Credo. Everybody seems to make up their own, depending on their own beliefs. You can go online and search "American Credo" and find conservative and liberal versions. You can find religious versions that declare the United States is a Christian nation and you can find versions that include freedom from religion as an essential part of the American Credo. Some versions include fairness and opportunity for all. Some include the words on the Statue of Liberty, that the United States is the place for all people to come to be lifted out of bondage, poverty, oppression, and to seek a welcoming nation filled with opportunity.

In the United States and in other parts of the world our civilizations and our political systems are under great strain. We seem restless and uncertain. We are not happy. Yet history shows this to be the normal state of things down through the centuries. There has never been a time in human history that has not been filled with anxiety and peril. Each generation must find its own way of coping with the social and political ills that it faces.

The forces that create our angst change over time. Margaret Atwood in her poem "The Loneliness of the Military Historian" said, "for every year of peace there have been 400 years of war." Think what our planet and our civilizations would be like if the ratio of war and peace was reversed.

What I have written so far is but a preface. I am trying to step back from the United States during the Trump administration. I am searching for a vantage point that may offer a better perspective. I am trying to recover my bearings about how I think about my country and its history in light of the criminal presidency of Donald Trump.

Even in the darkest days of Watergate, I never felt that the basic institutions of the United States were in jeopardy. What I saw with the congressional investigations into Watergate was Congress doing its job and protecting the Constitution. What I saw then in the American press was a diligent quest for the truth while cover-ups and lies were the order of the day. What I saw in Nixon was a greatly flawed president who ultimately bowed to the rule of law and stepped down. He faced the fact that his powers as president were not sufficient to place him above the law.

It is not that Donald Trump is the worst thing that has ever befallen the United States. It is that he represents the current worst thing. He is more troubling than Nixon and Watergate because he is defiant and far more corrupt than Nixon ever was. Nixon was a major American politician who went bad. Trump is a major American politician who started out bad and got worse.

Trump came into office as a fraud and a criminal. Nixon had to work at becoming one. Nixon, for all his faults, was a skilled American politician. Trump, for all his faults, is a complete disaster who does not know the first thing about how to govern. Nixon could still listen to members of his own party who told him it was time to resign.

Trump doubles down on lies and sends a formerly distinguished American, Rudy Giuliani, out into the public to accuse all of Trump's accusers of being liars. Nixon was a staunch anti-communist who rose to power fighting against communism and the Soviet Union. Trump is a stooge of the head of the Russian Federation who used to be the head of the dreaded Russian spy agency, the KGB. We have a president who is colluding with one of our leading adversaries in the world.

This nation fought a Civil War over slavery that killed more than 700,000 Americans and left many more maimed. We still divide ourselves over that war even though the war ended more than 150 years ago. We engaged in so many wars against the Native Americans who populated the continent before the arrival of Europeans and others that most of these wars have been forgotten. All the many Indian wars were about dispossessing those who held the land so that a new group could hold the land. It amounted to a 300-year war of land-grabbing and genocide.

How does two years of having a malevolent idiot in the White House compare to these larger forces in our history? It doesn't. We will overcome Trump. But right now, I am as anxious as everyone else regarding how it will play out and how much damage will be done to what we believe in, what we hold dear, and what we as a nation decide to do with our country going forward. We could, given current extreme politics, screw things up badly for a long time. Or, just maybe, we will come to our senses. Right now, I cannot predict the outcome, and this is the basis of my personal angst.

I too have my belief system. I believe in government as a vital component of civilization. Government is not evil, it is evil men and women in government who must be voted out of office. I look at history and see how many times the United States has reinvented itself after depressions, wars, and social upheavals. I see plenty in this history that is vile and disgusting. But I also see greatness. I also see promise. I see goodness, even though it is largely unfulfilled right now.

I want desperately to be proud of the United States again. The pride I have is in knowing that most of our institutions are still strong, that our military is strong, that our courts are strong, and that most Americans, whatever personal shortcomings we each may have, want to do better for the whole country, not just for a political party. I see problem solvers. I see people who roll up their sleeves and work. I guess I am just as hopelessly optimistic as was Ronald Reagan who looked at America and saw a shining city on a hill.

We still have the freedom and the power to be whatever we want to be in this country. For God's sake, let's decide we do not want to follow Donald Trump down the path of iniquity, down the path of fraud, and down the path of being absorbed with self-interest. Let's try once again to put country over party, for the long-range benefit of both political parties and the whole nation.

I cannot tell you how much I love the Congress of the United States. The years I worked there were a revelation to me. I saw politicians from both parties as three-dimensional people, not cardboard cutouts with labels on them. Congress is the first branch of government; the branch that best represents the people. It has never been perfect, but it is at its best when it becomes the place for all Americans to grapple with and shape the future of the nation.

The beauty of the system is that every two years We the People can change course. We can kick the "bums" out of office and try a new set of representatives. And if these newly elected people don't work out, two years later we can kick them out too. There are good solid people in both parties in the House and Senate. It is time they stood up to Trump.

It is time for all of us to work for America. We can limit the damage of Trump and Trumpism with a new Congress with a new majority. This is where we must act, no matter how long it takes for the wheels of justice to roll out verdicts in all the Trump scandals. November 2018 is when we take the country back, not for Democrats, not for Republicans, but for all Americans. We have a golden opportunity to reboot our democracy. This is as optimistic as it gets, folks. It is in your hands. Do not despair. Go out and vote. Make sure it is your vote, not one from Russia.

The House Shall Chuse Their Speaker

August 12, 2018

The current GOP vilification of former House Speaker Nancy Pelosi, the Democratic Leader of the House, is the latest version of something that has been going on since the Republicans decided to smear Speaker Tip O'Neill (D-MA) in TV ads during Ronald Reagan's campaign for president in 1980.

The Republicans put out an ad showing an old, bloated, bumbling character out of touch with the nation. In the ad, an actor looking like Tip was seen driving an old, overly-large American sedan, representing the Democratic Party. A younger Democrat in the car kept telling Tip they were running out of gas, and Tip would not believe it. Finally, the car ran out of gas and the screen said: The Democrats are Out of Gas: Vote Republican for a Change.

Tip had to shore up his image, even in this pre-Internet age, and one of the things he did was to hire Chris Matthews, then working as a speech writer for President Jimmy Carter, to be his press secretary and speech writer. It worked. The GOP strategy against Tip backfired, and Tip was able to hold his own, serve as Speaker another six years, and retire from the House in 1987 on top as a well-respected national leader who served as Speaker for ten consecutive years.

The 1980 election of Ronald Reagan was a huge victory for Republicans, but that success had nothing to do with the ad attacking the Speaker. Tip O'Neill and President Reagan were political rivals, not polarized enemies.

Any Democrats who may be wavering or may have fallen for the massive Republican propaganda campaign against Nancy Pelosi need a serious reality check. The Republican Party wants you to believe that Nancy Pelosi, the most successful Speaker in recent memory, has too much baggage, is too polarizing, and is too old to help the Democrats take back the House in 2018.

We always underestimate the power and the purpose of well-orchestrated, well-financed smear campaigns. We seldom think of the big money that is behind the big smears. Propaganda usually has two purposes. First, to keep the faithful believing the party line, and second, to plant enough doubt in the other party and among independent voters that some may either switch party allegiances or not vote.

In the 2018 Congressional elections, it has become a litmus test for Democrats in some districts to declare in advance where they stand on the election of Nancy Pelosi as Speaker. I cannot think of another time in American history where the election of a Speaker was a burning campaign issue. Even the old Tip O'Neill ads seem mild when compared with the steady stream of vitriol directed at Nancy Pelosi.

A massive GOP propaganda campaign, which will get worse as we get closer to the election, has made the election of the next Speaker a political issue. Democrats need to get tough and not be swayed by this manufactured attempt to divide the party.

Since all politics, especially House elections, are local, I can see why the GOP wants to make the Speaker's contest an issue. It gives Democrats and swing voters one more thing to worry about that has nothing to do with the economy, national security, the failures of the Trump administration, the immigration issue, jobs, education, and all the other serious issues before the nation. And for the GOP it gives them a face to focus on, when what is really at stake is 435 separate elections and 434 other faces besides that of Nancy Pelosi.

Perhaps it would help to remind everyone how a Speaker is elected. Here is the way it works. The Speaker is the highest-ranking constitutional office that is elected with the fewest votes. You may get elected to the House with a few hundred thousand votes in your district. Then, to be elected Speaker requires only a simple majority of the House, or 218 votes (less if there are absent members).

The Speaker is not on any national ballot like the president. Our local congressional elections have become nationalized and this is unfortunate because it detracts from the issues in each district that are important to a member's constituents. Whoever becomes Speaker must first be elected to the House in his or her own district. The majority party in the Congress that starts in 2019, will elect the Speaker from among their members just as the Constitution provides. The majority party and the minority party will place names in nomination. When the nominations are completed, the Clerk of the House oversees the election of the Speaker.

The Constitution states "The House shall chuse their Speaker." (that's no typo, just an old way of spelling choose). It does not say "The People shall chuse their Speaker." The "People," voting locally in 435 districts are voting for members of Congress. They are voting for people who will represent them in Washington. The entire House is elected every two years. Voters have no individual say in electing the Speaker.

Electing a Speaker is a process internal to the House and the majority party gets to elect the Speaker. There have been times when the election of the Speaker has dragged on for weeks or even months, but it is usually decided on the first ballot, or perhaps several ballots on the same day.

What does President Trump have to say about Nancy Pelosi? He says she backs the thugs in the MS-13 gangs. He says she is the GOP's "Secret Weapon." He said that under Democrats like Pelosi, immigrants will flood into the country and overwhelm the nation. He is full of the usual demagogic excesses, as if Nancy Pelosi will single-handedly take over the government and the president will have to go hide in a closet somewhere. President Trump had a kinder view of Nancy back in 2007, when she was elected Speaker. He wrote her a personal note, "Nancy, you're the best. Congrats, Donald."

Yesterday I got one of my many email messages from Nancy Pelosi that anyone gets who has contributed to the Democratic Party. This one warned of the coming smear campaign and this is how Nancy Pelosi sees it:

"… Republicans and the Kochs are spending millions on falsehoods about me. Why? Because I'm effective; and because I've made some very powerful, rich enemies who are anti-government in terms of the Affordable Care Act, pro-Wall Street, anti-climate, and anti-labor. I don't think we should allow Republicans in Washington to choose the leaders of the Democratic Party. Yet that's what they're trying to do."

This is precisely what is going on. The campaign is directed mostly at weak-kneed Democrats. The GOP fears Nancy Pelosi as Speaker because she is so good at the job. Listen to the rhetoric about her on Fox News, on Rush Limbaugh, and from the president's lips and tweets to see the lengths the GOP will go to smear her.

Even worse, you can hear doubts about Nancy Pelosi from a few House Democrats who are arguing that the House needs new leadership. But until the elections are over, and we learn which party controls the House, it would be smart for Democrats to keep their powder dry if they want a change in leadership. If they support Nancy Pelosi, they should not be afraid to say so, as many have. If not, they should wait until the November elections are over. There will be two months between the election results and the swearing in of the new Congress. That would be the proper time to launch any campaigns for Speaker. To do so now only plays into Republican propaganda against Democrats.

There is a good deal of hypocrisy among those Democrats who bring up the new leadership issue now, when Nancy Pelosi is out on the hustings raising money for Democrats across the country like no one else in the House. She is working hard to elect Democrats. She is a very effective fundraiser, and even more importantly, we will need her kind of serious experience in governance during a very pivotal election.

We have an amateur president. We need an experienced Speaker. We need a Speaker that can challenge Trump, but one who also loves the institution of the House and is not afraid to work across the aisle to do the people's business. It would be nice to have a Speaker who understands the Constitution and her role as a party leader and as a leader for the entire nation.

In all the uncertainty in this election cycle, I feel totally confident, all the slings and arrows aside, that Nancy Pelosi is the best person to take the Democrats forward in the House; she is the best fundraiser for House elections, and the best person to help stabilize an unstable, dysfunctional Congress.

I started working for the House under Tip O'Neill's leadership in 1983. So, when Nancy Pelosi arrived in 1987, I was able to watch her work on behalf of the Democrats from day one. She came as a freshman member but already with many years of experience with the Democratic National Committee in California. She worked harder than any member at being a great member of Congress. She grew up in a political family. Her father was a congressman and the mayor of Baltimore. She saw politics as the noble calling it should be.

The three Speakers I worked for all knew that Nancy Pelosi was a natural leader and they were not wrong. Her best days as Speaker are yet to unfold, if the Democrats come to their senses, and if the Democrats can agree that taking back the House is the single most important political act that is needed to help restore good government in the United States.

Frenzied Commentary

August 16, 2018

President Trump, in a petty gesture to silence one of his most prominent and effective critics, has revoked the security clearance held by former CIA Director John Brennan. This will not stop Director Brennan from being critical of the president. He sees his current duty to his country to speak out about the president's incompetence to hold the office. Trump is waging open warfare on his critics both inside and outside of government. He has no respect for the distinguished service to this country of many of his critics, who under normal circumstances would stay out of the political fray.

Trump, through his spokesperson Sarah Huckabee Sanders, announced he was revoking Brennan's clearance because of his "increasing frenzied commentary" against the president. This was a unilateral action taken by the president without consulting anyone else in the intelligence community. It was within the president's powers to do this, but no president has ever abused his power this way, other than Richard Nixon.

I have seen nothing "frenzied" in John Brennan's much needed critique of Trump as a danger to national security. We need more John Brennans, people of great stature, who know how our government and the world works, to step up to the plate and speak out against the dangerous acts and untenable autocratic policies of our president. This is sorely needed given the fact that we have a GOP-controlled House and Senate with their heads in the sand when it comes to Trump.

I wonder what kind of dastardly deeds Trump is using, or plans to use, against his critics. Is he, like Nixon before him, using confidential government information to go after his enemies? Nixon gained access to income tax records of his enemies. This was one of the charges in the articles of impeachment against him that were never used, under the abuse of power category. Among Nixon's crimes was that he ran a shake down operation against prominent corporate leaders that could have been in trouble with the IRS unless they gave big money to the president's re-election committee. This was pure blackmail. Nixon had a long list of enemies and a variety of strategies to figure out how to "screw" them. This orchestrated plan to screw his enemies was something that came out in the Watergate hearings, when John Dean, the president's attorney, exposed this to the investigators.

We have never had a president like Trump who so distrusted his own staff that he would require them to sign non-disclosure agreements (NDAs). It will be interesting to see just how extensive this policy has been used and for what reasons. Trump survived in private business and kept the worst aspects of his shady dealings quiet by using NDAs with a lot of people, including Stormy Daniels. In private life, for a celebrity like Trump, who was in court all the time for one thing or another, an NDA was a useful business tool. But he is President of the United States now. There are laws of disclosure and transparency that are required of all presidents since Nixon. The U.S. Congress revised some laws after Watergate to help prevent Nixon's abuse of power from happening again.

A new Presidential Records Act declared that a president's official papers were owned by the public, not by the president. The law requires that papers be preserved, protected, and eventually made public after the passage of time, or through the Freedom of Information Act, passed in 1967, to allow the press and researchers access to government information. When you go to the FOIA website it says: "The basic function of the Freedom of Information Act is to ensure informed citizens, vital to the functioning of a democratic society." This could have been written by James Madison, who believed that informed citizens were essential for democracy to survive. Madison said that if the people did not have good information about what government was doing, it could lead to a "farce or tragedy, or both." We are living that farce and that tragedy right now and our president is trying to plug all the leaks and silence those who work in his White House with non-disclosure agreements. This is the very antithesis of Madisonian principles.

I wonder who is paying for the salaries the current and former White House staff who are getting upwards of $15,000 a month to keep from saying anything critical about Trump, his family, and Mike Pence and his family. If it is coming from campaign funds it is likely to be a violation of the law unless the recipients of the hush money are earning the money working full time for the campaign. And just whose campaign is it? Trump's former personal body guard is apparently drawing down this amount for working on security for the 2020 campaign, while he is living in Florida.

The whole thing with the non-disclosure business stinks to high heaven. I would find it hard to believe Trump is paying for these NDAs out of his own pocket. The only other source would be private donors. If this is where the money is coming from, who are these people and what are they getting for their "donations"? The public has the right to know about this arrangement and who is paying for it.

Stories about how the president spends his time in the White House are emerging and it is not a pretty picture because a substantial part of each day he is doing things in private with no record of his actions. He apparently does not like to hold meetings until 11 am each day. The time from 8 am to 11 am is called "executive time." This is when Trump is watching TV, looking at certain newspapers, tweeting, and making phone calls. We do not know who he is calling and for what purpose. There should be a record of everyone the president talks to. We do have a record of his tweets and it is one of the most damning indictments of bad behavior and ignorance ever recorded about any president. Trump is extremely public with his Twitter account, so public that all his lies and many of his autocratic and mean decisions, and even his obstruction of justice, are well documented in his own words. The president apparently tires of being president about 4 pm each day and goes back into "executive time," probably to watch how he's doing on the evening news.

Enter Omarosa Manigault Newman, the arch-villain of Trump's TV series, and recently fired White House staff member. For a long time, there was Stormy Daniels and her aggressive and media savvy lawyer Michael Avenatti. Stormy and Michael have receded so fast in our consciousness, that Avenatti is now thinking of running for president to get back in the news. Omarosa is the latest of Trump's White House staff members to smite their former boss. Reality TV meets the White House and makes every soap opera in the history of television, every other reality show, and every episode of "House of Cards," pale by comparison. This is Omarosa's moment. She is driving our president to complete distraction and frenzy, and she has tapes to back up her disclosures about the president.

Her most explosive charge is that the president knew in advance that Hillary Clinton's server had been hacked. When he said during the campaign, "Russia, are you listening, if you can find Hillary's

30,000 emails…" according to Omarosa the president already knew. If this is true, and we don't know if she is lying or not, then everything the president has done since regarding the Russian probe is one giant coverup, one giant conspiracy to collude with Russians to affect the outcome of the 2016 election.

My copy of Omarosa's book, "*Unhinged: An Insider's Account of the Trump White House*," arrives later today. Why did I buy this? Why do I contribute to the sales of a book that is so self-serving, and probably 90% gossip, that will make Omarosa a million dollars? I do it because I follow this stuff. I read as much as I can from all sources. I have already pre-ordered Bob Woodward's book *Fear: Trump in the White House*, due out next month. I expect Woodward's book to be far more substantive. But I am not sure if it will not be someone like Omarosa, someone who Trump himself invented in the world of reality TV, who will be the one that leads to his downfall.

And finally, with all of this going on, we still have 30 to 40% of Americans who are either oblivious to Trump's faults or are in complete denial. There are many Americans who think, as Trump does, that the Mueller investigations are a witch hunt. There are plenty of Americans who simply will not accept any criticism of Trump any more than he can. As Steve Schmidt put it so eloquently, there are too many Americans who have "surrendered their intellectual sovereignty" to Donald Trump. They choose not to think for themselves about what is truth and what is lies. Many have become Trump's True Believers, no matter what evidence is presented.

Trump as Unindicted Co-Conspirator

August 22, 2018

The double-barreled shotgun blast of news yesterday that President Trump's campaign manager, Paul Manafort, was found guilty of eight counts of federal crimes, followed by the guilty plea of President Trump's personal lawyer, Michael Cohen, who pleaded guilty to eight counts of federal crimes, was the beginning of a major unraveling of a criminal conspiracy involving the President of the United States.

In his plea, Michael Cohen went out of his way to implicate directly the President of the United States in the payment of hush-money to two women with whom he had sexual affairs. Cohen said the payments were made "in coordination and at the direction of a candidate for federal office." Other documents described this candidate for federal office as "individual-1" and then made clear that "...individual-1, who at that point had become the President of the United States."

Some of the president's lies are worse that others. It was merely bizarre braggadocio that he lied about the size of his inauguration crowd. But when he lied publicly in his statement to the press on Air Force One that he new nothing about any payments to Stormy Daniels (woman-2 in the records) and that the press should talk to Michel Cohen about this, he was engaged in covering up a criminal conspiracy that he fully knew about at the time.

Court documents show that not only did Trump order hush-money in the amount of $130,000 to be paid to woman-2, but that Trump paid a handsome fee to Cohen for this service. During Trump's first year in office, a Trump company paid Cohen a "legal fee" of $35,000 every month until the Stormy Daniels hush money and Cohen's bonus were paid in full. The amount was $420,000.

Recently a friend asked me to explain how all this stuff about hush-money to cover up sexual affairs had anything to do with Special Counsel Mueller's mandate to investigate Russian activity in the 2016 presidential election. I told him that the mandate of the Justice Department to the Special Counsel gave the federal prosecutors the right to bring indictments for any crimes that they uncovered during the investigation.

In important ways the Mueller team is using the process widely used in federal prosecutions under the RICO Act, (Racketeer Influenced and Corrupt Organizations Act) to charge smaller fish in a criminal conspiracy and get them to spill the beans on higher-ups. Faced with many years in jail, Cohen finally opted to spill the beans on his client, the President of the United States.

In a related matter, the Special Counsel just postponed sentencing of General Michael Flynn, who pleaded guilty to lying about his contacts with Russians. Reports suggest that this delay in sentencing is to get more information from Flynn about the fact that he was ordered by Donald Trump to contact Russians. If this is true, then it might reduce Flynn's sentence even more. Mueller is putting additional pressure on Flynn. As some of the key players in the conspiracy start to fall, others see the chance to bail out too, while the information they have is still of value in reducing their sentences.

Russia is infused in all this unfolding drama. Paul Manafort was campaign chairman when the GOP changed its platform position which originally called for sending weapons to the Ukraine to fend off Russian aggression, to a milder position that took out reference to weapons. Manafort, in deep debt at the time, was hoping to have debts forgiven if he kept Russians apprised of the Trump campaign. Russia wanted sanctions eased. Nobody in the campaign had longer and deeper ties with the Ukraine and with Russian oligarchs and operatives. Manafort was a perfect patsy. A man deep in debt, looking for a way out, and turning to his associates in the Ukraine and Russia for help.

Paul Manafort's convictions yesterday is not directly about Russia. It is about his elaborate criminal behavior. But Manafort, even more so that Cohen, is up to his eyebrows in longstanding dealings with Russians. Mueller may not get Manafort to spill the beans on Russian connections because Manafort may be expecting Trump to pardon him. Yet Manafort faces another trial in less than a month. As his web of crime is exposed, he may not be saved by a pardon from the President because state charges are involved. Trump can only pardon someone for federal crimes.

Those who are looking for simple ways to blame the Mueller team for being on a broad-based fishing expedition that is not related to the main subject of investigation simply need to understand how difficult it is to prosecute an elaborate criminal conspiracy. This difficulty is compounded immensely by the fact that the President of the United States is now an unindicted co-conspirator.

Trump will fight as dirty as he can to cling to power. I don't think he can see himself as a loser, even though his consciousness of guilt is apparent in all his assaults on the American system of justice. We may see unprecedented attempts to indict the president, something that has never been done, and may need to go to the Supreme Court for a decision if it comes to an indictment. Congress is still sleepwalking though a minefield of evidence of corruption in high office. Impeachment is never easy and may be all but impossible to achieve.

Yesterday's guilty plea from Michael Cohen and the guilty verdict in the Paul Manafort trial take the investigations to a new level, but not enough to bring any semblance of closure. There is much left to unravel. Much truth that remains hidden. The next phase may very well involve the indictment of Donald Trump, Jr., and perhaps others who were at the infamous Trump Tower meeting back in June 2016. That meeting is prima facie evidence of collusion with Russian agents. It took place in Trump's own headquarters, with Trump's offices one floor up.

When did the president know about this meeting and what did he know? What we do know is that when Donald Trump, Jr. was told of the meeting with a representative of the Russian government to get dirt on Hillary, he said he loved it. Any decent person, or any person who was mindful of the law, would have immediately called the FBI. No one did. Hell, it was just a meeting about adopting Russian babies. A nothingburger.

Oh, Say Can You See

August 28, 2018

The Star-Spangled Banner was never used for lower, meaner, more self-serving purposes than it was earlier this week. The President of the United States took his long-standing personal feud with the late Senator John McCain to absurd and embarrassing depths. Donald Trump did not want the American flag on the roof of the White House lowered in honor of the passing of a distinguished American, a senator, a war hero, and twice a candidate for President of the United States.

Someone at the White House originally did the right thing by lowering the flag to half-staff on the day Senator McCain died. This is protocol. This is one important symbolic way we honor distinguished Americans at the time of their passing. Protocol is the word that describes the rules and practices of government in the formal conduct of the affairs of the nation. It is all about respect, it is about tradition, it is about common courtesy and decency.

The State Department has an Office of the Chief of Protocol, to advise the president and other government officials on matters relating to diplomatic practice with foreign dignitaries and heads of state. All three branches of the government have rules and traditions that add dignity and decorum to governmental affairs. Trump is the most impolite, undiplomatic, president in American history. He has a disdain for protocol. For him, protocol is a straight jacket. He has no respect for others but demands others to respect him.

We learned that White House staff urged President Trump to issue a statement honoring Senator McCain's service to the United States, but he decided a tweet was in order that sent "thoughts and prayers" to McCain's wife and family, without even mentioning the senator. When the president discovered the flag had been lowered to half-staff as a matter of protocol and respect, he immediately ordered it back up again. Then, with mounting public pressure from all quarters, including veteran's groups, the president reversed his decision, lowered the flag again, and issued a statement honoring the senator. It was probably the same statement his staff had prepared for him but that he had rejected.

Is there anyone in America, regardless of party affiliation, and regardless of the level of support one may have for President Trump, who cannot see at the dawn's early light that what the president did was so petty and small that it violated every aspect of human decency imaginable? Whatever differences the president may have had with Senator McCain, no matter how severe the personal animosity, there could be no excuse that can atone for the actions of the petulant child that occupies the White House.

The president used the American flag, a symbol that should unite us, not divide us, and turned it into a tool for his personal vendetta against one of our most distinguished citizens. He not only insulted Senator McCain and his family, he insulted all of us who respect the flag as a symbol of national unity. President Trump belittled the flag and trampled on the traditions of the nation because he didn't like Senator McCain.

When he attacked the peaceful, symbolic protest of kneeling NFL players who were calling attention to violations of civil rights, he inflamed passions and divided us. He called kneeling football players sons of bitches who should leave the country. Trump turned a protest to highlight unfair treatment of black citizens into an attack on the national anthem and the flag and questioned the patriotism and citizenship of the protesters.

This is what demagogues do best. They change the focus and get us fighting each other over the wrong issues. We should not allow a president who has exhibited no understanding of patriotism to be the one who tells us what patriotism is. John McCain's life was about patriotism. Maybe this is why Trump hates him so much. Trump instinctively knows he can't be the real thing.

He denigrated Senator McCain on many occasions for being captured by the enemy. He said he didn't like heroes who were captured. How can any citizen who ever wore the uniform of any branch of the armed services, or anyone who has worked for government as a civilian, or any citizen who has ever spoken up in protest against injustice in this country, ever be able to find a suitable excuse that would account for our president's insult to this nation when he abused the American flag that flies over the White House and in so doing insulted all American flags and all our symbols of unity.

Senator McCain's Last Battle

September 1, 2018

John McCain's last battle was not the one he had with cancer. It was with Donald Trump and the forces of self-interest and demagoguery versus the forces of American values, public service, patriotism, and democracy. The nation badly needed to reflect on the things that have always made the United States the great experiment in self-government that it is. *The New Yorker* said this gathering at the National Cathedral, in honor of John McCain, was the largest "resistance movement" against Trump yet. It certainly had that feeling. It was done both subtly, gently, but with sledgehammer power.

The past few days, as the nation has honored one of its true sons, we have all had a profound reminder of our best values and we have had a much-needed break from Trump's daily lies and bombast. I felt proud of the nation again, not that I have ever given in to the cynicism that is easy to come by in the Trump years. I felt cleansed by the display of bipartisanship, the references to our better traditions, and the shear decency and humanity of this very special funeral service. And I cried at times, because I mourned for Senator McCain and because I mourned for our nation that is so far off its traditional moorings right now.

President Trump was not invited to the magnificent service at the National Cathedral. He spent the day, as he has on so many days of his presidency, playing golf and avoiding TV coverage of the service. While his name was never mentioned, it was as if the entire service was a lecture to Donald Trump and to the whole nation that we are so much better than the shoddy venality of our current president.

While John McCain and Donald Trump both claimed to be members of the Republican Party they are worlds apart in their grasp of this nation's history and their service to it. I wonder if the Republican Party even exists anymore, or if it has been replaced by a hollow shell of the party that John McCain knew and fought for.

In his last major speech before the Senate, McCain proved that he loved and revered the institution and its special place in our three-branch government. He called on his colleagues in his own party to get back to "regular order," to make the Senate work again the way it does when it is at its best through compromise and consensus that goes across party lines in the interest of the whole nation. Politics is always a tough fight, it can get ugly and is often very unpleasant, but it needs to be fought with the understanding that your opponents are Americans, fellow citizens, not mortal enemies. The goal of government is to benefit the nation, not a single party.

The most powerful speech at the National Cathedral service was delivered by Senator McCain's daughter Meghan who said we did not need to make America great again when it had always been great. She never mentioned Trump, but she contrasted her father's service and sacrifice with those who have always led a life of comfort and privilege. She said of heroes that we raise them up not to put them on pedestals but to emulate them and learn from their example.

It was all the references and stories about McCain's character, his decency, his devotion to country, and his authentic patriotism that stood out in sharp contrast to our president who displays no character, no decency, and no patriotism. President Bush said McCain could not abide bigots and swaggering despots, and this reference could easily have meant foreign despots, but it hit home as a direct reference to the bigot and swaggering despot in the White House.

Eulogies are not a time to be critical of the departed. It is a time to exalt their virtues and praise their service to the nation. Mc-Cain made plenty of political mistakes in his time, and any full accounting of his life story and his history will explore these. Many have been explored already. Nobody at the service even suggested that John McCain was perfect, far from it. This was not a funeral service for a saint.

McCain and his campaign for president in 2008 unleashed on the world the totally unqualified Sarah Palin as his vice-presidential pick. She has been strangely silent and mostly unmentioned this week. McCain and his presidential campaign staff knew that selecting this demagogic personality for the ticket was a colossal mistake. It helped unleash the Tea Party, the acceleration to the far-right, the ideological hardening of the Republican Party, which has driven out most of its moderates. It left a GOP that was ripe for an even more outrageous demagogue like Trump.

But all of this cannot be laid at McCain's feet. Ironically, it was the election of Barack Obama that was even more important in eliminating moderate Republicans from office, as the GOP made it a firm policy to fight against anything Obama proposed and as the Republican Party allowed itself to succumb to the political power of racism and bigotry as vicious tools to use against our first African American president.

There will be plenty of time to analyze all of this. But for the last few days it has been so good to be reminded of our better angels, to hear again noble talk of duty to country, sacrifice, honor, honesty, decency, patriotism, and character. These are not clichés. These things, embodied in generation after generation of Americans, is what makes each of us the best citizens we can be. Let's hope that John McCain's last battle to save the honor of this nation is one he wins and that all of us win too.

Anonymous Bombshell

September 6, 2018

I wish the anonymous writer of the explosive op-ed piece in today's *New York Times* that reveals a dedicated inside-the-White House opposition to President Trump's amorality and his haphazard and dangerous policies, had thought ahead and signed the piece "Publius." Since the op-ed was released, it has become the hottest item of Breaking News, even overshadowing the Senate hearings on Judge Brett Kavanaugh for a seat on the Supreme Court.

If the op-ed had been signed Publius it would still be anonymous, but it would have a touch of class that referred back in time to the anonymous writings of the Federalist essays by three of the nation's founders, Alexander Hamilton, James Madison, and John Jay.

It would be doubly appropriate to make this connection with patriotism in the founding era of the nation. We sorely need patriots right now who can stand up for the country. Madison, Hamilton, and Jay, and many other of the founding generation, were worried that the Constitution might not survive. We have that same worry today.

Publius was a common first name in the Roman Empire. It basically means one of the people or could mean a citizen. It reminds us that the United States is a republic, where the people have the ultimate political power.

Anyone watching the Kavanaugh hearings has had a lesson in the Federalist essays, the eighty-five brilliant explorations of the meaning of the U.S. Constitution written in 1787-88. The goal of Hamilton, Madison and Jay was to convince voters in key states, especially New York, to ratify the Constitution.

They wrote anonymously so their writing would have to stand on its own merit, without any political baggage attached that would cause some readers to dismiss it out of hand because they may not have liked the authors. Sometimes anonymity avoids a reader's bias. It says, deal with the words of the op-ed, not with the individual writer. We know the media would immediately hound the author if they knew who it was.

Imagine if Woodward and Bernstein's "Deep Throat" source during Watergate had been exposed immediately as the Deputy Director of the FBI, Mark Felt. An early revelation would have shifted the focus from Nixon and the Watergate cover-up to a major investigation of the FBI. We know that Trump is very good at shifting the focus of news away from him and onto his critics. He does this every day. He has already accused the anonymous op-ed writer of treason and has started a witch hunt of his own to find culprits in the White House.

Anonymous or not, I found the op-ed one more compelling indictment of our unstable and unfit president. Many observers, including me, have long said that Trump is totally unqualified to be the president on many grounds including his general ignorance of the world and his total lack of experience in governance. When you add to this his unstable mental condition, his rants, his paranoia, and his lashing out at everyone who crosses him or fails to show loyalty, it is easy to see why a lot of us are looking seriously at ways to check his excesses.

I am glad there are some "adults" in the White House who keep an eye on the president, but I also take seriously the criticism of some that un-elected officials second guessing and undermining the president gets close to something like a coup. Trump corrupts everything, even the actions of good people trying to help the country.

We have whistle-blower laws that are supposed to protect federal employees who bring to public attention malfeasance in office, crimes, or otherwise dangerous situations. But they don't always work. Top federal officials who see crimes or amoral activity in the White House or other places in government, should be able to go to Congress, either publicly or privately, to air a grievance or report wrong-doing. But we have a compliant, dysfunctional Congress that seems incapable of acting, even when they know how bad the situation is with the president.

Senate Majority Leader Mitch McConnell is on the verge of delivering another conservative Justice to the Supreme Court, exactly the one he wants, and he is not going to jeopardize this nomination with an open fight with the president. McConnell prides himself on playing the long game for the conservative movement, and he has put everything into this court nomination. Senator Bob Corker thought the anonymous *New York Times* op-ed told us nothing new. He admitted that everyone knows we have a disaster in the White House, but his response was ho-hum, what else is new? Senator Lindsey Graham, unmoored from his late friend Senator John McCain, is now ingratiating himself to Trump. On the House side, Speaker Paul Ryan, who is retiring from the House, continues to play the role of the Mad Magazine character Alfred E. Neuman, famous for saying "What? Me Worry!"

Within this political context, what is a senior official inside the executive branch to do? The anonymous writer decided to go public, to go to the vast, unstable market of public opinion. To broadcast to the world that within the White House there are those who are trying to save the country and the world from a crazy president, even though this is in itself a crazy and unsatisfactory way of doing it.

Correcting Trump on the Gettysburg Address

September 8, 2018

It is a fool's errand for a historian to try to correct all the errors of historical fact and interpretation that emanate from the current President of the United States. But I cannot sit still while Trump re-writes the history of Lincoln at Gettysburg for his own selfish purposes.

This is what he said to his adoring fans at a rally in Billings, Montana, on Thursday, September 6.

> You know, when Abraham Lincoln made the Gettysburg Address speech, the great speech, do you know he was ridiculed? He was ridiculed.

> He took the horse and carriage up from the White House, he wrote it partially in that carriage and partially at a desk in the Lincoln Bedroom, which is incredible, by the way, in the White House. And he went up to Gettysburg, and he delivered that speech, the Gettysburg Address. And he was excoriated by the fake news. They had fake news then. He was excoriated.

> They said it was a terrible, terrible speech. They said it was far too short. It's not long. Many of us know it by memory. It was far too short, and it was far too flowery. It was too flowery, four score and seven years ago, right? Too flowery. And he died. Fifty years after his death, they said it may have been the greatest speech ever made in America.

Trump said all this to make the case that his speeches are not liked by the current fake-news press but that one day his speeches too would qualify for greatness. This was not the first time Trump has tried to put himself in the same league with Abraham Lincoln.

A more accurate view was that Lincoln's speech was very favorably received in some quarters and criticized in others, generally along partisan lines and along lines about the nature of race in American life. One critic, writing in the *Chicago Times*, shortly after Lincoln delivered the speech, attacked Lincoln for having the audacity to suggest that Negroes might be equal to whites. Racism was alive and well during the Civil War. The United States at the time of the address was at war with itself and partisan passions were as high as they could go, with Americans killing one another in unbelievable numbers.

Gettysburg was still a smelly mess four-and-a-half months after the battle when Lincoln spoke there. All the dead had not been re-interred. Residents of Gettysburg were still coming down with typhoid fever from the pollution caused by the dead, and from dead horses that remained unburied at the time of the cemetery's dedication, even though 5,000 dead horses had been burned before the dedication.

Reporters, like the one from the *Chicago Times*, who did not like the idea of equal rights for slaves, or for slavery to be abolished, criticized Lincoln for talking about equality in his speech. If they didn't like Lincoln to begin with, they called the speech boring, much the way Trump said he was bored and fell asleep listening to Barack Obama's speech yesterday.

In my book *Trump Tsumani*, I wrote a piece called "Trump's Gettysburg Address." Trump gave one of his final campaign speeches before the election, outlining what he would do in his first 100 days in office. He did this at Gettysburg, because he saw himself as the next Lincoln.

I began my piece on Trump's speech at Gettysburg this way: "Imagine, if you can, Abraham Lincoln announcing at Gettysburg that he was going to sue all the lying women who have accused him of sexual assault. This was indeed Trump's pronouncement in his speech on the hallowed ground of Gettysburg, which Trump mispronounced as 'hollowed' as he read it from his Teleprompter."

Trump's recent assertion that Lincoln's address was not popular at the time is contradicted by the coverage of the speech in the "failing fake-news" *New York Times*, a newspaper that was around when Lincoln was president and that will, I expect, be around to cover many more presidents, some yet unborn.

Lincoln's short, 272-word-speech, was not the featured address of the day, and was listed in the program as "remarks." It was interrupted five times by applause, with sustained applause when he finished. The *New York Times* reported that the speech was well received and delivered with a strong clear voice that could be heard by the large audience assembled for the occasion. Lincoln had a high-pitched shrill, nasal voice, that had a great advantage in the days before electronic amplification of being able to be heard by large crowds.

I would not expect Trump to know any of this historical context. I would not expect Trump to know that Lincoln took a train to Gettysburg, not a horse and carriage as he told the crowd in Billings last Thursday. Trump described Lincoln's speech as "too flowery." He should read Garry Wills, *Lincoln at Gettysburg: The Words that Remade America* to fully appreciate the powerful richness of Lincoln's carefully chosen, carefully crafted, and carefully rehearsed words. Lincoln knew the difference between "hallowed" and "hollowed." Lincoln did not go to Gettysburg to give a stream-of-consciousness talk, off the top of his head, and in incomplete sentences with inaccurate prose.

I suppose I should be glad that President Trump recognizes the Gettysburg Address as a great American speech. I do believe, however, that he is totally incapable of explaining its meaning to those who heard it in 1863, or to those who have gained inspiration from it all these years later.

What he did before the crowd in Billings was to wrap himself in Lincoln. It was not about Lincoln, it was about Trump's prediction that he will one day be recognized as a great president, just like Lincoln. Suffice it to say that I have read many of Lincoln's speeches and I have read many of Trump's speeches. Donald Trump is no Abraham Lincoln. And the passage of time, be it fifty years, or four score and seven years from now, will not change this assessment. Of this, I am most confident.

The Truth Emerges: Woodward's Book

September 13, 2018

This is not going to be a book review of Bob Woodward's, *Fear: Trump in the White House*. It will be instead my reaction and thoughts now that I have finished reading the book. This is not an easy book to read. Not that the language is a problem. Woodward's narrative on the chaos inside the Trump White House is top-notch professional reporting. We would expect nothing less from this distinguished journalist.

The book is hard to read because it is so painful. There is no let-up in the account of the president's ineptitude and lies. There is no comedy relief in this book. This story is an unmitigated tragedy. It is uncomfortable to read, even for those of us who follow the Trump presidency closely and think our hide has been toughened now that we are more than 600 days into the Trump presidency.

This is an important book that will stand among the best reporting on our flawed and fearful president. Students of the Trump presidency years from now will find this essential reading. It stands out in the growing literature on Trump as among the very best reporting. Bob Woodward passes no judgments, he offers no psychological profile, and shows no favoritism toward anyone in the book.

Woodward never says Trump is crazy, although some of the people he interviewed say it. And they call Trump an idiot and a moron. These epithets come from Trump's own hand-picked people, not his political enemies. Woodward reports what people tell him. He gets more than one source, and he benefits from the work of many other reporters covering the same beat, which he readily acknowledges.

In his book-tour interviews, Woodward cites his former boss at the *Washington Post*, Ben Bradlee, from the Watergate days, as saying "the truth emerges." It only emerges when you go looking for it, and it doesn't emerge easily.

We hear and read daily about the ineptitude of the president. We see it in his tweets. Today the *Washington Post* fact-checkers put Trump's lies and misleading statements at over 5,000. It wasn't that long ago that I wrote about his 3,000th lie. They keep mounting up like an embarrassing tower of shame, an enduring historical blemish on his presidency.

Trump seems incapable of shame. His lies don't bother him. He may not even see them as lies. And some of those Woodward interviewed believe Trump can't help himself. It seems to be in his DNA somewhere. Gary Cohn, Trump's economic adviser, until he left the White House, kindly called Trump a "professional liar." Trump's lawyer, John Dowd, used the vernacular. "Trump is a f**king liar."

The president's inability to separate fact from fiction and truth from lies is what caused John Dowd to quit the president. There was no longer any way to help him with a defense. Yet Woodward reports that John Dowd does not think Trump is guilty of collusion or obstruction of justice.

This book is not about the Mueller investigation, it is not about Trump's policies, even though these things are mentioned. It is what the subtitle says: "Trump in the White House." It is about the utter chaos, the back-biting, the constant turnover of top staff, and the utter shock that serious government people experience after being in high-level meetings with Trump and discovering that he is an ignorant, child-like man who has virtually no knowledge or experience in any of the major subjects expected of American presidents.

A few stories in Woodward's book quickly dispel the myth that America should be governed by a businessperson, especially one with no prior military or government experience, and one who is ignorant of macro-economics, or the independence of the Federal Reserve. During a discussion about the rising debt and the idea that interest rates would rise, Trump's idea was to have the government make money selling money. Buy while interest rates were low and sell the money when interest rates got higher. To offset growing debt Trump said, "Just run the presses—print more money." (page 56).

I came away from Woodward's book with a feeling that the inner circle of White House staff is really a relatively small group of people, many of whom are running around not knowing exactly what they are doing from day to day. One young staffer was supposed to recommend top people to work with Secretary of State Rex Tillerson. Tillerson reported that the people sent over to him were disastrously ill-equipped and unqualified.

Everyone in the White House was trying to avoid the minefield that Trump laid for them everyday with his tweets, lies, and flips over policy and other matters. Jared and Ivanka floated above all the staff as members of the royal family. At one point Steve Bannon chewed out Ivanka, reminding her that she was just a staff person. She replied that she wasn't staff, she was "the first daughter." (p.145). She didn't need to go through the White House chief-of-staff. Trump's family dynamics, this blatant nepotism, has been a constant irritant to the professionals trying to do their jobs.

The presidency is too big for one person. Even though we elect a single president, the Constitution assumed the president would delegate authority to "the principal Officer in each of the executive Departments...." From George Washington's time to the present we have had a cabinet of top executives. Many president's have picked friends and cronies to fill some of these top spots, but usually they were people with some knowledge of their agency, or prior experience in government or the military. Many of Trump's appointees have already left under various clouds of ineptitude and scandal.

Trump picked his top executives for loyalty first. He picked billionaires for many posts because he thought they could do anything because they were rich, like him. On his stump speeches he brags about his mental acumen to pick the best people and says he picks billionaires over poor people and other "non-rich" people because, and he often points to his own head, he is smart enough to know that rich people are better executives than poor people. He says this to audiences with poor people present and they applauded nonetheless, apparently not noticing the president has just insulted them, and portrayed himself and his cabinet as a monetary version of American royalty.

May the truth emerge about this president and his corrosive administration for the benefit of the nation and the world. In the meantime, there is plenty for all of us to fear, even without being overly paranoid about it. We can do better than this. We have the power to change things. Whatever fear and anxiety we may have about the current situation in the White House, we should never be afraid to be active citizens. This is where hope resides, and where truth will emerge. It's called the ballot box. Find one near you in November. Reboot American Democracy.

The Kavanaugh Hearings: A View from Cadillac Mountain

September 29, 2018

I missed the first-hand frenzy of the Brett Kavanaugh confirmation hearings in the Senate. I was vacationing in Maine with my wife Phyllis and some friends. We were on top of Cadillac Mountain in Acadia National Park, looking down on the town of Bar Harbor, while Washington, DC, and much of the nation were transfixed by the hearings. Our only worldly concern was finding a good place to have a lobster roll for lunch. We felt released from the machinations of politics. It was a very good feeling.

We were staying in a house that sits on the banks of the Bagaduce River as it empties into Penobscot Bay, a lovely retreat in a spectacular setting. The house has no television. You don't go there to watch television, you go to watch the tides, the changing of the light on water, and to experience the utter silence of the place, punctuated occasionally by the cry of a gull or the mournful note of a loon at sunset.

Still, we were not oblivious to what was going on in the seat of the American Empire. We had Internet service. We got news of the hearings. We did dip into the stories in the *Washington Post* and the *New York Times*, but we did not feel compelled or even interested in all the nuances and the frustrations and utter embarrassment of the proceedings on manly levels.

I engaged in a few exchanges on the Kavanaugh hearings with Facebook friends, but was not interested at the time in getting in too deep. When we returned to Washington, we once again entered the daily ebb and flow of political culture in the nation's capital, made exponentially more frustrating and maddening since the ascendancy of Trump to the presidency.

The Kavanaugh confirmation hearings seem to be playing out as a daytime soap opera. Despite plenty of good reportage and analysis, there has been considerable confusion among citizens and some of those commenting on TV and social media.

The President of the United States nominates judges for the Supreme Court. The Senate provides advice and consent and votes to confirm or reject the president's nominee. Read how simple the process is described in the Constitution. The process may be simple to explain, everything else about it is complicated, mainly due to extreme partisanship and hard-line ideology.

There is nothing in the Constitution that lists job requirements for the Supreme Court other than the president's nomination. You do not have to be a judge in a lower court to be nominated. You don't even need be a lawyer. We have had many justices who never received law degrees. The qualifications for the position are that the president nominates a single candidate and the Senate confirms or rejects that candidate.

I would argue that we have too many lawyers on the high court and not enough broad-gauged wise heads, men and women who understand more about human nature than can be found in a law book filled with precedents and where the human element is often completely subsumed under a fine point of law—and where real human beings become abstractions. Our current Supreme Court is all Ivy League-trained lawyers. It does not have to be this way. Don't assume that justices on our highest court need to be from Harvard or Yale, or any other elite law school.

The other mistake made by the public and some news coverage of the Kavanaugh hearings is that this is a trial. Brett Kavanaugh becomes a defendant on trial to prove his guilt or innocence of lies he may have told the Senate while under oath, or his guilt or innocence in acts of sexual aggression while drunk during his high school and college years.

The Senators in this scenario become judges not unlike the unflattering image of the Spanish Inquisition. I do not doubt the testimony of Professor Christine Blasey Ford any more than I doubted the testimony of Professor Anita Hill twenty-seven years ago, when she testified about the sexual attitudes of Clarence Thomas. But I again remind you that this is not a sexual harassment trial in a court of law. I do not know how the full United States Senate will respond to these serious allegations when the time comes to cast their votes.

The Senators are indeed judges in a confirmation process, just as they are judges in an impeachment. They do judge. But unlike any judge in a court of law, Senators can make their judgment for their own reasons and are not accountable to any law book. They operate on constitutional provisions and Senate rules and a big dose of hardball politics. They may decide to ram this through on a party-line vote even with public sentiment turning against Kavanaugh. The Senate does take the measurement of public sentiment, but they can choose to ignore it.

The Senate's decision to confirm cannot be overturned. There is no appeal once the Senate confirms a person to the Supreme Court. The only way a federal judge can be removed is by impeachment, and it is the Senate that votes on any judge who is impeached.

The history of Supreme Court nominees is a rich and colorful one that reveals that nominations to the high court do not automatically succeed. Nominees have been rejected. A handful have been withdrawn by the president after nomination. Some have simply failed to be confirmed and the nominations have expired at the end of a Congress. Most presidential nominees have been routinely approved by the Senate over the years. Senate rules up until 1925 did not require a candidate to appear before the Senate Judiciary Committee. Historically, most nominees were confirmed in short order with only a few hours of full Senate debate.

In modern times, especially in the era of increasing hard-core partisanship beginning in the 1980s, Supreme Court nominations have become more and more contentious and drawn out. Senate rules have changed regarding how many votes in the Senate it takes to confirm a justice. Both political parties are guilty of changing Senate rules for the advantage of one party. In 2013, Senate Democratic Leader Harry Reid, reduced the number of votes needed to confirm federal judges from 60 to 51, to help break the log-jam caused by Republican obstruction to President Obama's appointees to the federal bench. But this rule change, made by the Democratic Party majority, did not apply to the Supreme Court, which still required 60 votes. Last year Senate Republican Leader Mitch McConnell pushed through another rule change that only required 51 votes to confirm a Supreme Court justice.

Recent history shows that the nomination process for the Supreme Court has gotten more partisan than ever. The rise of ultraconservative law-oriented groups, especially the Federalist Society, have made this organization a favorite place for Republicans to groom judges who will tow a strict approach issues paramount to the conservative movement.

Both of President Trump's nominees have been taken from a list of acceptable candidates prepared by the Federalist Society.

President Trump apparently went down from the top of the list to pick Kavanaugh because of Kavanaugh's expansive views on presidential powers and his earlier role in working with Ken Starr on the Clinton impeachment. We know how much Trump likes anyone who is opposed to Bill or Hillary. Trump is probably expecting that his nominee will rule in his favor should aspects of the Mueller investigation reach the Supreme Court in 2019 or 2020.

No matter how frustrated you get, please constrain yourselves from magical thinking about how the Kavanaugh nomination can be stopped, or, if confirmed, how his role on the Supreme Court could be limited in some way. You will just waste your time and become even more frustrated. Social media is full of wild and wishful thinking to ease the pain of those who do not want to see Kavanaugh confirmed.

The lesson in all this is that elections have monumental consequences. The entire federal government is controlled by Republicans. A Republican president who knows nothing about the Constitution or how the Supreme Court works as a co-equal and separate branch of government, picks a name from a list from the Federalist Society. The name goes to the Senate. The Senate has enough votes to confirm Kavanaugh no matter what turns up in the FBI investigation.

The Senate is in full control of this matter now. Don't expect President Trump to suddenly have an attack of ethics and decency and withdraw Kavanaugh's name to quell the controversy.

Don't expect Mitch McConnell to change his mind about the nominee, no matter what turns up. He wants an ultraconservative Supreme Court that will keep conservatism and corporate America in the driver's seat in this one branch of government for the next 30 years. He plans to put Kavanaugh on the high court and he expects no defections from the Republican ranks. I do not know if he will succeed. If Kavanaugh becomes tainted further, the president could possibly withdraw his name, go back to the Federal Society list and pick another candidate from Column A or Column B.

My guess is that the Senate, up against the deadline of the November elections, will push Judge Kavanaugh through quickly to confirmation because they are worried they may not have a Senate majority next year. Senate Republicans will push Kavanaugh through and count on the American public to have a short attention span and an even shorter historical memory. They expect the American public to move on to the next circus act and forget that this nasty show ever played here at all.

The Supreme Court will embrace whomever is confirmed and that person will become an instant colleague in this very small, very exclusive, high-powered branch of government. We like to think that a lifetime appointment frees justices on the high court from the daily concerns of partisan politics. Brett Kavanaugh has shown that he has had trouble containing his partisanship and his cool during these hearings.

Word Rape

October 3, 2018

Last night before a screaming mob of thousands in Mississippi and before the whole nation, the President of the United States word raped Dr. Christine Blasey Ford. He mocked her unmercifully with vile cruelty. Donald Trump, true to form as the highest-ranking worst bully in American history, wanted to discredit her testimony against his nominee for the Supreme Court. He cannot control himself. But the mob loved it. The saddest part of it all was that American citizens at a rally allowed themselves to become a mob. They encouraged the president. They reverted to form and shouted "Lock her up. Lock her up." This chant, once reserved for another prominent woman, is apparently useful against any woman (or man) who disagrees with the president.

This was no campaign stump speech. This was uncontrolled vengeance. The fact that the crowd was so highly entertained by this public word raping, made me think back to the lynching of black people in America, where the crowds were often large and boisterous and highly entertained while the victim was tortured, murdered, and often burned. Sometimes pieces of the victim, like fingers and ears, were carted off as souvenirs.

We have seen this president mock virtually every kind of American, from a war hero, a disabled reporter, a Gold Star family, all the Republican and Democratic candidates for the presidency, the entire American press, (except for Fox News), the Democrats on the Judiciary Committee, the FBI, Mexican Americans, Muslim Americans, and African Americans. He browbeats and insults virtually anyone who, at any given moment, offends him. He has not limited his insults and bullying to Americans but has publicly disparaged heads of state including most of our allies in the world.

The United States Senate needs to take a hard look at what happened last night at that Mississippi rally. What we saw was unconscionable. The president has no right whatsoever to word rape any citizen for any reason. The whole world knows how badly Donald Trump has sullied the presidency. He should not be allowed to sully the Senate or the Supreme Court. If the Senate confirms Brett Kavanaugh after

Trump's behavior last night, it will condone misogyny, demagoguery, and outrageous cruelty.

This nomination is no longer about Brett Kavanaugh's fitness to be confirmed as a member of the Supreme Court. It is about the president's fitness to nominate anyone for this position if he is going to act in such unconscionably cruel ways. The Senate needs to show Trump that they don't have to confirm any nominee if the president is not going to play by the rule of law and common decency.

The citizens of this country will have to wait until election time to show Trump that he has crossed the line far too many times. We have power at election time. But the Senate, our duly elected Senators, our one hundred top representatives, two from each State in the Union, have the power to stop this nomination. This is far beyond partisan politics now. The moral standing of a nation is at stake. The Senate should tell the president to shut up.

The president should nominate someone else. And the Senate will take the new nominee under advisement, as it should, but in doing so the senators should put the president on notice that he can no longer engage in the character assassination of any witness before the Senate Judiciary Committee or any other committee. The Senate must defend its own constitutional prerogatives.

Later next month, at election time, we the people of this nation will have our say in this matter through the election process. A Senate vote on Brett Kavanaugh now is a vote to condone the president's vile behavior and to allow him to word rape anyone he pleases. Trump has no decency. We look to our senators to see if they have any.

Ceremonial Arrogance of Power

October 8, 2018

Donald Trump could not accept victory quietly, or gracefully. He had to rub it in. Justice Brett Kavanaugh was sworn in immediately after his confirmation. In an unusual nationally televised ceremonial swearing-in at the White House the President took the opportunity to gloat and campaign for next month's elections. Trump said the occasion was historic. There was nothing historic about it, except for the minor point that this was the first time a former Justice of the Supreme Court, was able to swear in one of his former law clerks.

It was retired Justice Anthony M. Kennedy who conducted the oath ceremony. Kavanaugh had clerked for him twenty-five years ago. I have no idea why Justice Kennedy was and is so outwardly friendly with Trump. Maybe it was because Kennedy's son, Justin, had dealings with the Trump Organization as an official of Deutsche Bank. Kennedy said he was retiring to spend more time with his family, a standard Washington cliché. It gave Trump the opportunity to appoint his second Supreme Court justice.

We will have to wait to see if Trump's campaign promise to appoint justices who would overturn *Roe* v. *Wade* comes to pass. If it is overturned, the only way to restore a woman's right to choose would have to come from a Congress controlled by Democrats. The Supreme Court may overturn established law, but if they do, Congress can re-establish it by rewriting the law to work around whatever reasons the court used to make their ruling.

Justice Kavanaugh called the Supreme Court the "crown jewel" of the Constitution. I beg to differ. It is Congress, yes Congress, not the Supreme Court or the presidency that was designed to be the leading branch of government and for most of American history this was the case. So those of you who think the Supreme Court has the last word on any matter, should recall that Congress writes the laws. If an old law is overturned, Congress can write a new one.

Justice Kavanaugh's speech this evening was just fine except for some grating moments that he was not sensitive enough to recognize. He did not make a political speech. He gave an instructional one about the role of the high court under the Constitution. He thanked everyone for their support.

There were no protesters in the East Room. This was the Republican establishment and Trump people, wall to wall. When the new justice thanked his friends in high school and college, it bothered me as a false note. I immediately thought of Dr. Christine Blasey Ford, his contemporary, if not a classmate. And I thought of his high school acquaintances with whom he got drunk, so drunk they had memory failure when the FBI came calling.

I was saddened to see the entire Supreme Court at this ceremonial swearing-in. They were there to welcome their newest colleague, someone they all knew. This was fitting and proper. But Trump used their presence as a prop. Perhaps they did not know that Trump would take this opportunity to divide the nation once more, with them in the room.

This event was the only time I ever heard Trump apologize for anything. And when he did, it was all wrong, it was ugly, and uncalled for. The president said that on behalf of the nation he apologized for the way that Brett Kavanaugh was treated during the hearings. Trump had no business declaring Justice Kavanaugh to be innocent of all the charges against him or to say that he was vindicated and proven innocent. He never once thought of apologizing to Dr. Ford, who has been humiliated by the Senate Judiciary Committee and the president.

The allegations of sexual impropriety brought against Kavanaugh at his hearings did not mean he was on trial for a crime. But these were serious allegations that needed to be investigated and instead we witnessed a ramrod job of pushing this nominee to confirmation before any of the allegations could be properly explored. We saw raw, arrogant power on the part of the GOP-controlled Congress, and we saw, on the part of the president, the manipulation of the FBI which was not allowed to conduct a proper inquiry.

It was Donald Trump's arrogance and his boastfulness and his complete lack of sensitivity to the feelings of the many protesters who objected to this nomination that was the ugly false note in this ceremony. The American citizens who went to the hearings and exercised their First Amendment rights and spoke out against Kavanaugh, had every right to do so. Those who interrupted the Senate debate were within their rights to do so. Yet the Republican Party to a man, and to a woman, have branded the protesters, mostly young women, as "an angry mob." Since when is it right to call American citizens a mob when they are exercising their right to protest the government?

Whatever is included in the judgment of history on the Trump years, it will note the fact that every time this president had a chance to heal the nation, he divided us further. Trump has found ways to sully not only the presidency, but all three branches of government.

Early in the Kavanaugh hearings President Trump called Dr. Ford a credible witness and described her as a nice person. As the hearings heated up, he mocked her shamelessly at campaign rallies and now calls her whole testimony, her personal anguish at coming forward, to be nothing but a hoax orchestrated by Democrats. Dear Dr. Ford, I humbly apologize to you for the way you were treated in your testimony and the way you have been so unfairly maligned by the President of the United States.

Whether we like it or not Brett Kavanaugh is now a justice on our high court. This battle is over. Those who think he should be immediately impeached are wasting their time. This battle is lost. It was won by the exercise of raw political power by a party that controls all three branches of government.

While this battle is lost for Democrats, Independents, as well as Republicans who don't like the daily embarrassment of Trump, I remind you that the war is not lost. We can all fight another day and every day. Politics is steady battle. You win some, you lose some, as the old saying goes. If you want to be a player in shaping the nation and fighting for your causes, you never stop fighting. There are plenty more battles to fight.

It will take many changes and fixes to restore decency to the White House and to achieve a better balance to the high court. Right now, corporate thinking and corporate America are on top. It is government of the rich, for the rich, by the rich. It is time for the people to get back their say in what America's future should be. It is time to remember that Lincoln said this was supposed to be government of the people, by the people, and for the people. We start with Congress. We start next month.

Trump on CBS's 60 Minutes

October 15, 2018

President Trump does not conduct press conferences in the manner of past presidents. He talks to the press on the fly, on the way to his helicopter, in the crowded confines of Air Force One, or at a White House conference room with the press jammed in at one side of the table and him, often with arms folded, badgering the press from the other side of the table.

He sends Sarah Huckabee Sanders out to face the White House Press Corps, where she lies, obfuscates, and tries to make sense of the president's lies and obfuscations. When the president himself has appeared on stage, or on the White House lawn with a visiting head of state, he is usually scripted. If he goes off script it is usually to cast an insult at the press or to deny something. He never explains his policy or his actions. When asked what the affects of his actions might be, he usually replies, "We will see what happens."

He has been interviewed a few times on television, on Fox News, and on CBS. Such was the case yesterday when the president sat down for a second interview with Leslie Stahl. I tried very hard to find any substance in his answers to her list of questions. It was a smorgasbord of questions, wide-ranging but also terribly shallow because there was no consistent follow-up when the president tossed a silly response back to her.

I looked for substance and then it dawned on me that perhaps the main take away that CBS was looking for was just another opportunity to show how limited the president is, how unprepared he is to give serious answers that are a paragraph or two long. Stahl asked questions that any other president would have been able to talk about in narrative fashion that showed a grasp of issues. Not all our presidents have been super-smart people, but they prepared for these interviews. They read briefing books. They often rehearsed such public appearances. Trump doesn't read and he doesn't prepare.

My takeaway from this interview is exactly what Gertrude Stein said in 1937, when she visited the site of her childhood home and found it completely gone: "There is no there there." The president runs on instinctive behavior and bragging. When it comes to detailed knowledge of the world, there is no there there. Had Leslie Stahl asked a complex question of the president, he would have been unable to handle it. She tried to get yes and no answers, only to get "Maybe," "Some people say that, I've said that," "We are looking into that."

The other revelation from this interview, that several commentators have picked up on is that Trump showed himself to be totally lacking in a moral dimension. I have written about this and so have many other observers, but this interview clarified it even more. When asked if Putin murdered people, Trump replied affirmatively but questioned what this proved. Trump brushed aside executions that happened elsewhere. Not our problem. So what?

This president has given away the moral leadership in the world that we once had. Not that we are a perfectly moral or ethical nation. But we stood for human rights, decency, the rule of law, and moral behavior and held these out as ideals. We made them an essential part of our foreign policy. Now our president has us down in the ditch with the tin-pot dictators he seems to like so much.

I was troubled by the lack of engagement in the president's answers to questions about the apparent murder and dismemberment of *Washington Post* reporter Jamal Khashoggi at a Saudi consulate in Turkey. Trump was reluctant to say what he knew. He said Jared Kushner had called the Saudi leader Prince Mohammed bin Salman, who denied having anything to do with it. Trump had no reason to doubt him.

President Trump's first foreign visit was to Saudi Arabia, where the Prince treated Trump and his family as American Royalty. Lavish parties, a ceremonial sword dance, projecting Trump's image on tall buildings, all made Trump very happy. He and son-in-law Kushner have had business dealings with the Saudis for years. Trump has hotels and owns apartments there. During the campaign he made a disclosure that he had eight companies operating in Saudi Arabia. Once again, Trump could not think of raising a moral question about this murder. He could lose business there. It could cost him millions of dollars to get tough with Saudi Arabia. When money is everything, we end up with a compromised president trapped by his own money interests in foreign countries. The president cannot express empathy for a murdered journalist, because he has no empathy.

Did Kim Jong Un starve his people and did he use slave labor, and did he kill his half-brother, Stahl asked, and Trump replied probably so, but I love the guy and we have a great relationship and the United States has no more worries about his nuclear program. When Stahl asked if North Korea was still building nuclear weapons, Trump at first said the North Koreans were tearing down facilities, then he said no one knows for sure, and finally he said maybe they were still building nukes, but nobody knew for sure. It was clear the president did not know for sure about anything and once again he ignored any mention of what his own intelligence agencies were telling him about North Korea.

Trump's complete lack of historical knowledge was on display in one of the most telling responses of the evening. Stahl asked him about how he was treating our traditional allies in the European Union and in NATO. Trump shot back, "The E.U. was founded to take advantage of us on trade." Ponder this off-handed quip from the leader of the free world. If this is what he really thinks, and there is no reason to doubt it, he just threw under the bus one of the greatest diplomatic and economic achievements of the 20th Century.

The European Union was created to end the kind of economic strife that kept European nations at war. It was designed to bring economic stability and peace to Europe and it has worked very well since its early iterations following World War II. Trump doesn't like the E.U. because he sees it as globalism. He wants the whole world to be economically subservient to the needs of the United States. There is no way he can understand things in the world without attaching a price tag to them. What is the price of peace? In 2012 the European Union received the Nobel Peace Prize.

Trump continued his attack on the press during the interview saying how badly the press has treated him since he became president. He described Washington, DC as a vicious, vicious place but offered no plan to make it less vicious. He said he thought the world of real estate developers was vicious but politics in Washington is much worse. Yet when Stahl asked him if he liked being president he said he had grown into it and at first was surprised by it all, but now he feels very comfortable. He reminded Stahl at one point in the interview "I'm the president, and you're not."

I almost fell out of my chair when the president expressed his view on global warming that he was suspicious of the political agenda of scientists predicting dire consequences. But the part that almost threw me to the floor was Trump's admission that, sure, the world's climate was changing but that it would change back! I never heard anyone say this before. When will it change back? How many thousands of years do we need to wait for the climate to improve? Trump was worried that any attempt to save the Earth's temperature from rising would cost people jobs and money. How about loss of humans as a species? No need to worry about jobs when humans are extinct.

Finally, when Leslie Stahl asked the president if he would pledge not to shut down the Mueller investigations, Trump shot back "I don't pledge anything." It was a stark remark but not surprising for a man who never admits regretting anything and prefers loyalty and trust to be a one-way street headed toward him.

I thought of the pledge Trump did take at his inauguration, the Oath of Office. It is the one time he made a pledge. He swore to "faithfully execute the Office of the President of the United States, and will to the best of my ability, preserve, protect, and defend the Constitution of the United States." Donald Trump may be doing this to the best of his ability. Unfortunately, his ability is woefully inadequate for the job. This much was crystal clear from his sit down with CBS and Leslie Stahl.

Hatred in the Digital Age: A Perfect Storm

October 27, 2018

Hate is part of the human condition. It is one of the terrible flaws of our species. We are warlike too, even though we talk peace all the time. Humans have been at war far more often than at peace for the full history of our species. All the civilizations of the world have known about hate and written about it in various ways. We try to mitigate its worst aspects, with laws, customs, diplomacy, manners, and teaching the common decency. We have asked in many languages at many times in history the same question Rodney King, a black citizen of Los Angeles, asked after he was brutally beaten by white police officers, "Can we all get along?"

While hate is not new, it has a new friend: social media. Never in the history of the world has it been easier to spew hatred than in the digital age. All of us who use social media see it every day. We see it among our friends who post outrageous statements, often couched in cynicism. We use extreme language because ordinary language doesn't attract attention. We share memes of ugly caricatures of politicians we don't like. Many of us who are not part of any hate group have helped spread hate when we share something hateful to point out how hateful it is.

But a more serious aspect of this new level of hatred is the thousands upon thousands of specialized hate sites in social media, where people go to learn how to hate or to have their hate reinforced. Young impressionable people, largely white men of all ages, go to these sites and find them exciting. They learn how to hate in more focused ways and in doing so find acceptance in the group. These sites are easy to identify, and they specialize in hating government, or particular parties, religious and ethnic groups, races, and sexual orientation. They may espouse an ideology, they may take on the style of previous hate-mongers like Nazis and the KKK.

Many of these hate groups have existed long before social media came along. But the haters had a hard time breaking into a large audience. Their pamphlets, flyers, and local demonstrations had a pathetically limited audience, only occasionally magnified by the press, when the group did something that peaked national interest as news. Now, through social media, they can be everywhere in the world, instantly. They can form alliances with hate groups in other countries. They get magnified. Social media is the best propaganda device ever invented. It makes true the adage that a Lie can spread half way around the world before the Truth can put on its shoes.

We have created a digital monster. Social media is big business run by billionaires to make money gathering data about its users. It has been a wide-open, unregulated frontier of hate, conspiracy theories, false stories, fake news, and massive propaganda, all jumbled together with healthy, positive sites that contain valuable and useful information, and where truth-seekers can be found. We have not learned how to harness this awful beast. And it is not just social media. It is the proliferation of cable television with niche markets, where you can get news and commentary that suits your own views.

Enter Donald Trump, another new friend of hate, the master self-brander, the most famous tweeter in the world, the demagogic, deeply-flawed president of the United States, who rose to power by smearing, insulting, and degrading his opponents, by saying nasty things about people based on their religion, their ethnicity, their sex, and their race. More specifically the president's anti-immigrant stance, his obvious hatred of Muslims, has fueled a 900% increase in hate groups since he began running for president. Most of the new hate groups are against immigration because it spells the end of white power and white supremacy in America. The largest new group of haters focuses on anti-Muslim immigration.

Trump feeds these hate groups a daily dose of red meat. They are an important part of his base supporters. The hate-group graph shot through the roof in 2016, during the Trump campaign. Thousands of new hate groups joined Twitter, the president's social medium of choice, according to a study based on data from the Southern Poverty Law Center that was reported in major newspapers in 2017. One such hate group, with the bland and governmental think-tank name of Federation for American Immigration Reform (FAIR) was the largest single hate group on Twitter with 72,000 followers.

We would be blind to reality to suggest, as the president does, that he does not incite hate. He does not just incite it, he thrives on it. He campaigns on it. His fear campaign is predicated on the big lie that if Democrats get elected our borders will cease to exist and we will be overrun by alien hordes.

While pipe bombs are sent to prominent Americans by one of Trump's most ardent followers, the president calls this "bomb stuff" a distraction from his campaign, and he points far away in another direction to the "national emergency" of 5,000 men, women, and children who are months away from the U.S.-Mexico border, marching for political asylum.

The president has issued no plan to combat hate of the kind expressed by the mail bomber, but he has mobilized National Guard and regular U.S. troops to go to the border, as if this marching caravan is the biggest threat to this nation. The president wants us to hate the people in that caravan as a faceless mass before we even know who they are or what story each of them will tell about their plight. The president said there were Middle Eastern types infiltrating the caravan. He had no evidence for this other than to spew more hate, by suggesting there are Muslims trying to sneak into the United States by pretending they are from Honduras.

To be this hateful, the president must lie to make his case, and by now there should be no sane American who cannot see how this president has built his entire career on a fabric of lies. I am sure his supporters would deny what I just said as simply another "liberal lie." The official story from the White House is that President Trump has been vilified and criticized more than any other president in our history and that this criticism is unfair and unprecedented. The truth is that no president from George Washington to Donald Trump has been free of constant criticism. The White House statement is just one more lie that depends on the public's ignorance of history for it to be believed.

The president was asked today about another hate crime, the killing of eleven people in a Pittsburgh synagogue, by a man armed with an AR-15 type long gun. He expressed dismay at the loss of life, but then focused on the fact that the people in the synagogue should have had an armed guard to stop the shooter. It made me cringe to think he could be so insensitive at such a time to blame the synagogue and not the perpetrator of the crime. Later, in a scripted statement, the president did condemn this heinous crime for what it was and said that mass murderers were bad people.

Donald Trump did not invent hatred. He did not invent bigotry or any of the other long-standing ills of humankind. Ironically, he has found ways to thrive on these negatives and in doing so, with him as the voice of the United States, with him as the leader of the free world, we have a perfect storm for raging hatred in the United States and the world. He is a major hate enabler. He has the loudest hate megaphone on the planet. He stands in the eye of this perfect storm, oblivious to the damage being done all around him.

It's the Republic, Stupid!

November 5, 2018

On the day before one of the most important off-year elections in American history, I have turned off the constant news about polls that may or may not reflect what will happen at polling places across America in less than twenty-four hours. To say that I am apprehensive is an understatement.

I really have no sense of how things will turn out. I have been following politics for a long time and this election remains a complete mystery. The economic issues, as they affect specific states and localities across the county, most often dominate our elections, so much so that we have an expression for it: "It's the Economy, Stupid." But this does not seem to apply this time around.

Never has an American president thrust himself into the mid-terms to the extent that Donald Trump has done. He is a campaigner. It is about all that he does. He has tried to make all elections in all fifty states, whether they for state offices or federal offices, about him. He has declared himself the embodiment of the Republican Party. A vote for any Republican is a vote for him, he tells us repeatedly. If this is so, then I offer that a vote for any Democrat is a vote against Trump. Elections are never this simple, but Trump is trying to make it so.

Even though Trump is not on the ballot, the election is playing out as a referendum on Donald Trump's first two years in office. This will be the first opportunity American voters have to either sanction the conduct of his presidency or to send a signal that the Trump administration needs some checks and balances on its excesses.

Trump cares nothing for the many local and state issues that are at play, and should be, in these off-year elections. When he speaks at rallies it is all about him. He seldom speaks about the economy. He often uses the economy as a throw-away line. He takes credit for good economic indicators and goes right back to the caravan of immigrants hundreds of miles south of our border with Mexico.

Trump has never had a vision for the future. His campaign was predicated on returning America to a time when white men (and white men only) ran the nation. His campaign was about the past. He never defends or explains his policies, like his trade wars. What he does is to divide us with white-heat rhetoric about how this country will be ruined if Democrats win. Don't even mention his administration's assaults on healthcare. We are under attack from people south of our border who the president has called animals, criminals, and disease carriers. He is sending American soldiers to save us from being overrun. They are ridiculously laying barbed wire for the TV-cameras to keep out the Hispanic Hordes. This is an embarrassment to the good men and women of our armed forces. What is so disturbing is that this demagoguery on the border resonates with many voters.

I fear for our republic. I fear we may be losing it because Donald Trump and his enablers in the Republican Party have bought into extreme division rather than much-needed unity to win elections at any cost.

My fears are not new. They were the same fears that the founding generation had. It is the same fear that was expressed by Ben Franklin when, on the day the Constitution was signed in 1787. A woman asked him what kind of government the delegates had given us. Franklin replied, "A republic, if you can keep it." The founders knew that human nature contained both nobility of thought as well as depraved greed. When the people lose their virtue, when they hate their government and revert to tribal behavior, all could be lost in short order. Governments are more fragile than most people realize.

The American republic that existed in the early 1790s consisted of about four million people, of whom 700,000 were slaves. Native Americans were not counted until 1860. By the time of the drafting of the Constitution, the Native American population was already decimated by more than two centuries of exposure to European diseases and to extensive warfare in the colonies. "Democratic" elections then were elections held by and for property-owning white men. About 6% of the population made up the eligible voters. That is not a republic we want to return to. But the Enlightenment ideals that shaped our early republic are still worth fighting for.

For more than 230 years we have managed to keep our republic intact through times of economic boom and bust, through civil war, and through world wars. We have seen the United States go from a small band of English colonies to a nation of 327 million souls spanning the entire continent. We have slowly and painfully broadened the base of those eligible to vote. With increased size, diversity, and complexity came new kinds of problems for maintaining the American republic. The founders of our republic were fully aware of how fragile this concept could be. Many of the founders had read the classics. They knew about the ideas of Plato going back 2,000 years. They wondered if the United States could survive as a republic when it reached from sea to sea.

Plato described five stages of government: aristocracy (rule by an enlightened elite, such as a philosopher king); timocracy (rule by land-owners or those controlling wealth or land, such as a military power); oligarchy (rule by a small group or groups, usually wealthy or otherwise powerful); democracy (rule by the people through direct or indirect elections, with the emphasis on liberty); and tyranny (rule by a leader or group that has usurped all law and institutions and exercises power unilaterally with cruel methods). Plato predicted that governments would tend to go through all these stages unless checked by "the good," which meant people who believed in justice and happiness, rather than injustice and unhappiness.

Our founders talked a lot about virtue as an essential ingredient to successful government. Virtuous behavior was needed to check greed, selfishness, and avarice. Our Constitution was designed to check the worst tendencies of human nature. But in 2018 the checks seem hard to come by. We go along with a flawed demagogue in charge and with half of those running for office and probably half the voters willing to align themselves with him.

Can our big, sprawling, multi-racial, multi-ethnic, multi-religious, multi-corporation, multi-oligarchic country hold onto common ground? Can our teaming cities, suburbs, and vast stretches of emptiness be contained in one republic? How big can a republic get before it collapses of its own weight? What does it take for us to keep alive the idea of e pluribus unum, out of many, one?

We take polls to show how college educated Americans differ in political preferences from those with no college education. It is but one way we define our growing separation. We disunite ourselves with talk about elites as the enemy of the people, who, I presume are the non-elites. Is it so tragically simple that the easiest way to define the "many" in e pluribus unum, is to decide which ones to hate?

Can we find common ground in a rapidly-changing technological world with the nature of the workplace changing faster than each generation can adapt to change? Can we continue to seek solutions to racial and sexual inequities in the workplace? Will we ever be able to distribute wealth more equitably to all citizens instead of constantly promising tax cuts that benefit the rich? Can we become something more than a nation where everyone seems armed to the teeth and itching for a fight?

Are we ready for the monumental challenges of global warming? It is coming faster than most of us realize. It is here now. It will get steadily worse in our lifetimes and in the lifetimes of those yet unborn. We worry about our lack of a comprehensive immigration policy, as we should, but we don't even consider the new class of migrants that is appearing now and will grow into the hundreds of millions in the next 75 years, people who are fleeing the ravages of climate change. There are no laws on the books to protect such migrants. They cannot qualify for asylum. There will be wars fought over water rights and access to arable land. A demagogic leader in the United States and in other nations of the world will have plenty of new people to hate when we see worldwide migrations in the millions.

When I think of President Trump in relation to all these questions that are troubling me on the eve of this vital election, I see a leader who is tearing us apart for his own personal gain. I see Americans who seem willing to be torn apart, caught up in hatred and confusion and seemingly oblivious to what will happen if we cannot find common ground.

I see a president who is willing to be a dictator, willing to take us to the final phase of Plato's cycle of governments that is tyranny. I see a president who thrives on continued use of the ancient wounds of racism which remains this nation's greatest single flaw. I see in him the very definition of tyranny, which is the rejection of the law and the institutions of civilization. I see a man without virtue.

With this as my vision on the eve of this election, the many local, state, and federal issues that desperately need to be addressed fall away into insignificance when compared to the threat to the American republic posed by President Trump and the Trumpism he has unleashed in this nation. This election has indeed turned into the frightening single issue: It's the Republic, Stupid.

Tomorrow's elections may provide a clue to answers to the questions Ben Franklin and other founders posed so long ago. Can we keep this republic? Can we make it work? Can we be one nation?

The Winter of Trump's Discontent

November 13, 2018

Former CIA director John O. Brennan's critiques of President Trump are so insightful that Trump took away his security clearance last August and threatened to have him investigated. The president said Brennan was being erratic. It is now one week after the most significant midterm elections in a half century and John Brennan sees Donald Trump as a brooding, sulking man who seems incapable of functioning as president. Whatever chaos that existed inside the White House before the elections has been doubled now that the results are in.

The president went to Paris to join other world leaders in commemoration of the 100th anniversary of the end of World War I. Unfortunately, he could not muster enough energy to go to an American cemetery where more than 6,000 American soldiers, mostly Marines, are buried in sweeping semi-circles of white crosses interspersed with rose bushes. These honored dead were the casualties of the Battle of Belleau Wood about 50 miles from Paris during the month of June 1918. President Trump blamed his absence on the rainy weather. Somehow other world leaders got there just fine. Later he blamed his protocol people for not telling him that a no-show was bad for his image.

When the president returned to the United States he could not focus on his ceremonial role as commander-in-chief long enough to visit Arlington Cemetery on Veteran's Day. He sent his chief of staff and the Chairman of the Joint Chiefs in his place. This same president who castigates the patriotism of NFL players who kneel during the playing of the National Anthem in protest of African American civil rights violations could not muster the strength to visit Arlington Cemetery, just 2.1 miles from the White House, on Veteran's Day. Clearly, the president is distracted by other things right now. Supposedly this is the week he and his lawyers are answering written questions from the Special Counsel.

This is the winter of Trump's discontent. His presidency is falling apart around him. Members of his family may soon be indicted. He tried to make the midterm elections a referendum on his personal popularity rather than any other issue facing the nation. He extended his desire for a referendum on his performance to include all elections for the House and Senate and even extended his ego-trip to local and state elections.

He expected to have his presidency vindicated. He expected the elections to show how popular he was with the people. What he discovered was a shrinking base and a dissipation of his allure. He has been weakened politically and he does not know how to deal with it.

More people voted in this midterm election than at any time in our history. There was a Blue Wave that changed the majority of the House to the Democratic Party. Democrats picked up seats in state legislatures and in governorships, with some of these contests still being counted as I write this. Even in red states, where Republican candidates prevailed, the races were much tighter than they were in the presidential election two years ago.

Most presidents who have faced big losses in the midterms take it in stride. No president likes it when his party loses. But Trump, true to form, declared victory and blamed those Republicans who lost for not "embracing" him more.

President Trump used demagogic tactics to frighten voters. There was a caravan of foreigners invading our country. He ordered American soldiers to the border with Mexico to be video-taped laying barbed wire. He said a vote for Democrats was a vote to open the flood gates to a massive invasion of illegal aliens and criminals. It did not work with most voters. As soon as the elections were over, the breathless talk about the caravan ceased. But the president still clings to the Mexico border wall as his most important priority.

Trump is in full battle mode and can think of nothing else. He is grumpy. He lashes out even more than ever. One day after the elections he fired Attorney General Jeff Sessions. More firings are coming as the president hunkers down for warfare with House Democrats and the Mueller Investigations.

Today Melania Trump apparently fired the deputy national security adviser. By what authority I have no idea. Melania Trump is not a government official. How can she fire a government employee?

Rumors are flying that Chief-of-Staff John Kelly may be next. The Secretary of Homeland Security, Kirstjen Nielsen, may soon be out the door. Other heads may roll.

The president's choice to replace the Attorney General is a former Iowa state's attorney, Matthew Whitaker, who the president discovered by watching TV. Whitaker has made appearances on Fox News and CNN, where he has spouted some of the strangest positions imaginable. He said the Supreme Court is the inferior of the three branches of government. He said judges should judge with the New Testament in mind and they should be Christian. He did not think Jews, Muslims or atheists should be appointed as judges. He claims a state can nullify a federal law. This idea hasn't been around since John C. Calhoun used nullification as a justification for slavery and state's rights, an idea that helped lead the nation toward civil war.

Trump sees Whitaker as an asset in the upcoming battles with Special Counsel Mueller and with any investigations launched by House committees next year. It is one more way for the president to undermine the morale and the integrity of the Justice Department. Trump's hiring of Matthew Whitaker may be unconstitutional. Several law suits are pending on this subject. Trump is no doubt thinking hard about firing Robert Mueller, something that has never been far from his mind. The question is how to do it. Whitaker suggests cutting Mueller's funds. Trump may give his new man at Justice a chance to do it.

The president's gloomy discontent appears to be focusing on immediate survival and on gearing up for re-election in 2020. The rumor mill is churning out stories of more indictments coming soon possibly including members of Trump's family and his longtime friend Roger Stone.

Trump has campaign operatives working on lists of derogatory nicknames for the new Democrats in the House leadership. Just as his first campaign had nasty nicknames for Republicans as well as Democrats, Trump is at it again. It is what demagogues and bullies do. It strikes me as the kind of thing we read about when mobsters are apprehended. We had Crooked Hillary, Heartless Hillary, Lyin' Ted Cruz, Little Rubio, Cheatin' Obama, Sleepy Joe Biden, Crazy Joe Biden, Low Energy Jeb Bush, Wild Bill Clinton, Lyin' James Comey, Slippery James Comey, Slimeball James Comey, Pocahontas (Senator Elizabeth Warren), and many others. We can all look forward to more slimy insults from our president as the cast of his perceived enemies grows.

While the recent elections have made Trump sad, sullen, and discontented, they have given me hope. What I see is a new generation of leaders, a new generation of Americans willing to step into the arena of national politics and find ways to serve their country. This is a diverse group of men and women who demonstrate the strength that is America's diversity. And all the wonderful women!

When I was the Historian of the House of Representatives back in the 1980s and 90s, my office published a book, "Women in Congress, 1917 to 1990." It was published in 1991. The book had biographies of 115 women who served in the House and another 16 who had served in the Senate (including 2 that served in both chambers) over more than 80 years, since the first woman, Jeannette Rankin, served in the House from Montana beginning in 1917. Then, the very next year, 1992, saw the election of 27 women to the House and Senate. It was such an increase that the press called it "The Year of the Woman."

Now look what just happened in 2018. We have 120 women elected to the House and Senate in one election cycle, from both parties, with a predominance among Democrats. This bodes very well for the future of Congress, where women have been under-represented for far too long.

I find hope in the fact that the House will now act as a constitutional check on the president's worst tendencies. This election was not a mandate to impeach the president, even though I think there are reasons to go forward with an impeachment. With the House in Democratic Party control, Congress now has another voice to remind the president that he is not above the law and to remind him that Congress can and should function as an independent co-equal branch of government.

The Republicans in Congress protected the president and since Trump knew nothing about how Congress is supposed to work, he thought Congress was his rubber stamp. Recently the president warned the incoming House committee chairs not to investigate him because "two can play that game." He said he would get the Senate to investigate the House if the House investigated him.

This revealed how little the president knows about the constitutional roles of the House and Senate. The Senate does not investigate the House and the House does not investigate the Senate. Each body is the sole judge of its members and whether or not they are conducting themselves properly. Individual members of the House and Senate, are, of course, not above the law either, and individual members of the House or Senate can be charged with crimes and tried in courts of law. But Trump cannot lead an investigation of House investigators or order the Senate to lead such investigations related to the work of House committees.

Anyone who plans to rest on their laurels and retreat from political activism until the next election would be making a big mistake. The next few months, especially this lame duck period between now and January 3, when the new Congress is sworn in, needs our constant vigilance. Trump may very well be planning to heat up the constitutional crisis that already exists in this country.

An Argument for Impeachment Now

November 26, 2018

K aren Tumulty of the *Washington Post* started her piece in to-day's newspaper with the observation that Donald Trump's presidency has been "a civics lesson in reverse." She wasn't writing about impeachment but her opening line got me to thinking about one argument for impeachment that may just be the one to use. Perhaps we should consider impeachment as a much needed civics lesson for the nation. Most Americans simply do not know enough civics to be properly informed. It's time for the House of Representatives to do some public education in the most dramatic manner possible.

The idea would be to have the House impeach the president primarily for the purpose of formally presenting the articles of impeachment and debating them sufficiently to instruct the public on the nature of the president's transgressions. The House Judiciary Committee would determine the various articles. The list of possible high crimes and misdemeanors and dereliction of duty would be a long one. Once the Judiciary Committee passed the articles to the full House for a vote, a proper and lengthy debate would take place that would further educate the public about the seriousness of the charges.

Whether the House voted to impeach the president on a long list of grievances or a short one, the Senate would be required to conduct a trial, even if the Republican majority had no interest in convicting the president and removing him from office. The American public needs to know, in stark terms, exactly how this president has abused the power of his office and how he has violated various laws. The impeachment process does not have to result in the removal of the president from office for it to be an effective civics lesson to the nation.

We should remember that in the two cases where presidents have been impeached, neither was removed from office. In the case of President Nixon, the threat of impeachment led to his resignation. No president has ever been removed from office by the impeachment process. But the process itself might well be a deciding factor in limiting the president to one term in office. The impeachment process would inform voters who would decide on removal in the election of 2020.

This proposal fits a very legitimate use of the impeachment process that is well within the thinking of the Founders on the nature of impeachment. It serves as a check and a balance on the conduct of the president. It is in harmony with the whole constitutional structure of the federal government as co-equal branches that have powers to check abuses of power. The debates on impeachment at the Federal Convention of 1787, and Alexander Hamilton's explanation in *Federalist 65*, show that the Founders saw impeachment as a necessary check on corruption and malfeasance in the presidency. We still debate the meaning of "high crimes and misdemeanors" in deciding when impeachment might be justified. We can thank James Madison for this imprecise language. In debate, and in English law, a better term was "maladministration." But regardless of academic debates on the subject, which are legion, impeachment begins with a political process, not a legal one. It begins with a recognition that the president may be abusing his power, engaging in corrupt practices, violating laws, or being derelict in his duty to faithfully defend the Constitution.

The main thing the Founders believed in was that most decisions about how the government was being conducted would not be decided within the checks and balance system, or by impeachment. The conduct of the government and its elected officials would be tested at election time, where the voters would decide on the worthiness of elected officials. This is still the best practice. It is why we have frequent elections. This argument holds that the people need to be better informed about the nature of the Trump administration and that impeachment is a vital tool for us to become better informed citizens. Impeachment is not an extreme measure. It is a reasonable part of the process of informing the public between election cycles. It should not be used cavalierly or for partisan gain. It should be used to alert and inform the electorate. Even though we are in a hyper-partisan atmosphere, where charges of partisanship are constantly in the air, we cannot let this poisonous atmosphere hamstring Congress from doing its duty.

This impeachment should begin now, even before the final report of the Mueller investigations and the final disposition of other investigations being conducted at the state level. We still do not know for sure if the Mueller investigations can be properly protected and concluded without interference from the president and from his handpicked controversial new Acting Attorney General. Congress, especially the Senate, has been reluctant to protect the Mueller team from the president's meddling. Should Acting Attorney General Matthew Whitaker take his orders from President Trump and engage in various efforts to undermine or dismantle the Mueller investigations, this would constitute a crime. But much of the damage could be done behind closed doors, by denying Mueller subpoena power, or reigning in aspects of the investigation. The public could be kept in the dark about closed-door machinations until long after the 2020 presidential election. We cannot be kept in the dark going into the 2020 election.

No one knows for sure when and how any final report of the Mueller investigations may be forthcoming. We hear daily rumors that the investigations are nearing completion. Will the Justice Department decide not to release the Mueller report? Will it go to Congress under seal, only to be selectively leaked to the public? Will the American people get a watered-down summary that only confuses issues that desperately need clarity? The proceedings of an impeachment are conducted in the open. The records of the process are open and available for public scrutiny.

All voters, regardless of party affiliation, should witness a transparent impeachment process. The press, the legal profession, the political scientists, the historians, and the ever-present pundits, will analyze the impeachment in fine detail and report all of it to the public as it happens.

This president needs to be impeached just to get his attention. He needs to understand that he cannot act like an unbridled dictator. He must be held accountable so that future presidents will be reminded that no president is above the law. Our presidents, of all our elected officials, must conduct themselves within the laws and regulations, and within the time-honored and well-honed traditions and protocols of decency, diplomacy, and adherence to the Constitution.

This essay does not mention any specific high crimes or misdemeanors that the president might be charged with that would constitute a list of Articles of Impeachment. Readers can supply their own suggestions ranging from obstruction of justice related to the Russian interference in the presidential campaign, violations of the emoluments clause of the Constitution, misuse of Trump's foundation for campaign finances, attempts to order the Justice Department to prosecute the president's political enemies, conspiracy with a foreign power to undermine the campaign of Hillary Clinton, and profiting personally while in office. I have not mentioned the president's chronic lies, because unless they are under oath, they are not a crime. They are simply abysmally wrong.

Presidents do not have to be guilty of anything to be impeached. The Senate determines the guilt after the House brings the charges. Impeachment puts the burden on members of the House to seriously define the nature of the charges against the president. It would, of course, be easier for the House if there was a final report from the Mueller investigations. But the House (and Senate) have investigative powers of their own. They can and should act independently. Given President Trump's abuses of the Justice Department and the FBI from the very beginning of his presidency, we need all the independence we can find. The new House of Representatives that will be sworn in on January 3, 2019, has the potential to be a bolster to the Mueller investigations and a new independent check on the president by launching an impeachment, even if it does not result in the president's removal from office until 2020, when the voters again will have the final word. We have a system. We should have the courage to use it.

If I Was President and the Congress Called My Name

December 7, 2018

It was 1973 in the middle of the Watergate Scandal that Paul Simon's song "Loves Me Like a Rock" made it to number 2 on the pop charts. It captured the disillusionment and the angst of those years, when we discovered that our president was a crook. The third verse of the song hit me like a rock on the head at the time. It seemed so perfect. Now, 45 years later, Simon's song still resonates.

If I was President
And the Congress called my name
I'd say "now who do . . .
Who do you think you're fooling?"

I've got the presidential seal
I'm up on the presidential podium
My mama loves me, she loves me
She get down on her knees and hug me
And she loves me like a rock
She rock me like the rock of ages....

We all knew that Richard Nixon was hiding behind the presidential seal. He and his lawyers kept using the concept of "executive privilege," to avoid complying with the investigations of special prosecutors and the House Judiciary Committee and the Supreme Court, that eventually brought him down. When I heard the song in those days, I always pictured Nixon hiding behind the presidential podium, peaking out to see if anyone was after him. Only a mother's love could save him or forgive him.

President Donald J. Trump is about to have several powerful entities call his name. Starting in January, Congress, in the guise of several major House committees, could call his name, and Trump, no doubt, will hold up the Presidential Seal and hope it has the power of Kryptonite to weaken the resolve of Congress to take him on. But will the Presidential Seal and the Presidential Podium be enough to stop the investigations of Special Counsel Robert Mueller? Or will Trump be able to ward off prosecutors in the Southern District of New York and other places, where investigations and lawsuits are pending?

While many of us have concluded from ample public evidence, much of it coming from the president's own mouth in hundreds of videotapes and thousands of tweets, that our president is a crook, the evidence is not arranged carefully enough to suit courts of law. The president said he fired the FBI director James Comey to end the Russian investigation. Even worse, he invited the Russian ambassador to the White House the next day to brag about it. How is this not obstruction of justice?

But today, in a sentence filing for the president's long-time lawyer and business associate Michael Cohen, we can see enough to conclude that Donald Trump committed a felony when he seriously violated campaign finance laws by ordering his lawyer to pay off two women with whom he had sex, a porn film actress and a Playboy Bunny. What was illegal was the reason he paid them off. He did it to affect the outcome of a presidential election. He used hundreds of thousands of dollars of his own money and this is an illegal, unreported, campaign expense. This direct connection to the president was established earlier when Cohen pleaded guilty. Today it is spelled out even more explicitly.

Former Secretary of State Rex Tillerson in a CBS interview in Houston, Texas, yesterday minced no words in describing his rocky relationship with the president. He said that on many occasions Trump had to be talked out of taking actions that were clearly violations of law. Trump has always operated on his own gut, as he tells us, and then he leaves it to his lawyers to determine if what his gut said was legal.

Tonight, on MSNBC, several former prosecutors said that from what we know about crimes committed by the president, that any other government official, a big city mayor, a member of the House or Senate, the governor of a state, would have already been charged and sentenced. It is a monstrous irony that the President of the United States, who was successfully sued for fraud before he was elected, is the one person in the whole country who has a level of immunity held by no other person in the country. He is the one man, in the one office, where it is not completely clear if he can be indicted while still in office. Everyone engaged in the various investigations that lead back to the president and members of his family are being extremely cautious.

Each day, it seems, we learn new sordid details. A month after Trump's inauguration, the Saudi government paid for 500 rooms at the Trump International Hotel in DC for a program to bring U.S. servicemen and women to DC. Once in the luxury hotel the guest were sent to Capitol Hill to lobby against a bill the Saudis opposed. The Trump International Hotel, owned by the president, netted $270,000 for this program. No one has charged the president with violations of the emoluments clause of the Constitution, where accepting anything of value from a foreign government is forbidden. But add this to the list of high crimes and misdemeanors that could become Articles of Impeachment in 2019.

The new Democratic majority in the House is sending cautious signals to the public. There are no plans to impeach the president. Democrats will not rush to judgment, they say. And, of course, they should be cautious. But if the list of crimes and potential crimes continues to grow, and if the House, in exercising its constitutional duty to provide oversight of the executive branch, turns up more violations of law, at some point impeachment will have to be put on the table, at least long enough for the Judiciary Committee to weigh the accumulated evidence.

No man is above the law. Not even the president. I realize, however, the dicey position we are in and the absolute necessity of the Mueller investigations, the upcoming House investigations, the prosecutions in state courts, to dot all the I's and cross all the T's as the case against the president grinds on.

Whatever Kryptonite the president thinks he may have to ward off the law, Congress, and the federal courts, including the Supreme Court, will be found to be insufficient in the end. He is already isolated, frustrated, acting crazier all the time, and tweeting more incoherently.

This is not a situation that makes me gleeful or righteous. I feel only sorrow for the nation and embarrassment that we have such a defective person in our highest office. He continues to corrode the federal government and the rule of law. We can do so much better and I hope we will in 2020. President Trump, who has never stopped campaigning since he was elected, has supposedly amassed $100 million already for his re-election. I hope somebody is keeping a close eye on that money to make sure it is not used to pay his lawyers, or that he does not take it with him when he leaves office on, or before, January 20, 2021.

Walled In

December 22, 2018

T he President of the United States has walled himself inside a dysfunctional White House, where, by all accounts, he rages and tweets and rages and tweets. Tonight, he issued one of his White House taped video clips reminding Americans that it is dangerous out there with drugs and criminals flooding into the country. We need a wall. Which of late he has been calling a slat fence. Congress, as dysfunctional as it is, was trying to get through this last few weeks of the session by finding a way to keep the government from shutting down.

But the president continued to change his mind on what he expected to get from the continuing resolution for his Mexico wall. As I write this the government has gone into a partial shutdown that will cause several hundred thousand government workers to be furloughed, or, if they are required to, they will continue to work without pay. This is the third time in the Trump presidency that the government has been shut down. What kind of government allows itself to shut down? The job of our elected officials is to run the government. Only abject political failure can account for this unacceptable and, I believe, unconstitutional act. Shutting down the government is dereliction of duty, pure and simple.

A few days ago, it looked like a deal had been cut to send Congress home for the holidays and send the President down to his golf course in Florida. The government would be funded until February 8, 2019, but the deal did not include any funds to build Trump's wall. Because Trump agreed to such a bill, the right-wing media mavens, Laura Ingraham, Anne Coulter, Rush Limbaugh, and others who make their fortunes from extreme political commentary, all jumped on the president for reneging on his promise to build the wall.

I would not give a plug nickel for the views of any of these propagandists, but, unfortunately, our president lives and acts on what they say to him. So, a handful of right wingers on radio, TV, and through Twitter got the president stewing in his own pot again. And he backed out of the agreement he had to keep the government funded.

It was probably Anne Coulter who hit the president the hardest in his soft underbelly, where he makes decisions. She said if Trump didn't get the wall built, no Republican president might ever be elected again. She said, "it'll just have been a joke presidency who scammed the American people, amused the populists for a while, but he'll have no legacy whatsoever." In Congress, members of the House Freedom Caucus, the most rabid of the right, led by Jim Jordan (R-Ohio), also jumped on the president and told him he must build that wall at all costs.

We may never fully understand the interior world of this flawed man to figure out why a few right-wing pundits have more sway with him than his entire cabinet, the members of the House and Senate (other than a few hardliners), or polls showing public disapproval of the Mexico wall. Whatever the final verdict on the president's mental health, we are faced with the reality that his presidency is in free fall.

He has lost his chief of staff and could not find a good replacement. He settled for an acting chief of staff, Mick Mulvaney, the former Freedom Caucus House member, who is currently director of the Office of Management and Budget and does not plan to give up that position.

The worst news this week, other than the shutdown of government, is the resignation of the Secretary of Defense General James Mattis. He resigned in protest because of his many disagreements with Trump on national defense. His letter of resignation will become one of the significant documents of the Trump presidency. The straw that broke this general's back was the arbitrary, capricious, and unilateral announcement that the president was withdrawing our military force from Syria. He followed this up soon afterwards with an equally arbitrary decision to start pulling troops out of Afghanistan.

The Pentagon was caught flat-footed. Congress was not consulted. We don't know who put this bug in the president's bonnet. The entire world learned of these decisions when the president tweeted them. These are the actions of a petty dictator, not a president of the United States. The last adult between the president and the armed forces of the United States will be gone by February.

The president's erratic behavior is linked, of course, to the investigations swirling around him. The Mueller investigation may be completed by mid-February. But regardless of what is revealed, Trump and his adult children face potential criminal charges in the use of the

Trump Foundation for illegal purposes. Trump was forced to close the Foundation earlier this week. He apparently used it as a slush fund for his own purposes.

There are new investigations into what the Trump Inaugural Committee did with the record amount of money it raised. How was that money used? Where did it come from? If it came from foreign governments we have a problem with the emoluments clause of the Constitution. Ivanka Trump played a central role in the inaugural committee and may be called to testify on this subject.

In a matter of weeks, the 116th Congress will convene with Democrats in control of all House committees. The best news for the American people that may come from this is the opportunity to learn more about how the Trump presidency works. There will be numerous oversight hearings on how agency heads ran their agencies. Some of the cabinet members have already left government service, with investigations pending. I hope that most of the hearings the House conducts are open to public scrutiny.

The greatest disservice the GOP-controlled Congress has foisted on us is the way they have covered up information that should have been made public. We don't expect to know about the Mueller investigations until they are over. The professionalism of the Mueller investigations, which only reveals information when they go to court, is a model of how these operations should be run. But one of the important roles of Congress is to inform the American people of how government is working. We have a right to know. Oversight of the executive branch is an important constitutional duty of Congress. It has the power to investigate for the purposes of writing better laws and to keep government accountable to the American people.

The Trump presidency is almost two years old, but we have been getting mostly one side of what is going on in the White House and in the agencies of government. There has been too little accountability and too little public information. The president has dominated the news and the media with his daily tweets, which the press has dutifully pointed out to be daily lies. We have watched the president malign the Justice Department and other agencies, malign Congress, and blame Democrats for everything, including the government shutdown.

It is hard to be rational about what this walled in, trapped, and failing president might do. But the events of this third week of December 2018, contain enough signs of total collapse that the new Congress may find that impeachment moves to the top of the list of priorities. I hope it doesn't because I want us all to have more information, so we can grasp the situation better. The impeachment process might be the best way to get the information out to the public. But I would rather see some systematic public hearings on these troubling matters before making a final judgment about whether the president should be removed from office.

James Madison's famous quotation from a letter he wrote in 1822 is appropriate for all seasons. It is even more relevant at this time in our history when we are bombarded with falsehoods in new ways through social media and when we have been denied information the public needs to help us understand what is going on. This is what Madison wrote:

"A popular Government, without popular information, or the means of acquiring it, is but a Prologue to a Farce or a Tragedy; or, perhaps both. Knowledge will forever govern ignorance: And a people who mean to be their own Governors, must arm themselves with the power which knowledge gives."

If the people of the United States want a republican form of government, where the ultimate power of government resides with the people; if we want our system of representative democracy to work; it is essential that we act as knowledgeable voters and participants in the political process. If we don't have the "popular information" we need to make informed decisions, we could be open to all kinds of problems, not the least of which is a government that dispenses false information designed to suit a certain political party or a certain leader.

I don't expect miracles from the new Congress or the new Democratic majority in the House. We have yet to see hyper-partisanship decrease. Trump won't let it decrease and neither will Mitch McConnell's GOP-controlled Senate and the political nihilists in the House Freedom Caucus. But I do expect the new House majority to conduct investigations that shed much needed light on a government that has been run too much in darkness and without accountability. Investigations, more so than legislation, may be the greatest legacy of the 116th Congress.

Democracy Awakens

January 7, 2019

The significance of the 2018 congressional elections may well be looked upon someday as a major watershed in American history, a turning point in a long period of dysfunctional government and ideological hyper-partisanship. Speaker Nancy Pelosi, in her first address to the 116th Congress said "Our nation is at an historic moment. Two months ago, the American people spoke, and demanded a new dawn."

Whatever the final verdict, the immediate result is that for the first time since the election of Donald Trump as president, a part of Congress, the House of Representatives, now has the power to conduct oversight of all the agencies of the executive branch, to subpoena witnesses, and conduct hearings on a full range of topics related to the Trump administration. The so-called "Blue Wave" of victories of Democratic Party candidates for the House materialized and resulted in the Democrats gaining control of the chamber for the first time in eight years. The turnover of 40 seats was the largest Democratic Party gain since the Watergate era of the 1970s. The *New York Times* said "… the Democrats' House takeover represented a clarion call that a majority of the country wants to see limits on Mr. Trump for the next two years of his term." [Nov. 6, 2018].

The Republican Party had been in complete control of the executive and legislative branches of government and an already conservative Supreme Court added two new justices, nominated by President Trump. It became the openly-expressed position of the GOP-controlled House and Senate to do everything in their power to limit Obama to one term in office and when he was re-elected the GOP continued to conduct a steady congressional opposition to the Obama administration, spending vast amounts of legislative time in attempts to repeal President Obama's signature achievement, the Affordable Healthcare Act.

Senate Majority Leader Mitch McConnell and the Republican majority in the Senate changed Senate rules to make it easier to approve justices of the Supreme Court once Trump was in office. This was after Leader McConnell had held up President Obama's nominee, Merrick Garland, for over a year and prevented the nominee from receiving a vote in the Senate. There was nothing illegal in this process. It was, however, a blatant partisan move to put the interests of the Republican Party over the previous Senate rules and procedures for approval of justices to the Supreme Court.

President Trump has had the luxury of a compliant and supportive Republican-led Congress for the first two years of his administration. The president's pronouncements to Congress often reflect his view that Congress is a rubber stamp. House and Senate committees, controlled by Republicans, dragged their feet on serious investigations related to the Russian influence in the 2016 presidential election. In the House, Congressman Devin Nunes, chairman of the Permanent Select Committee on Intelligence, took actions to protect the president from his committee's own investigation. These antics forced his temporary removal from the chairmanship.

The election of a Democratic Party majority in the House changes the power of Congress dramatically. Whatever President Trump may do to undermine the investigations of Special Counsel Robert Mueller, including the possibility of firing Mueller, the president will not be able to control any investigations launched by the committees of the House of Representatives.

It is too soon to predict how well the new House will take up its constitutional duty to investigate troubling aspects of the Trump administration. But the good news is that an important door was opened as a result of the House elections.

"Checks and balances" is not a hollow phrase from a high school civics lesson. It is one of the most important concepts contained in the U.S. Constitution. It is essential that each branch of government can check the excesses and wrong-doings of the other branches. Checks and balances keep government from corruption. Oversight hearings and investigations, when done right, lead to better laws, better policy, and better national security. They lead also to exposure and correction of wrong-doing in all the agencies of the federal government. They could lead to the impeachment of the president.

The other aspect of the House elections for the 116th Congress is the new diversity and the number of women elected to serve. This is a sign that a new generation of leaders is emerging. The House is the place where change can take place first, because only the House has all its members elected every two years. The House is the fulcrum of the democratic process. It is where the people can speak the loudest for change.

Whether the new House leaders can find common ground to move major legislation in a bipartisan manner remains to be seen. On the first day of the new Congress, Speaker Pelosi said she would seek bipartisan support to move major legislation. She named areas where agreement already exists, in infrastructure, reducing prescription drug costs, background checks for firearm sales, protection against future cyberwar and terrorism. Despite fierce partisanship, both parties have long expressed interest in these areas and others.

The year 2019 is shaping up to be pivotal in terms of the new Congress, the completion or extension of existing investigations from the Special Counsel and with several states attorneys looking into a variety of areas related to the president, his campaign, his inauguration committee, and the demise of the Donald J. Trump Foundation on charges that it was not a charity but a slush fund for the president.

Perhaps this will be the year that we see progress in determining if the president has violated the emoluments clause of the Constitution, which prohibits government officials from receiving anything of value from foreign governments. While there is at least one lawsuit pending on this topic, I see this area as one of the important unexplored areas.

The president opted not to establish a blind trust for his many holdings during his term as president. I recall a staged session early in his presidency, where the president's lawyer, standing in front of a long table filled with stacks of documents, declared that the president did not need to establish a blind trust. In 2017, we learned from a story first reported by ProPublica that the General Services Administration approved a filing that allowed President Trump to draw down money from hundreds of Trump businesses whenever the president requested the money, or whenever the president's son deemed it appropriate. This story was in the *Chicago Tribune* on April 3, 2017, and in most major newspapers. We have a president who continues to function as head of his business empire with a slight arm's-length of separation that reaches to the president's nearby son.

The masthead of the *Washington Post* has included the phrase "Democracy Dies in Darkness" since the ascendency of Donald Trump to the White House. From the elections of 2018, I see a ray of light penetrating that darkness. I see Democracy Awakening.

Acknowledgments

Many thanks to the vibrant and dynamic members of the free press of the United States, practicing in print, online, and on network and cable TV. Collectively, you have kept me informed and engaged in the process of following the Trump presidency.

Fake news does exist. Partisan news analysis is commonplace. But the free press and the First Amendment of the U. S. Constitution is alive and well and doing its job of informing citizens. Those who throw up their hands and say all news is biased and fake, are only fooling themselves and playing into the hands of demagogues and propagandists. While lies travel faster than truth, we better hope that truth prevails.

My thanks to friends and colleagues, some on social media, who have been my first readers of many of these essays. Your encouragement as well as your critiques and corrections of errors have sustained me. A special note of thanks to Richard Bernstein, Don Ritchie, Richard A. Baker, Matt Simek, Joe Famulary, Mike Donaghue, Jim Lane, Allida Black, Charlene Bickford, Mark Kohut, and Rick Shenkman of the History News Network.

Thanks also to the intellectual community of Shepherd University and the town of Shepherdstown, West Virginia, which has encouraged my writing on President Trump. A special thank you to the good people at the Four Seasons Bookstore in Shepherdstown who made my book *Trump Tsunami* their fifth bestselling non-fiction title in 2018, where Bob Woodward's *Fear: Trump in the White House*, was fourth on the list with just 13 more sales than mine. Thank you Kendra Adkins and Leigh Koonce.

Thanks also to the newspaper editors in our area who have carried my writing, especially, Mike Chalmers of the *Observer*, Steve Altman of the *Good News Paper*, and Rob and Christine Snyder of the *Spirit of Jefferson*.

The book layout was designed by Rachel Fields of Hedgesville, West Virginia. She chose Baskerville as the typeface without even knowing it was my favorite font! It is a good partnership.

Phyllis Smock, my dear wife, has encouraged and supported my writing and research for almost 60 years. I am a lucky guy.

About the Author

Ray Smock was the first official historian of the U.S. House of Representatives serving from 1983 to 1995. He received his Ph.D. in American History from the University of Maryland in 1974. He is the author of *Trump Tsunami: A Historian's Diary of the Trump Campaign and His First Year in Office*. He is a biographer of Booker T. Washington and co-editor of the 14-volume *Booker T. Washington Papers*. He co-edited a two-volume work: *Congress Investigates: A Critical History with Documents* and edited *Landmark Documents on the U.S. Congress*. He was a historical consultant to the National Constitution Center in Philadelphia, and senior consultant to a 20-part TV series "Biography of America," produced by WGBH, Boston Public Television. He has made frequent appearances on C-SPAN and is a contributor to the History News Network. For sixteen years, he was director of the Robert C. Byrd Center for Congressional History and Education at Shepherd University, in Shepherdstown, West Virginia. He resides with his wife Phyllis in Martinsburg, West Virginia, 75 miles from Washington, DC.

53959587R00145

Made in the USA
Columbia, SC
23 March 2019